FREE Test Taking Tips DVD Offer

To help us better serve you, we have developed a Test Taking Tips DVD that we would like to give you for FREE. **This DVD covers world-class test taking tips that you can use to be even more successful when you are taking your test.**

All that we ask is that you email us your feedback about your study guide. Please let us know what you thought about it – whether that is good, bad or indifferent.

To get your **FREE Test Taking Tips DVD**, email freedvd@studyguideteam.com with "FREE DVD" in the subject line and the following information in the body of the email:

    a. The title of your study guide.

    b. Your product rating on a scale of 1-5, with 5 being the highest rating.

    c. Your feedback about the study guide. What did you think of it?

    d. Your full name and shipping address to send your free DVD.

If you have any questions or concerns, please don't hesitate to contact us at freedvd@studyguideteam.com.

Thanks again!

TExES 231 English Language Arts and Reading 7-12 Study Guide

TExES ELAR 7-12 Test Prep and
Practice Exam Questions [2nd Edition]

Written and edited by TPB Publishing.

TPB Publishing is not associated with or endorsed by any official testing organization. TPB Publishing is a publisher of unofficial educational products. All test and organization names are trademarks of their respective owners. Content in this book is included for utilitarian purposes only and does not constitute an endorsement by TPB Publishing of any particular point of view.

Interested in buying more than 10 copies of our product? Contact us about bulk discounts:
bulkorders@studyguideteam.com

ISBN 13: 9781628459784
ISBN 10: 1628459786

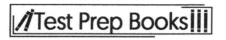

Table of Contents

Quick Overview

As you draw closer to taking your exam, effective preparation becomes more and more important. Thankfully, you have this study guide to help you get ready. Use this guide to help keep your studying on track and refer to it often.

This study guide contains several key sections that will help you be successful on your exam. The guide contains tips for what you should do the night before and the day of the test. Also included are test-taking tips. Knowing the right information is not always enough. Many well-prepared test takers struggle with exams. These tips will help equip you to accurately read, assess, and answer test questions.

A large part of the guide is devoted to showing you what content to expect on the exam and to helping you better understand that content. In this guide are practice test questions so that you can see how well you have grasped the content. Then, answer explanations are provided so that you can understand why you missed certain questions.

Don't try to cram the night before you take your exam. This is not a wise strategy for a few reasons. First, your retention of the information will be low. Your time would be better used by reviewing information you already know rather than trying to learn a lot of new information. Second, you will likely become stressed as you try to gain a large amount of knowledge in a short amount of time. Third, you will be depriving yourself of sleep. So be sure to go to bed at a reasonable time the night before. Being well-rested helps you focus and remain calm.

Be sure to eat a substantial breakfast the morning of the exam. If you are taking the exam in the afternoon, be sure to have a good lunch as well. Being hungry is distracting and can make it difficult to focus. You have hopefully spent lots of time preparing for the exam. Don't let an empty stomach get in the way of success!

When travelling to the testing center, leave earlier than needed. That way, you have a buffer in case you experience any delays. This will help you remain calm and will keep you from missing your appointment time at the testing center.

Be sure to pace yourself during the exam. Don't try to rush through the exam. There is no need to risk performing poorly on the exam just so you can leave the testing center early. Allow yourself to use all of the allotted time if needed.

Remain positive while taking the exam even if you feel like you are performing poorly. Thinking about the content you should have mastered will not help you perform better on the exam.

Once the exam is complete, take some time to relax. Even if you feel that you need to take the exam again, you will be well served by some down time before you begin studying again. It's often easier to convince yourself to study if you know that it will come with a reward!

Test-Taking Strategies

1. Predicting the Answer

When you feel confident in your preparation for a multiple-choice test, try predicting the answer before reading the answer choices. This is especially useful on questions that test objective factual knowledge. By predicting the answer before reading the available choices, you eliminate the possibility that you will be distracted or led astray by an incorrect answer choice. You will feel more confident in your selection if you read the question, predict the answer, and then find your prediction among the answer choices. After using this strategy, be sure to still read all of the answer choices carefully and completely. If you feel unprepared, you should not attempt to predict the answers. This would be a waste of time and an opportunity for your mind to wander in the wrong direction.

2. Reading the Whole Question

Too often, test takers scan a multiple-choice question, recognize a few familiar words, and immediately jump to the answer choices. Test authors are aware of this common impatience, and they will sometimes prey upon it. For instance, a test author might subtly turn the question into a negative, or he or she might redirect the focus of the question right at the end. The only way to avoid falling into these traps is to read the entirety of the question carefully before reading the answer choices.

3. Looking for Wrong Answers

Long and complicated multiple-choice questions can be intimidating. One way to simplify a difficult multiple-choice question is to eliminate all of the answer choices that are clearly wrong. In most sets of answers, there will be at least one selection that can be dismissed right away. If the test is administered on paper, the test taker could draw a line through it to indicate that it may be ignored; otherwise, the test taker will have to perform this operation mentally or on scratch paper. In either case, once the obviously incorrect answers have been eliminated, the remaining choices may be considered. Sometimes identifying the clearly wrong answers will give the test taker some information about the correct answer. For instance, if one of the remaining answer choices is a direct opposite of one of the eliminated answer choices, it may well be the correct answer. The opposite of obviously wrong is obviously right! Of course, this is not always the case. Some answers are obviously incorrect simply because they are irrelevant to the question being asked. Still, identifying and eliminating some incorrect answer choices is a good way to simplify a multiple-choice question.

4. Don't Overanalyze

Anxious test takers often overanalyze questions. When you are nervous, your brain will often run wild, causing you to make associations and discover clues that don't actually exist. If you feel that this may be a problem for you, do whatever you can to slow down during the test. Try taking a deep breath or counting to ten. As you read and consider the question, restrict yourself to the particular words used by the author. Avoid thought tangents about what the author *really* meant, or what he or she was *trying* to say. The only things that matter on a multiple-choice test are the words that are actually in the question. You must avoid reading too much into a multiple-choice question, or supposing that the writer meant something other than what he or she wrote.

5. No Need for Panic

It is wise to learn as many strategies as possible before taking a multiple-choice test, but it is likely that you will come across a few questions for which you simply don't know the answer. In this situation, avoid panicking. Because most multiple-choice tests include dozens of questions, the relative value of a single wrong answer is small. As much as possible, you should compartmentalize each question on a multiple-choice test. In other words, you should not allow your feelings about one question to affect your success on the others. When you find a question that you either don't understand or don't know how to answer, just take a deep breath and do your best. Read the entire question slowly and carefully. Try rephrasing the question a couple of different ways. Then, read all of the answer choices carefully. After eliminating obviously wrong answers, make a selection and move on to the next question.

6. Confusing Answer Choices

When working on a difficult multiple-choice question, there may be a tendency to focus on the answer choices that are the easiest to understand. Many people, whether consciously or not, gravitate to the answer choices that require the least concentration, knowledge, and memory. This is a mistake. When you come across an answer choice that is confusing, you should give it extra attention. A question might be confusing because you do not know the subject matter to which it refers. If this is the case, don't eliminate the answer before you have affirmatively settled on another. When you come across an answer choice of this type, set it aside as you look at the remaining choices. If you can confidently assert that one of the other choices is correct, you can leave the confusing answer aside. Otherwise, you will need to take a moment to try to better understand the confusing answer choice. Rephrasing is one way to tease out the sense of a confusing answer choice.

7. Your First Instinct

Many people struggle with multiple-choice tests because they overthink the questions. If you have studied sufficiently for the test, you should be prepared to trust your first instinct once you have carefully and completely read the question and all of the answer choices. There is a great deal of research suggesting that the mind can come to the correct conclusion very quickly once it has obtained all of the relevant information. At times, it may seem to you as if your intuition is working faster even than your reasoning mind. This may in fact be true. The knowledge you obtain while studying may be retrieved from your subconscious before you have a chance to work out the associations that support it. Verify your instinct by working out the reasons that it should be trusted.

8. Key Words

Many test takers struggle with multiple-choice questions because they have poor reading comprehension skills. Quickly reading and understanding a multiple-choice question requires a mixture of skill and experience. To help with this, try jotting down a few key words and phrases on a piece of scrap paper. Doing this concentrates the process of reading and forces the mind to weigh the relative importance of the question's parts. In selecting words and phrases to write down, the test taker thinks about the question more deeply and carefully. This is especially true for multiple-choice questions that are preceded by a long prompt.

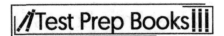

9. Subtle Negatives

One of the oldest tricks in the multiple-choice test writer's book is to subtly reverse the meaning of a question with a word like *not* or *except*. If you are not paying attention to each word in the question, you can easily be led astray by this trick. For instance, a common question format is, "Which of the following is...?" Obviously, if the question instead is, "Which of the following is not...?," then the answer will be quite different. Even worse, the test makers are aware of the potential for this mistake and will include one answer choice that would be correct if the question were not negated or reversed. A test taker who misses the reversal will find what he or she believes to be a correct answer and will be so confident that he or she will fail to reread the question and discover the original error. The only way to avoid this is to practice a wide variety of multiple-choice questions and to pay close attention to each and every word.

10. Reading Every Answer Choice

It may seem obvious, but you should always read every one of the answer choices! Too many test takers fall into the habit of scanning the question and assuming that they understand the question because they recognize a few key words. From there, they pick the first answer choice that answers the question they believe they have read. Test takers who read all of the answer choices might discover that one of the latter answer choices is actually *more* correct. Moreover, reading all of the answer choices can remind you of facts related to the question that can help you arrive at the correct answer. Sometimes, a misstatement or incorrect detail in one of the latter answer choices will trigger your memory of the subject and will enable you to find the right answer. Failing to read all of the answer choices is like not reading all of the items on a restaurant menu: you might miss out on the perfect choice.

11. Spot the Hedges

One of the keys to success on multiple-choice tests is paying close attention to every word. This is never truer than with words like almost, most, some, and sometimes. These words are called "hedges" because they indicate that a statement is not totally true or not true in every place and time. An absolute statement will contain no hedges, but in many subjects, the answers are not always straightforward or absolute. There are always exceptions to the rules in these subjects. For this reason, you should favor those multiple-choice questions that contain hedging language. The presence of qualifying words indicates that the author is taking special care with his or her words, which is certainly important when composing the right answer. After all, there are many ways to be wrong, but there is only one way to be right! For this reason, it is wise to avoid answers that are absolute when taking a multiple-choice test. An absolute answer is one that says things are either all one way or all another. They often include words like *every*, *always*, *best*, and *never*. If you are taking a multiple-choice test in a subject that doesn't lend itself to absolute answers, be on your guard if you see any of these words.

12. Long Answers

In many subject areas, the answers are not simple. As already mentioned, the right answer often requires hedges. Another common feature of the answers to a complex or subjective question are qualifying clauses, which are groups of words that subtly modify the meaning of the sentence. If the question or answer choice describes a rule to which there are exceptions or the subject matter is complicated, ambiguous, or confusing, the correct answer will require many words in order to be expressed clearly and accurately. In essence, you should not be deterred by answer choices that seem excessively long. Oftentimes, the author of the text will not be able to write the correct answer without offering some qualifications and modifications. Your job is to read the answer choices thoroughly and completely and to select the one that most accurately and precisely answers the question.

13. Restating to Understand

Sometimes, a question on a multiple-choice test is difficult not because of what it asks but because of how it is written. If this is the case, restate the question or answer choice in different words. This process serves a couple of important purposes. First, it forces you to concentrate on the core of the question. In order to rephrase the question accurately, you have to understand it well. Rephrasing the question will concentrate your mind on the key words and ideas. Second, it will present the information to your mind in a fresh way. This process may trigger your memory and render some useful scrap of information picked up while studying.

14. True Statements

Sometimes an answer choice will be true in itself, but it does not answer the question. This is one of the main reasons why it is essential to read the question carefully and completely before proceeding to the answer choices. Too often, test takers skip ahead to the answer choices and look for true statements. Having found one of these, they are content to select it without reference to the question above. Obviously, this provides an easy way for test makers to play tricks. The savvy test taker will always read the entire question before turning to the answer choices. Then, having settled on a correct answer choice, he or she will refer to the original question and ensure that the selected answer is relevant. The mistake of choosing a correct-but-irrelevant answer choice is especially common on questions related to specific pieces of objective knowledge. A prepared test taker will have a wealth of factual knowledge at his or her disposal, and should not be careless in its application.

15. No Patterns

One of the more dangerous ideas that circulates about multiple-choice tests is that the correct answers tend to fall into patterns. These erroneous ideas range from a belief that B and C are the most common right answers, to the idea that an unprepared test-taker should answer "A-B-A-C-A-D-A-B-A." It cannot be emphasized enough that pattern-seeking of this type is exactly the WRONG way to approach a multiple-choice test. To begin with, it is highly unlikely that the test maker will plot the correct answers according to some predetermined pattern. The questions are scrambled and delivered in a random order. Furthermore, even if the test maker was following a pattern in the assignation of correct answers, there is no reason why the test taker would know which pattern he or she was using. Any attempt to discern a pattern in the answer choices is a waste of time and a distraction from the real work of taking the test. A test taker would be much better served by extra preparation before the test than by reliance on a pattern in the answers.

FREE DVD OFFER

Don't forget that doing well on your exam includes both understanding the test content and understanding how to use what you know to do well on the test. We offer a completely FREE Test Taking Tips DVD that covers world class test taking tips that you can use to be even more successful when you are taking your test.

All that we ask is that you email us your feedback about your study guide. To get your **FREE Test Taking Tips DVD**, email freedvd@studyguideteam.com with "FREE DVD" in the subject line and the following information in the body of the email:

- The title of your study guide.
- Your product rating on a scale of 1-5, with 5 being the highest rating.
- Your feedback about the study guide. What did you think of it?
- Your full name and shipping address to send your free DVD.

Introduction

Function of the Test

The Texas Examination of Educator Standards (TExES) English Language Arts and Reading 7-12 test is one of dozens of TExES tests used as part of the certification process for teachers in the state of Texas. Texas law requires every person seeking certification as an educator in Texas to pass comprehensive examinations appropriate to the area in which they wish to teach. The TExES tests have been developed gradually since 2002 as the means by which prospective educators can meet this requirement.

The TExES tests are intended to identify individuals who have the appropriate level of knowledge to teach in Texas public schools. They are governed by the Texas State Board for Educator Certification and the Texas Education Agency. These state agencies have contracted with Educational Testing Service (ETS) to assist in development and deployment of the tests. All TExES tests are based on Texas Essential Knowledge and Skills, the required curriculum for all Texas public school students.

The test evaluates prospective teachers' skills and preparedness for teaching 7th through 12th grade English. The test is not used for purposes other than determining whether the test taker qualifies for certification. Understandably, it is almost exclusively taken in Texas, by individuals seeking employment as public educators in Texas. In the 2015-2016 year, the test was taken by 3,000 test takers, of whom 64% passed.

Test Administration

Prospective exam candidates must first get approval to take the test from their Educator Preparation Program (EPP). Once a candidate receives approval from their EPP, he or she can register to take the test through ETS, either online or by phone.

The test is administered by computer at test centers throughout Texas and at selected test centers in states bordering Texas and elsewhere. The test takes five hours, and may be taken in either a morning or afternoon testing session. Candidates taking multiple TExES tests may take tests in both sessions in one day.

As with all computer-based TExES tests, Texas law requires that a test taker who does not pass the TExES English Language Arts and Reading 7-12 exam must wait 45 days before retaking the test. A test taker may attempt the test for a maximum of five total administrations (the original plus four retakes).

In accordance with the Americans with Disabilities Act, individuals with documented disabilities can receive testing accommodations. Such individuals must register for their test through ETS and have their desired accommodations approved prior to the testing day.

Test Format

Test takers should arrive at their computer testing center with an admission ticket and appropriate identification. After signing in at the test center, test takers are given the opportunity to secure personal belongings in a locker and then they are assigned a computer. The test consists of 100 multiple-choice questions and two constructed-response questions. The questions cover four domains of knowledge in the field of English Language Arts instruction.

These domains, and the approximate percentage of the test content they comprise, are as follows:

Domain	Approximate Percentage of Test
Integrated Language Arts, Diverse Learners and the Study of English	15%
Literature, Reading Processes and Skills for Reading Literary and Nonliterary Texts	40%
Written Communication	30%
Oral Communication and Media Literacy	15%

Scoring

All TExES tests are criterion-referenced, meaning they designed to measure each performance against a reference baseline rather than in relation to other test takers. Raw scores are based on the number of multiple-choice questions answered correctly, with no penalty for guessing incorrectly, along with scores given by two scorers for the constructed-response questions. The raw score is then scaled to enable comparison between results on different forms of the test. Scaled scores range from 100 to 300, with a passing score set at 240. The average score in the 2015-2016 year was 243.01.

Score reports include both the pass/fail result and the test taker's raw score information broken down by subject matter within the test, for the purpose of aiding preparation for a potential retake attempt. Scores are posted within seven days of the test date.

Recent/Future Developments

The limit of a maximum five total attempts to pass was instituted effective September 1, 2015. All attempts taken before that date count as one total attempt. No other substantial recent or prospective changes have been announced.

Integrated Language Arts, Diverse Learners, and the Study of English

Integrating Language Arts Education

One of the keystone roles of a middle or high school level English Language Arts instructor is helping with the development of each student's academic language and literacy competencies. The ability for students to comprehend and communicate in an academic tone fluently and effectively is one of the principle goals of any education program, and the Texas school system is no exception. Academic language can be considered a second language that native English Language learners must gain proficiency with, separate from conversational or social language. This represents a third language that non-native English speakers must master. In fact, studies have demonstrated that a new student's mastery of social English language is usually attained in two years or so of immersion in an English-speaking school and community, while academic language mastery takes an average of seven years. It is the great responsibility of English Language Arts educators to facilitate this learning for all students, regardless of background, to poise them to be effective communicators and able to critically understand and evaluate the many types of academic texts they will encounter in their education and career.

Perhaps somewhat unique to English Language arts over other disciplines is the importance of a student's ability to transfer knowledge gained in the language arts discipline to curricular areas outside of language arts. For example, writing can be improved through explicit reading instruction and practiced within language arts, while comprehension of social studies texts or the skill in writing science lab reports can also be augmented through transferring learning from English classes.

With this in mind, it is possible to consider the integration of English language arts in two different ways. The first context takes the form of integration within the English classroom by learning each of the language arts relative to the others. Writing can be improved by drafting ideas orally or by reading and editing peer projects, reading can be improved through writing and oral read alouds, and oral language ability can also be improved through complex reading and writing tasks. In this context, it is important to emphasize that each mode of language is not an isolated discipline, but rather a component of the integrated whole of academic language. The second type of integration involves developing English language ability while engaging in studies in other content areas, such as math and science. In this context, educators are employing the "language-across-the-curriculum" model.

In the first integration method, it is often not sufficient to provide a variety of speaking, listening, reading, and writing tasks for students. Explicit instruction and dedicated activities designed to help scaffold the blending and transferability of skillsets is necessary to develop students' appreciation of and fluency between the variety of modes of language. For example, educators can provide blended assignments and activities. Peer-reviewing writing drafts incorporates critical reading and writing. Oral reports with written assessments also integrate careful listening and language processing skills. Similarly, writing and delivering verbal reflections in small discussion groups after reading assignments integrates a variety of modes. Although these complex tasks require purposeful designing, they provide rich opportunities for students to make connections between the different components of academic language as a whole.

Integrating across the curriculum is equally important for a student's academic success. Lagging English language arts skills will significantly hinder comprehension and mastery in other core curricular areas;

students who struggle to use an academic tone in writing will perform more poorly on history or science reports, students who cannot deliver eloquent or logical oral responses will contribute less successfully to discussions or debates, students who have not developed critical listening skills will fail to gather all necessary information and connections from lectures or discussions, and those who struggle with reading comprehension will be unable to attain the expected knowledge from textbook readings and other reading assignments. Working on these skills as they pertain to literature or in isolation in language arts-related content is no substitute for developing the abilities to read, write, speak, and listen in broader academic and real-life communicative settings. It is imperative that educators draw upon resources and topics from other core curricular areas, such as shifting the focus of the English class to the Industrial Revolution and then exploring the topic within the mode of language. Again, it is important in these activities to blend the modes together as part of a whole, rather than focusing on them in fragmented entities.

Finally, it should be noted that guiding students to form relationships among language arts and other areas of their academic and personal lives will help enrich their learning experience both within the classroom and beyond. In competitive economies, it is the prepared, well-rounded, and fluent communicator who is poised for flexibility and success within his or her career aspirations. English language arts educators are instrumental in developing these important skills. As such, they are responsible for and expected to stay informed of the Texas Essential Knowledge and Skills (TEKS) language arts standards for students in grades 7–12. These standards and skills are specifically designed for the development of critical language arts skills in middle and high school students. Texas language arts educators are responsible for adhering to the necessary competencies laid out in the TEKS by building their curriculum and activities in a thoughtful manner to promote such skills in their students.

Teaching Diverse Students

Understanding Students' Various Perspectives, Cultures, and Backgrounds

Planning Instruction Responsive to Students' Individual and Group Needs
It can be difficult as a teacher to be mindful of the varying individual and group identities present in the classroom. Every adult has internalized beliefs that he or she has learned through experience or was taught as a child. To encourage cultural understanding and dismantle stereotypes, an essential part of the curriculum should be devoted to teaching students tolerance of themselves and others.

One thing teachers should keep in mind is that although students may share similar group identities—race, nationality, socioeconomic status—they also contain differing individual identities. They may have different religions, different ancestry, or different languages. These differences will present themselves in everything the students do, from curricular activities, such as reading and writing, to social interaction in speaking and listening.

To incorporate cultural awareness into classroom instruction, the teacher must first express interest in the cultural backgrounds of his or her students. If the instructor is closed off against certain identities, the students will echo these viewpoints, being reserved in expression and also harboring the same reservations towards cultures different than their own. Therefore, the first step in planning instructions that tailors to the cultural needs of the students is to be interested in their identities. This can be done in many ways, but one sure way that a teacher can show he or she cares is by engaging in diversity activities, such as introduction cards or online questionnaires that students can fill out about themselves.

These may include the following categories:

- Where they or their ancestors are from
- Their age
- Their primary and secondary languages, if applicable
- Their religious or spiritual beliefs
- Their race
- Their gender, what they identify as
- Any other information they feel comfortable introducing to the class

These are only a few examples of the information that can be gathered on index cards or questionnaires. Teachers can have the students go around the room and introduce themselves, while displaying curiosity about the backgrounds of their classmates. The information may then be kept throughout the year for reference and will also help the teacher collect a sort of census on the different cultural backgrounds their students possess.

Another proven way to show interest in the students and instill a sense of cultural awareness in the classroom is to assign a family survey project in which the students report on their heritage, the special customs or holidays that they practice in their home, the languages they speak, or anything they wish to share about their families and identities. These projects can be completed on PowerPoint presentations, poster boards, or video interviews, and students should be encouraged to bring items of cultural significance to share with their classmates.

The knowledge gained from these sorts of activities will greatly help the teacher to create a curriculum of instruction that encourages tolerance. For example, in reading about historic events involving horrendous crimes against a certain race or culture, teachers should try to read texts that contain both perspectives—e.g., texts from German, American, and Jewish voices related to the Holocaust. Discussions such as these can be taught in very compassionate and empathetic ways, while still recognizing the horrors of the crimes committed. Students can also consider historical and contemporary texts to see how perspectives have evolved on significant cultural issues throughout history.

It is also important to create a curriculum in which all students see themselves, their race, their genders, and their religions represented in their studies. The curriculum should not focus on the achievements of one particular group, such as only teaching history related to Christian Caucasian culture. Further, teachers should be ready and willing to alter the curriculum to respond to the needs of the students.

To instill a sense of tolerance in the classroom, students can complete worksheets on the kinds of behavior and diction that are acceptable when they encounter differences in cultures or belief systems. They can create a play or scene where they write out such an encounter and how they would approach it to build understanding between people from different backgrounds. Monitoring the interactions between the students and pointing out any situation or comment that unintentionally conveys intolerance will help make them more aware. Students should be educated on stereotypes. Most importantly, teachers should always lead by example by being as open and impartial as possible.

Strategies for Creating a Safe Environment

There are countless different strategies for creating a culturally-safe environment in which reading, writing, speaking, and listening can take place. First, the classroom should be clean and orderly to minimize distractions. It should reflect cultural diversity or impartiality. The classroom should be arranged with resources readily available and easily accessible so that a teacher never has to turn his or her back on their students. Secondly, the classroom should be arranged in a way that makes interaction with fellow students easy. The classroom environment also must convey a sense of emotional safety where students feel comfortable expressing themselves without fear of bullying or prejudice. This means teachers should be modeling respectful behavior for students, establishing rules of respectful interaction between students, and addressing any instances of disrespectful speech or behavior. Once the classroom has been set up safely, the following strategies are effective ways to incorporate cultural awareness into the curriculum:

Reading

- Choosing texts that reflect multicultural perspectives and include different cultures
- Clarifying that chosen texts may contain culturally and racially-sensitive language and pointing out the intolerance in such texts—e.g., the excessive use of racial slurs in Mark Twain's *Huckleberry Finn* and what they suggested of cultural intolerance at the time
- Trying not to choose texts that talk about an entire race or religion in general, but specific aspects of the race or religion to avoid sweeping generalizations or stereotypes about a group— e.g., choosing books on certain Native American tribes, rather than books solely on Native Americans, texts that offer specifics about a particular religion
- Choosing texts that are both fun and serious, such as texts on cultural festivities and fun, as well as those about wars and hardships
- Choosing texts that are historically accurate and up-to-date
- If allowing students to choose their own books, encouraging them to explore texts that are culturally different than their own

Writing

- Requiring that students complete a project, such as a presentation or examination of a famous figure, who represents a culture or religion or philosophy that differs from their own
- Monitoring student writing, checking for the presence of stereotypes and intolerance, and holding one-on-one conferences with students whenever concerns arise
- Instructing students on the appropriate vocabulary, diction, and phrasing when writing on culturally or racially sensitive subjects
- Encouraging students to write together via collaborative discussion boards, blogs, or group projects
- Assigning students to groups with varying cultural, religious, racial, or socioeconomic backgrounds
- Having students write on personal experiences where they have encountered intolerance against themselves or others

Speaking

- Holding frequent group discussions in which students can learn how to converse with people of different backgrounds, which may include inviting guest speakers
- Arranging chairs in circles or allowing students to remain at their desks in a way that demonstrates equality among all participants
- Monitoring student behavior during such discussions, calling attention to any inappropriate dialogue, use of stereotypes, or displays of intolerance the moment they occur

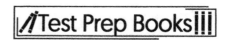

- Leading by example by treating all races, religions, cultures, genders and gender identities with tolerance and respect
- Beginning every discussion with a reminder to be accepting and tolerant of differing perspectives and beliefs and asserting that offensive language or behavior will not be tolerated

Listening

- Encouraging active listening by allowing students to take notes and ask questions
- Asking students to summarize what they heard
- Discouraging interruptions or non-verbal negative responses, such as eye-rolls, sighs, or noises of disgust, to reduce disrespectful behavior during discussion
- Allowing enough time for all students to speak so that others may listen and giving everyone an equal amount of time to speak without letting any one person dominate discussion

When an instructor is knowledgeable in a subject, demonstrates passion for the work, and creates an environment of respect, students will learn a great deal from him or her as a mentor, both in real-world situations and in academics.

Research-Based Approaches for Diverse Learners

Commonly Used Research-Based Strategies

For the vast majority of people, native language acquisition comes about naturally in childhood. From the time they are born, babies are usually surrounded by the language use of their parents or caregivers. The human brain is hardwired to learn language, meaning that babies do not have to put conscious effort into unraveling the intricacies of grammar or pronunciation; it is something that happens automatically as they are exposed to language. Furthermore, caregivers do not have to formally teach first language skills to babies.

First language acquisition in infancy and early childhood passes through several predictable stages. Babies begin by crying to express a range of emotions like hunger or discomfort. By the time they are two months old, they then begin cooing to convey other emotions, such as happiness and satisfaction. In later months, infants start to experiment with different sounds like babbling and gurgling by repeating simple syllables like "goo goo goo" and "ma ma ma" and show signs of comprehending certain full words. A baby's first word often occurs around one year of age, and for the next six months, the baby can conduct simple communication through one-word expressions like "Daddy," "milk," and "cat."

After they reach eighteen months, young children begin to use two- and three-word utterances to express more complex meaning, such as "Mommy go?" "Don't want to!" and "Where juice?" By the time they are two and a half years old, toddlers enter the telegraphic stage of language where they begin using the grammatical structure of their native language, although not without some problems. A common error is "I goed to school," instead of "I went to school." However, even though young children do make mistakes in their language usage, it is nevertheless remarkable that they achieve functional mastery of a language in such a short amount of time, generally without any formal instruction.

Although acquisition of a first language is largely a natural process of childhood development, *second language acquisition* in older children or adults is quite different. This is partially linked to the critical period hypothesis, which states that language acquisition only occurs readily and naturally during the first few years of life; language acquisition that happens later, perhaps after puberty, is much more difficult and less successful. Children who are not exposed to any language before the age of five or so will have extreme difficulty learning a language later. This seems to indicate that the brain is primed to learn language from birth, but this readiness quickly diminishes after the critical period has been passed.

Although scientists continue to debate the exact significance of a critical period on second language development, learning a second language later in life clearly presents different challenges than learning a first language. In linguistics, *L1* refers to a speaker's native language and *L2* refers to a second language.

L2 acquisition follows different stages from that of L1. L2 acquisition begins with *preproduction*, also known as the *silent stage*, during which the learner is exposed to the new language, but lacks the skills to communicate and may only use body language or other non-verbal expressions. During the early production stage, the L2 learner begins using simple expressions and has limited comprehension ability.

Next is *speech emergence*—the low-intermediate stage. At this point, the language learner can form simple sentences although he or she makes frequent errors in grammar and usage. L2 learners then pass to *intermediate fluency*, where they begin to gain skills in academic or idiomatic language, demonstrate a much higher level of comprehension, and make fewer mistakes in their expressions.

Finally, the learner reaches *advanced fluency*, exhibiting near-native expressive and comprehensive skills. It is worth noting that even with near-native skills, after many years of advanced fluency, L2 learners may continue to speak with a different accent or use certain idiosyncratic expressions that are markedly different from native speakers. Nevertheless, they are certainly fluent.

In 2013, the Census Bureau reported that one in five Americans are speaking a language other than English at home, so language arts instructors will encounter a mixture of native speakers and second language learners in the classroom. In both cases, though, certain goals and strategies remain the same. The purpose of a language arts class is not to teach students language from scratch, but rather to further develop their preexisting knowledge and increase their awareness of how to use language for more effective and meaningful communication.

For both native and non-native English speakers, the exposure to written and spoken language that they receive outside of school impacts their future performance in school. In a notable 1995 study, researchers observed children in low- and high-income families and found that those in high-income households were exposed to 30 million more words during their childhood than those from families on welfare. When researchers followed up on these children in third grade, those who had been exposed to more words early on showed greater success in measures of reading comprehension and vocabulary.

As the early stages of both L1 and L2 acquisition show, learners need language input before they can achieve language output. Providing students with a variety of language resources, both formally and informally, can give them valuable exposure to new means of expression. In class, this exposure can include daily assignments, a classroom library, or a bulletin board with news for students. Educators can also get students in the habit of accessing resources outside of the classroom such as visiting the school or public library, watching, reading, or listening to the news, or reading informally from magazines, blogs, or other sources of interest.

This exposure also relates to two different forms of vocabulary acquisition—through incidental learning or direct instruction. *Incidental learning* occurs when students naturally encounter new vocabulary in context during daily life whereas *direct instruction* occurs through structured lessons and assignments in an academic setting.

In vocabulary development in particular, when it comes to direct instruction, there are several approaches to teaching new words to students.

One is the *three-tier approach*, which states that vocabulary can be classified into three levels as shown in the graphic below.

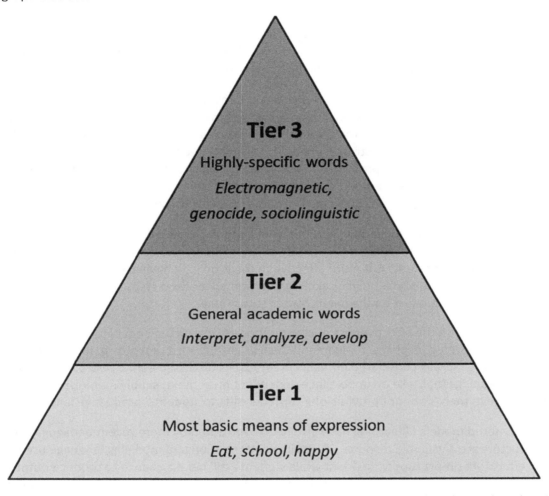

Tier 3

Highly-specific words

Electromagnetic, genocide, sociolinguistic

Tier 2

General academic words

Interpret, analyze, develop

Tier 1

Most basic means of expression

Eat, school, happy

Tier three words should be taught within the subjects that they are directly related to rather than in a language arts class. Instead, language arts instruction should focus on tier two words that are broadly applicable to a range of subjects and, therefore, more practical for students.

Another theory of vocabulary development is learning language through chunks or groups of related words. By learning words in context along with other connected words, students are better able to connect vocabulary to areas of prior knowledge and more effectively store new words in their long-term memory. Students also gain a more complete set of tools with which to form new expressions, rather than simply learning new words in isolation. Learning in *semantic chunks*—clusters of five to ten words forming a connected phrase or sentence—is particularly useful for L2 learners in gaining familiarity with how to manipulate vocabulary and combine words to build meaning.

Vocabulary learning can also be conducted through a variety of media, combining visual, auditory, and active cues. One strategy is known as the *total physical response*, where students learn to associate a word with a certain physical reaction. For example, in response to the word *circumference*, students might use their finger to draw a circle in the air. Students can also watch videos related to the vocabulary topic they are learning about or look at visual representations of new words through a picture dictionary. By activating different styles of learning, instructors can provide students with more opportunities to acquire new language skills.

Evaluating the Effectiveness of Specific Strategies

New research on teaching strategies is emerging all the time, and it is important for instructors to stay abreast of new developments while evaluating when and how to implement any changes in their classroom. Instructors should also consider the pros and cons of different approaches to teaching.

In terms of encouraging students to seek outside language resources (noted the section above), the effectiveness differs greatly depending on students' background and home life. Students who must work after school to support themselves or their families may not have much time to stop by the public library or to read for leisure; in this case, instructors need to maximize in-class instruction time. According to another strategy, the three-tier approach, tier two words are most important in a language arts classroom. However, some L2 students in the early production or intermediate fluency stages may lack basic tier one skills and struggle with understanding more advanced academic vocabulary.

Also, the integrated approach to learning vocabulary in a group of related words calls on instructors to present words as they are actually used in context, which might involve using some tier three words related to specific fields of study. Is it more effective to focus only on having a broad base of general vocabulary or to spend some time building skills in different specialized areas? This question might be answered differently depending on the needs of students in class.

As they experiment with the effectiveness of new methods of instruction, educators can also move beyond outdated learning practices. Assignments such as getting a list of words to look up in the dictionary are not generally considered effective methods. As discussed earlier, words contain a multitude of meanings that take on importance dependent on context; simply memorizing words outside of context, then, does not provide long-term benefits to students' productive language skills.

Instructor-centered models of learning have also been overturned by more recent pedagogical research. While instructors are a valuable resource of providing information and modeling language use for students, educators simply supply the input while students still need a chance to produce output. This means giving students ample opportunity to practice and apply new vocabulary, calling on students' prior knowledge when introducing new vocabulary, and demonstrating how students can use language skills outside of the classroom.

Interpreting Research and Applying it to Language Challenges

For instructors, pedagogical research is only as valuable as its real-life application in the classroom. Educators need to be able to use research-based strategies to tackle issues that arise while teaching.

One challenge may be the gap that exists between students who come to class with a high degree of literacy and language skills and students who have had fewer opportunities to develop those skills before entering the classroom. For example, some students have no access to a computer or the Internet at home or have a limited/nonexistent home library. Closing the gap through basic media literacy—perhaps in collaboration with a school media specialist—can empower students to know how to access language resources through the library, Internet, or other sources and how to utilize these resources for both learning and leisure. The concept of vocabulary development through incidental learning holds that students will benefit from any reading material, so instructors can encourage

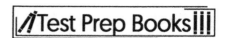

students to pursue their own interests through reading if they seem disinterested in textbook offerings. Asking students to keep a personal reading log or daily journal can encourage them to make reading and writing part of their everyday lives.

Another common problem in language instruction is students forgetting new vocabulary as soon as they learn it. Repetition and reinforcement is key to creating lasting knowledge. Also, as many studies point to the importance of learning vocabulary in context, utilizing contextual learning strategies can help students build onto prior knowledge rather than treat every new word as something strange and unfamiliar. This can be done by prompting students for what they already know when a new concept is introduced in class, introduce possible unfamiliar words that they might encounter in a text, and encourage them to use context clues as they read to make logical guesses about how unknown words are connected to known ones. These strategies further empower learners to utilize the knowledge that they already possess.

Incorporating multimedia resources can also be a powerful tool for providing meaningful instruction for students with a variety of learning styles. If students struggle to remember new vocabulary words, strategies such as total physical response or recognizing a picture associated with the word can provide students with different tools to secure information in their long-term memory.

In terms of research specific to L2 learning, knowledge of the stages of development can help instructors handle frustrations that may arise during second language learning. For example, teachers may worry that students understand nothing during the silent period, but students are absorbing the basic linguistic information that they will need to start forming utterances. Rather than giving up and getting discouraged from the start, instructors can continue providing basic communication information that students will be ready to use within the first few weeks or months of being exposed to a new language.

Identifying Dialect and Diction

Identifying Variation in Dialect and Diction

Language arts educators often seem to be in the position of teaching the "right" way to use English, particularly in lessons about grammar and vocabulary. However, all it takes is back-to-back viewings of speeches by the queen of England and the president of the United States or side-by-side readings of a contemporary poem and one written in the 1600s to come to the conclusion that there is no single, fixed, correct form of spoken or written English. Instead, language varies and evolves across different regions and time periods. It also varies between cultural groups depending on factors such as race, ethnicity, age, and socioeconomic status. Students should come away from a language arts class with more than a strictly prescriptive view of language; they should have an appreciation for its rich diversity.

It is important to understand some key terms in discussing linguistic variety.

Language is a tool for communication. It may be spoken, unspoken—as with body language—written, or codified in other ways. Language is symbolic in the sense that it can describe objects, ideas, and events that are not actually present, have not actually occurred, or only exist in the mind of the speaker. All languages are governed by systematic rules of grammar and semantics. These rules allow speakers to manipulate a finite number of elements, such as sounds or written symbols, to create an infinite number of meanings.

A *dialect* is a distinct variety of a language in terms of patterns of grammar, vocabulary, and/or *phonology*—the sounds used by its speakers—that distinguish it from other forms of that language. Two dialects are not considered separate languages if they are *mutually intelligible*—if speakers of each dialect are able to understand one another. A dialect is not a subordinate version of a language. Examples of English dialects include Scottish English and American Southern English.

By definition, *Standard English* is a dialect. It is one variety of English with its own usage of grammar, vocabulary, and pronunciation. Given that Standard English is taught in schools and used in places like government, journalism, and other professional workplaces, it is often elevated above other English dialects. Linguistically, though, there is nothing that makes Standard English more correct or advanced than other dialects.

A *pidgin* is formed when speakers of different languages begin utilizing a simplified mixture of elements from both languages to communicate with each other. In North America, pidgins occurred when Africans were brought to European colonies as slaves, leading to a mixture of African and European languages. Historically, pidgins also sprung up in areas of international trade. A pidgin is communication born of necessity and lacks the full complexity or standardized rules that govern a language.

When a pidgin becomes widely used and is taught to children as their native language, it becomes a *Creole*. An example is Haitian Creole, a language based on French and including elements of West African languages.

An *accent* is a unique speech pattern, particularly in terms of tone or intonation. Speakers from different regions tend to have different accents, as do learners of English from different native languages. In some cases, accents are mutually intelligible, but in other cases, speakers with different accents might have some difficulty in understanding one another.

Colloquial language is language that is used conversationally or familiarly—e.g., "What's up?"—in contrast to formal, professional, or academic language—"How are you this evening?"

Vernacular refers to the native, everyday language of a place. Historically, for instance, Bibles and religious services across Europe were primarily offered in Latin, even centuries after the fall of the Roman Empire. After the revolution of the printing press and the widespread availability of vernacular translations of the Bible in the fifteenth and sixteenth centuries, everyday citizens were able to study from Bibles in their own language without needing specialized training in Latin.

A *regionalism* is a word or expression used in a particular region. In the United States, for instance, examples of regionalisms might be *soda, pop,* or *Coke*—terms that vary in popularity according to region.

Jargon is vocabulary used within a specialized field, such as computer programming or mechanics. Jargon may consist of specialized words or of everyday words that have a different meaning in this specialized context.

Slang refers to non-standard expressions that are not used in elevated speech and writing. Slang creates linguistic in-groups and out-groups of people, those who can understand the slang terms and those who can't. Slang is often tied to a specific time period. For example, "groovy" and "far out" are connected to the 1970s, and "as if!" and "4-1-1-" are connected to the 1990s.

A language arts classroom should demonstrate the history and evolution of language, rather than presenting fixed, unchangeable linguistic regulations. Particularly for students who feel intimidated or excluded by Standard English, instructors can make lessons more relatable or inclusive by allowing students to share or explore their own patterns of language. Students can be encouraged to act as linguists or anthropologists by getting involved in projects. Some examples include asking them to identify and compare slang in their generation to slang from their parents' generation, to exchange information about their dialect with students who come from different cultural backgrounds, or to conduct a linguistic survey of their friends, family, or neighbors. Language arts class can also be integrated with history topics by having students research unfamiliar slang or words that have shifted in meaning from the past until now—a type of study particularly useful when reading a text from a past era.

Understanding Dialect and its Appropriateness

While students should come away from class feeling supported in their linguistic diversity, the reality is that certain forms of language are viewed differently depending on the context. Lessons learned in the classroom have a real-life application to a student's future, so he or she should know where, when, and how to utilize different forms of language.

For students preparing for college, knowledge of the conventions of Standard English is essential. The same is true for students who plan to enter professional job fields. Without necessarily having a word for it, many students are already familiar with the concept of *code-switching*—altering speech patterns depending upon context. For example, a person might use a different accent or slang with neighborhood friends than with coworkers or pick up new vocabulary and speech patterns after moving to a new region, either unconsciously or consciously. In this way, speakers have an innate understanding of how their language use helps them fit into any given situation.

Instructors can design activities that help students pay attention to their language use in a given context. When discussing a novel in class, students might be encouraged to spend a few minutes freewriting in a journal to generate ideas and express their unedited thoughts. Later, though, students will then be asked to present those thoughts in a formal writing assignment that requires adherence to Standard English grammar, employing academic vocabulary and expressions appropriate to literary discussions. Alternatively, students might design an advertisement that appeals to teenagers and another one that appeals to adults, utilizing different language in each. In this way, students can learn how to reformulate their thoughts using the language appropriate to the task at hand.

Awareness of dialect can also help students as readers, too. Many writers of literary fiction and nonfiction utilize dialect and colloquialisms to add verisimilitude to their writing. This is especially true for authors who focus on a particular region or cultural group in their works, also known as *regionalism* or *local color literature*. Examples include Zora Neale Hurston's *Their Eyes Were Watching God* and the short stories of Kate Chopin. Students can be asked to consider how the speech patterns in a text affect a reader's understanding of the characters—how the pattern reflects a character's background and place in society. They might consider a reader's impression of the region—how similar or different it is from the reader's region or what can be inferred about the region based on how people speak. In some cases, unfamiliar dialect may be very difficult for readers to understand on the page but becomes much more intelligible when read aloud—as in the reading of Shakespeare.

Reading passages together in class and then finding recordings or videos of the dialect presented in the text can help familiarize students with different speech patterns. And of course, students should also consider how use of dialect affects the audience or if it is directed to a specific audience. Who was the intended audience for *Their Eyes Were Watching God*, a novel that recreates the speech patterns of African Americans in early 1900s Florida? How might the novel be understood differently by readers who recognize that dialect than by readers who are encountering it for the first time? What would be

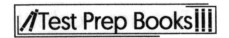

lost if the characters didn't converse in their local dialect? Being alert to these questions creates students who are attuned to the nuances of language use in everyday life.

The Structure and Development of the English Language

Word Parts

By analyzing and understanding Latin, Greek, and Anglo-Saxon word roots, prefixes, and suffixes one can better understand word meanings. Of course, people can always look words up if a dictionary or thesaurus, if available, but meaning can often be gleaned on the spot if the writer learns to dissect and examine words.

A word can consist of the following:

> root
> root + suffix
> prefix + root
> prefix + root + suffix

For example, if someone was unfamiliar with the word *submarine* they could break the word into its parts.

> prefix + root
> sub + marine

It can be determined that *sub* means *below* as in *subway* and *subpar*. Additionally, one can determine that *marine* refers to *the sea* as in *marine life*. Thus, it can be figured that *submarine* refers to something below the water.

Roots

Roots are the basic components of words. Many roots can stand alone as individual words, but others must be combined with a prefix or suffix to be a word. For example, *calc* is a root but it needs a suffix to be an actual word (*calcium*).

Greek, Latin, and Anglo-Saxon Roots

Understanding the meaning of a part of a word can aid in understanding the meaning of the entire word. Knowledge of Greek, Latin, and Anglo-Saxon roots and affixes can help students to decode the meaning of unfamiliar words and build vocabulary. Some examples follow:

Greek Root	Meaning	Latin Root	Meaning	Anglo-Saxon Root	Meaning
cosm	universe	bene	good	ber	carry
dec	ten	clar	clear	kno	skill
macro	large	ject	throw	tru	faithful
poli	city	mot	move	ward	guard

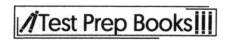

Prefixes

A *prefix* is a word, letter, or number that is placed before another. It adjusts or qualifies the root word's meaning. When written alone, prefixes are followed by a dash to indicate that the root word follows. Some of the most common prefixes are the following:

Prefix	Meaning	Example
dis-	not or opposite of	disabled
in-, im-, il-, ir-	not	illiterate
re-	again	return
un-	not	unpredictable
anti-	against	antibacterial
fore-	before	forefront
mis-	wrongly	misunderstand
non-	not	nonsense
over-	more than normal	overabundance
pre-	before	preheat
super-	above	superman

Suffixes

A suffix is a letter or group of letters added at the end of a word to form another word. The word created from the root and suffix is either a different tense of the same root (*help* + *ed* = *helped*) or a new word (*help* + *ful* = *helpful*). When written alone, suffixes are preceded by a dash to indicate that the root word comes before.

Some of the most common prefixes are the following:

Suffix	Meaning	Example
-ed	makes a verb past tense	wash*ed*
-ing	makes a verb a present participle verb	wash*ing*
-ly	to make characteristic of	love*ly*
-s/es	to make more than one	chair*s*, box*es*
-able	can be done	deplor*able*
-al	having characteristics of	comic*al*
-est	comparative	great*est*
-ful	full of	wonder*ful*
-ism	belief in	commun*ism*
-less	without	faith*less*
-ment	action or process	accomplish*ment*
-ness	state of	happi*ness*
-ize, -ise	to render, to make	steril*ize*, advert*ise*
-cede/ceed/sede	go	con*cede*, pro*ceed*, super*sede*

Here are some helpful tips:

- When adding a suffix that starts with a vowel (for example, *-ed*) to a one-syllable root whose vowel has a short sound and ends in a consonant (for example, *stun*), double the final consonant of the root (*n*).

  stun + ed = stun*n*ed

- Exception: If the past tense verb ends in *x* such as *box*, do not double the *x*.

  box + ed = boxed

- If adding a suffix that starts with a vowel (*-er*) to a multi-syllable word ending in a consonant (*begin*), double the consonant (*n*).

  begin + er = begin*n*er

- If a short vowel is followed by two or more consonants in a word such as *i+t+c+h = itch*, do <u>not</u> double the last consonant.

  itch + ed = itched

- If adding a suffix that starts with a vowel (*-ing*) to a word ending in *e* (for example, *name*), that word's final *e* is generally (but not always) dropped.

  name + ing = naming

  exception: manage + able = manag*e*able

- If adding a suffix that starts with a consonant (-*ness*) to a word ending in *e* (*complete*), the *e* generally (but not always) remains.

    complete + ness = completeness

    exception: judge + ment = judgment

- There is great diversity on handling words that end in *y*. For words ending in a vowel + y, nothing changes in the original word.

    play + ed = played

- For words ending in a consonant + *y*, change the *y* to *i* when adding any suffix except for –*ing*.

    marry + ed = married
    marry + ing = marrying

Context Clues

Context clues help readers understand unfamiliar words, and thankfully, there are many types.

Synonyms are words or phrases that have nearly, if not exactly, the same meaning as other words or phrases

    Large boxes are needed to pack *big* items.

Antonyms are words or phrases that have opposite definitions. Antonyms, like synonyms, can serve as context clues, although more cryptically.

    Large boxes are not needed to pack *small* items.

Definitions are sometimes included within a sentence to define uncommon words.

    They practiced the *rumba*, a *type of dance*, for hours on end.

Explanations provide context through elaboration.

    Large boxes holding items weighing over 60 pounds were stacked in the corner.

Here's an example of *contrast*:

    These *minute* creatures were much different than the *huge* mammals that the zoologist was accustomed to dealing with.

Word Usage

Word usage: the way and manner in which writers choose to use words (or phrases). This is a vital consideration in order to create excellence in writing. Context plays a role in the selection of words, as does simple choice.

Correct word usage can be as basic and imperative as making the right grammatical choice.

> Incorrect: I never *seen* that play
> Correct: I never *saw* that play.

Seen (past participle of see) in place of *saw* (the correct past tense of *see*) is a relatively common and grievous mistake.

> Incorrect: *There* going to the store with *there* parents.
> Correct: *They're* going to the store with *their* parents.

There (adverb) mistaken for *they're* (contraction for "they are") and *there* (adverb) for *their* (pronoun) are also frequent grammatical errors.

Correct word usage can be as simple as choosing between synonyms. For instance, determining whether to say *for instance* or *for example*! Would it be better to use the word *incongruous* or *inappropriate* for *unsuited,* or when the woman is *uncouth,* would *redneck, uninformed,* or *illiterate* better define her?

Correct word usage can also be as simple as knowing how to access and make good use of dictionaries, thesauruses, grammar correction software, and search engines on computers, tablets, and smartphones.

Understanding the Effect of Word Choice

An author's choice of words—also referred to as *diction*—helps to convey his or her meaning in a particular way. Through diction, an author can convey a particular tone—e.g., a humorous tone, a serious tone—in order to support the thesis in a meaningful way to the reader.

Connotation and Denotation

Connotation is when an author chooses words or phrases that invoke ideas or feelings other than their literal meaning. An example of the use of connotation is the word *cheap,* which suggests something is poor in value or negatively describes a person as reluctant to spend money. When something or someone is described this way, the reader is more inclined to have a particular image or feeling about it or him/her. Thus, connotation can be a very effective language tool in creating emotion and swaying opinion. However, connotations are sometimes hard to pin down because varying emotions can be associated with a word. Generally, though, connotative meanings tend to be fairly consistent within a specific cultural group.

Denotation refers to words or phrases that mean exactly what they say. It is helpful when a writer wants to present hard facts or vocabulary terms with which readers may be unfamiliar. Some examples of denotation are the words *inexpensive* and *frugal*. *Inexpensive* refers to the cost of something, not its value, and *frugal* indicates that a person is conscientiously watching his or her spending. These terms do not elicit the same emotions that *cheap* does.

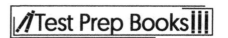

Authors sometimes choose to use both, but what they choose and when they use it is what critical readers need to differentiate. One method isn't inherently better than the other; however, one may create a better effect, depending upon an author's intent. If, for example, an author's purpose is to inform, to instruct, and to familiarize readers with a difficult subject, his or her use of connotation may be helpful. However, it may also undermine credibility and confuse readers. An author who wants to create a credible, scholarly effect in his or her text would most likely use denotation, which emphasizes literal, factual meaning and examples.

Technical Language
Test takers and critical readers alike should be very aware of technical language used within informational text. *Technical language* refers to terminology that is specific to a particular industry and is best understood by those specializing in that industry. This language is fairly easy to differentiate, since it will most likely be unfamiliar to readers. It's critical to be able to define technical language either by the author's written definition, through the use of an included glossary—if offered—or through context clues that help readers clarify word meaning.

Understanding the Conventions of Standard English

Parts of Speech
The English language has eight parts of speech, each serving a different grammatical function.

Verb
Verbs describe an action—e.g., *run, play, eat*—or a state of being—e.g., *is, are, was*. It is impossible to make a grammatically-complete sentence without a verb.

He *runs* to the store.

She *is* eight years old.

Noun

Nouns can be a person, place, or thing. They can refer to concrete objects—e.g., chair, apple, house—or abstract things—love, knowledge, friendliness.

Look at the *dog*!

Where are my *keys*?

Some nouns are *countable*, meaning they can be counted as separate entities—one chair, two chairs, three chairs. They can be either singular or plural. Other nouns, usually substances or concepts, are *uncountable*—e.g., air, information, wealth—and some nouns can be both countable and uncountable depending on how they are used.

I bought three *dresses*.

Respect is important to me.

I ate way too much *food* last night.

At the international festival, you can sample *foods* from around the world.

Proper nouns are the specific names of people, places, or things and are almost always capitalized.

Marie Curie studied at the *Flying University* in *Warsaw, Poland*.

Pronoun

Pronouns function as substitutes for nouns or noun phrases. Pronouns are often used to avoid constant repetition of a noun or to simplify sentences. *Personal pronouns* are used for people. Some pronouns are *subject pronouns*; they are used to replace the subject in a sentence—I, we, he, she, they.

Is *he* your friend?

We work together.

Object pronouns can function as the object of a sentence—me, us, him, her, them.

Give the documents to *her*.

Did you call *him* back yet?

Some pronouns can function as either the subject or the object—e.g., you, it. The subject of a sentence is the noun of the sentence that is doing or being something.

You should try it.

It tastes great.

Possessive pronouns indicate ownership. They can be used alone—mine, yours, his, hers, theirs, ours—or with a noun—my, your, his, her, their, ours. In the latter case, they function as a determiner, which is described in detail in the below section on adjectives.

This table is *ours*.

I can't find *my* phone!

Reflexive pronouns refer back to the person being spoken or written about. These pronouns end in -*self/-selves.*

> I've heard that New York City is gorgeous in the autumn, but I've never seen it for *myself.*

> After moving away from home, young people have to take care of *themselves.*

Indefinite pronouns are used for things that are unknown or unspecified. Some examples are *anybody, something,* and *everything.*

> I'm looking for *someone* who knows how to fix computers.

> I wanted to buy some shoes today, but I couldn't find *any* that I liked.

Adjective

An adjective modifies a noun, making it more precise or giving more information about it. Adjectives answer these questions: What kind? Which one?

> I just bought a *red* car.

> I don't like *cold* weather.

One special type of word that modifies a noun is a *determiner.* In fact, some grammarians classify determiners as a separate part of speech because whereas adjectives simply describe additional qualities of a noun, a determiner is often a necessary part of a noun phrase, without which the phrase is grammatically incomplete. A determiner indicates whether a noun is definite or indefinite, and can identify which noun is being discussed. It also introduces context to the noun in terms of quantity and possession. The most commonly-used determiners are articles—a, an, the.

> I ordered *a* pizza.

> She lives in *the* city.

Possessive pronouns discussed above, such as *my, your,* and *our,* are also determiners, along with *demonstratives*—this, that—and *quantifiers*—much, many, some. These determiners can take the place of an article.

> Are you using *this* chair?

> I need *some* coffee!

Adverb

Adverbs modify verbs, adjectives, and other adverbs. Words that end in –ly are usually adverbs. Adverbs answer these questions: When? Where? In what manner? To what degree?

> She talks *quickly.*

> The mountains are *incredibly* beautiful!

> The students arrived *early.*

Please take your phone call *outside*.

Preposition

Prepositions show the relationship between different elements in a phrase or sentence and connect nouns or pronouns to other words in the sentence. Some examples of prepositions are words such as *after, at, behind, by, during, from, in, on, to,* and *with*.

Let's go *to* class.

Starry Night was painted *by* Vincent van Gogh *in* 1889.

Conjunction

Conjunctions join words, phrases, clauses, or sentences together, indicating the type of connection between these elements.

I like pizza, *and* I enjoy spaghetti.

I like to play baseball, *but* I'm allergic to mitts.

Some conjunctions are *coordinating*, meaning they give equal emphasis to two main clauses. Coordinating conjunctions are short, simple words that can be remembered using the mnemonic FANBOYS: for, and, nor, but, or, yet, so. Other conjunctions are *subordinating*. Subordinating conjunctions introduce dependent clauses and include words such as *because, since, before, after, if,* and *while*.

Interjection

An *interjection* is a short word that shows greeting or emotion. Examples of interjections include *wow, ouch, hey, oops, alas,* and *hey*.

Wow! Look at that sunset!

Was it your birthday yesterday? *Oops*! I forgot.

Errors in Standard English Grammar, Usage, Syntax, and Mechanics
Sentence Fragments

A *complete sentence* requires a verb and a subject that expresses a complete thought. Sometimes, the subject is omitted in the case of the implied *you*, used in sentences that are the command or imperative form—e.g., "Look!" or "Give me that." It is understood that the subject of the command is *you*, the listener or reader, so it is possible to have a structure without an explicit subject. Without these elements, though, the sentence is incomplete—it is a *sentence fragment*. While sentence fragments often occur in conversational English or creative writing, they are generally not appropriate in academic writing. Sentence fragments often occur when dependent clauses are not joined to an independent clause:

Sentence fragment: Because the airline overbooked the flight.

The sentence above is a dependent clause that does not express a complete thought. What happened as a result of this cause? With the addition of an independent clause, this now becomes a complete sentence:

Complete sentence: Because the airline overbooked the flight, several passengers were unable to board.

Sentences fragments may also occur through improper use of conjunctions:

I'm going to the Bahamas for spring break. And to New York City for New Year's Eve.

While the first sentence above is a complete sentence, the second one is not because it is a prepositional phrase that lacks a subject [I] and a verb [am going]. Joining the two together with the coordinating conjunction forms one grammatically-correct sentence:

I'm going to the Bahamas for spring break and to New York City for New Year's Eve.

Run-ons

A *run-on* is a sentence with too many independent clauses that are improperly connected to each other:

This winter has been very cold some farmers have suffered damage to their crops.

The sentence above has two subject-verb combinations. The first is "this winter has been"; the second is "some farmers have suffered." However, they are simply stuck next to each other without any punctuation or conjunction. Therefore, the sentence is a run-on.

Another type of run-on occurs when writers use inappropriate punctuation:

This winter has been very cold, some farmers have suffered damage to their crops.

Though a comma has been added, this sentence is still not correct. When a comma alone is used to join two independent clauses, it is known as a **comma splice**. Without an appropriate conjunction, a comma cannot join two independent clauses by itself.

Run-on sentences can be corrected by either dividing the independent clauses into two or more separate sentences or inserting appropriate conjunctions and/or punctuation. The run-on sentence can be amended by separating each subject-verb pair into its own sentence:

This winter has been very cold. Some farmers have suffered damage to their crops.

The run-on can also be fixed by adding a comma and conjunction to join the two independent clauses with each other:

This winter has been very cold, so some farmers have suffered damage to their crops.

Parallelism

Parallel structure occurs when phrases or clauses within a sentence contain the same structure. Parallelism increases readability and comprehensibility because it is easy to tell which sentence elements are paired with each other in meaning.

Jennifer enjoys cooking, knitting, and to spend time with her cat.

This sentence is not parallel because the items in the list appear in two different forms. Some are *gerunds*, which is the verb + ing: *cooking, knitting*. The other item uses the *infinitive* form, which is to + verb: *to spend*. To create parallelism, all items in the list may reflect the same form:

> Jennifer enjoys cooking, knitting, and spending time with her cat.

All of the items in the list are now in gerund forms, so this sentence exhibits parallel structure. Here's another example:

> The company is looking for employees who are responsible and with a lot of experience.

Again, the items that are listed in this sentence are not parallel. "Responsible" is an adjective, yet "with a lot of experience" is a prepositional phrase. The sentence elements do not utilize parallel parts of speech.

> The company is looking for employees who are responsible and experienced.

"Responsible" and "experienced" are both adjectives, so this sentence now has parallel structure.

Dangling and Misplaced Modifiers

Modifiers enhance meaning by clarifying or giving greater detail about another part of a sentence. However, incorrectly-placed modifiers have the opposite effect and can cause confusion. A *misplaced modifier* is a modifier that is not located appropriately in relation to the word or phrase that it modifies:

> Because he was one of the greatest thinkers of Renaissance Italy, John idolized Leonardo da Vinci.

In this sentence, the modifier is "because he was one of the greatest thinkers of Renaissance Italy," and the noun it is intended to modify is "Leonardo da Vinci." However, due to the placement of the modifier next to the subject, John, it seems as if the sentence is stating that John was a Renaissance genius, not Da Vinci.

> John idolized Leonard da Vinci because he was one of the greatest thinkers of Renaissance Italy.

The modifier is now adjacent to the appropriate noun, clarifying which of the two men in this sentence is the greatest thinker.

Dangling modifiers modify a word or phrase that is not readily apparent in the sentence. That is, they "dangle" because they are not clearly attached to anything:

> After getting accepted to college, Amir's parents were proud.

The modifier here, "after getting accepted to college," should modify who got accepted. The noun immediately following the modifier is "Amir's parents"—but they are probably not the ones who are going to college.

> After getting accepted to college, Amir made his parents proud.

The subject of the sentence has been changed to Amir himself, and now the subject and its modifier are appropriately matched.

Inconsistent Verb Tense

Verb tense reflects when an action occurred or a state existed. For example, the tense known as *simple present* expresses something that is happening right now or that happens regularly:

> She *works* in a hospital.

Present continuous tense expresses something in progress. It is formed by to be + verb + -ing.

> Sorry, I can't go out right now. I *am doing* my homework.

Past tense is used to describe events that previously occurred. However, in conversational English, speakers often use present tense or a mix of past and present tense when relating past events because it gives the narrative a sense of immediacy. In formal written English, though, consistency in verb tense is necessary to avoid reader confusion.

> I traveled to Europe last summer. As soon as I stepped off the plane, I feel like I'm in a movie! I'm surrounded by quaint cafes and impressive architecture.

The passage above abruptly switches from past tense—*traveled, stepped*—to present tense—*feel, am surrounded*.

> I *traveled* to Europe last summer. As soon as I *stepped* off the plane, I *felt* like I was in a movie! I *was surrounded* by quaint cafes and impressive architecture.

All verbs are in past tense, so this passage now has consistent verb tense.

Split Infinitives

The *infinitive form* of a verb consists of "to + base verb"—e.g., to walk, to sleep, to approve. A *split infinitive* occurs when another word, usually an adverb, is placed between *to* and the verb:

> I decided *to simply walk* to work to get more exercise every day.

The infinitive *to walk* is split by the adverb *simply*.

> It was a mistake *to hastily approve* the project before conducting further preliminary research.

The infinitive *to approve* is split by *hastily*.

Although some grammarians still advise against split infinitives, this syntactic structure is common in both spoken and written English and is widely accepted in standard usage.

Subject-Verb Agreement

In English, verbs must agree with the subject. The form of a verb may change depending on whether the subject is singular or plural, or whether it is first, second, or third person. For example, the verb *to be* has various forms:

> I <u>am</u> a student.

> You <u>are</u> a student.

She <u>is</u> a student.

We <u>are</u> students.

They <u>are</u> students.

Errors occur when a verb does not agree with its subject. Sometimes, the error is readily apparent:

We is hungry.

Is is not the appropriate form of *to be* when used with the third person plural *we*.

We are hungry.

This sentence now has correct subject-verb agreement.

However, some cases are trickier, particularly when the subject consists of a lengthy noun phrase with many modifiers:

Students who are hoping to accompany the anthropology department on its annual summer trip to Ecuador needs to sign up by March 31st.

The verb in this sentence is *needs*. However, its subject is not the noun adjacent to it—Ecuador. The subject is the noun at the beginning of the sentence—students. Because *students* is plural, *needs* is the incorrect verb form.

Students who are hoping to accompany the anthropology department on its annual summer trip to Ecuador *need* to sign up by March 31st.

This sentence now uses correct agreement between *students* and *need*.

Another case to be aware of is a *collective noun*. A collective noun refers to a group of many things or people but can be singular in itself—e.g., family, committee, army, pair team, council, jury. Whether or not a collective noun uses a singular or plural verb depends on how the noun is being used. If the noun refers to the group performing a collective action as one unit, it should use a singular verb conjugation:

The family is moving to a new neighborhood.

The whole family is moving together in unison, so the singular verb form *is* is appropriate here.

The committee has made its decision.

The verb *has* and the possessive pronoun *its* both reflect the word *committee* as a singular noun in the sentence above; however, when a collective noun refers to the group as individuals, it can take a plural verb:

The newlywed pair spend every moment together.

This sentence emphasizes the love between two people in a pair, so it can use the plural verb *spend*.

The council are all newly elected members.

The sentence refers to the council in terms of its individual members and uses the plural verb *are*.

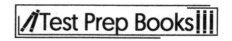

Overall though, American English is more likely to pair a collective noun with a singular verb, while British English is more likely to pair a collective noun with a plural verb.

Grammar, Usage, Syntax, and Mechanics Choices
Colons and Semicolons

In a sentence, *colons* are used before a list, a summary or elaboration, or an explanation related to the preceding information in the sentence:

> There are two ways to reserve tickets for the performance: by phone or in person.

> One thing is clear: students are spending more on tuition than ever before.

As these examples show, a colon must be preceded by an independent clause. However, the information after the colon may be in the form of an independent clause or in the form of a list.

Semicolons can be used in two different ways—to join ideas or to separate them. In some cases, semicolons can be used to connect what would otherwise be stand-alone sentences. Each part of the sentence joined by a semicolon must be an independent clause. The use of a semicolon indicates that these two independent clauses are closely related to each other:

> The rising cost of childcare is one major stressor for parents; healthcare expenses are another source of anxiety.

> Classes have been canceled due to the snowstorm; check the school website for updates.

Semicolons can also be used to divide elements of a sentence in a more distinct way than simply using a comma. This usage is particularly useful when the items in a list are especially long and complex and contain other internal punctuation.

> Retirees have many modes of income: some survive solely off their retirement checks; others supplement their income through part time jobs, like working in a supermarket or substitute teaching; and others are financially dependent on the support of family members, friends, and spouses.

Its and It's
These pronouns are some of the most confused in the English language as most possessives contain the suffix –'s. However, for *it*, it is the opposite. *Its* is a possessive pronoun:

> The government is reassessing *its* spending plan.

It's is a contraction of the words *it is*:

> *It's* snowing outside.

Saw and Seen
Saw and *seen* are both conjugations of the verb *to see*, but they express different verb tenses. *Saw* is used in the simple past tense. *Seen* is the past participle form of *to see* and can be used in all perfect tenses.

> I seen her yesterday.

This sentence is incorrect. Because it expresses a completed event from a specified point in time in the past, it should use simple past tense:

I *saw* her yesterday.

This sentence uses the correct verb tense. Here's how the past participle is used correctly:

I *have seen* her before.

The meaning in this sentence is slightly changed to indicate an event from an unspecific time in the past. In this case, present perfect is the appropriate verb tense to indicate an unspecified past experience. Present perfect conjugation is created by combining *to have* + past participle.

Then and Than

Then is generally used as an adverb indicating something that happened next in a sequence or as the result of a conditional situation:

We parked the car and *then* walked to the restaurant.

If enough people register for the event, *then* we can begin planning.

Than is a conjunction indicating comparison:

This watch is more expensive *than* that one.

The bus departed later *than* I expected.

They're, Their, and There

They're is a contraction of the words *they are*:

They're moving to Ohio next week.

Their is a possessive pronoun:

The baseball players are training for *their* upcoming season.

There can function as multiple parts of speech, but it is most commonly used as an adverb indicating a location:

Let's go to the concert! Some great bands are playing *there*.

Insure and Ensure

These terms are both verbs. *Insure* means to guarantee something against loss, harm, or damage, usually through an insurance policy that offers monetary compensation:

The robbers made off with her prized diamond necklace, but luckily it was *insured* for one million dollars.

Ensure means to make sure, to confirm, or to be certain:

Ensure that you have your passport before entering the security checkpoint.

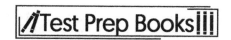

Accept and Except

Accept is a verb meaning to take or agree to something:

> I would like to *accept* your offer of employment.

Except is a preposition that indicates exclusion:

> I've been to every state in America *except* Hawaii.

Affect and Effect

Affect is a verb meaning to influence or to have an impact on something:

> The amount of rainfall during the growing season *affects* the flavor of wine produced from these grapes.

Effect can be used as either a noun or a verb. As a noun, *effect* is synonymous with a result:

> If we implement the changes, what will the *effect* be on our profits?

As a verb, *effect* means to bring about or to make happen:

> In just a few short months, the healthy committee has *effected* real change in school nutrition.

Components of Sentences

Clauses

Clauses contain a subject and a verb. An *independent clause* can function as a complete sentence on its own, but it might also be one component of a longer sentence. *Dependent clauses* cannot stand alone as complete sentences. They rely on independent clauses to complete their meaning. Dependent clauses usually begin with a subordinating conjunction. Independent and dependent clauses are sometimes also referred to as *main clauses* and *subordinate clauses*, respectively. The following structure highlights the differences:

> Apiculturists raise honeybees because they love insects.

Apiculturists raise honeybees is an independent or main clause. The subject is *apiculturists*, and the verb is *raise*. It expresses a complete thought and could be a standalone sentence.

Because they love insects is a dependent or subordinate clause. If it were not attached to the independent clause, it would be a sentence fragment. While it contains a subject and verb—*they love*—this clause is dependent because it begins with the subordinate conjunction *because*. Thus, it does not express a complete thought on its own.

Another type of clause is a *relative clause*, and it is sometimes referred to as an *adjective clause* because it gives further description about the noun. A relative clause begins with a *relative pronoun*: *that, which, who, whom, whichever, whomever,* or *whoever*. It may also begin with a *relative adverb*: *where, why,* or *when*. Here's an example of a relative clause, functioning as an adjective:

> The strawberries that I bought yesterday are already beginning to spoil.

Here, the relative clause is *that I bought yesterday*; the relative pronoun is *that*. The subject is *I*, and the verb is *bought*. The clause modifies the subject *strawberries* by answering the question, "Which strawberries?" Here's an example of a relative clause with an adverb:

The tutoring center is a place where students can get help with homework.

The relative clause is *where students can get help with homework*, and it gives more information about a place by describing what kind of place it is. It begins with the relative adverb *where* and contains the noun *students* along with its verb phrase *can get*.

Relative clauses may be further divided into two types: essential or nonessential. *Essential clauses* contain identifying information without which the sentence would lose significant meaning or not make sense. These are also sometimes referred to as *restrictive clauses*. The sentence above contains an example of an essential relative clause. Here is what happens when the clause is removed:

The tutoring center is a place where students can get help with homework.

The tutoring center is a place.

Without the relative clause, the sentence loses the majority of its meaning; thus, the clause is essential or restrictive.

Nonessential clauses—also referred to as *non-restrictive clauses*—offer additional information about a noun in the sentence, but they do not significantly control the overall meaning of the sentence. The following example indicates a nonessential clause:

New York City, which is located in the northeastern part of the country, is the most populated city in America.

New York City is the most populated city in America.

Even without the relative clause, the sentence is still understandable and continues to communicate its central message about New York City. Thus, it is a nonessential clause.

Punctuation differs between essential and nonessential relative clauses, too. Nonessential clauses are set apart from the sentence using commas whereas essential clauses are not separated with commas. Also, the relative pronoun *that* is generally used for essential clauses, while *which* is used for nonessential clauses. The following examples clarify this distinction:

Romeo and Juliet is my favorite play *that Shakespeare wrote*.

The relative clause *that Shakespeare wrote* contains essential, controlling information about the noun *play*, limiting it to those plays by Shakespeare. Without it, it would seem that *Romeo and Juliet* is the speaker's favorite play out of every play ever written, not simply from Shakespeare's repertoire.

Romeo and Juliet, which Shakespeare wrote, is my favorite play.

Here, the nonessential relative clause—"which Shakespeare wrote"—modifies *Romeo and Juliet*. It doesn't provide controlling information about the play, but simply offers further background details. Thus, commas are needed.

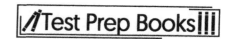

Phrases

Phrases are groups of words that do not contain the subject-verb combination required for clauses. Phrases are classified by the part of speech that begins or controls the phrase.

A *noun phrase* consists of a noun and all its modifiers—adjectives, adverbs, and determiners. Noun phrases can serve many functions in a sentence, acting as subjects, objects, and object complements:

> *The shallow yellow bowl* sits on the top shelf.

> Nina just bought *some incredibly fresh organic produce.*

Prepositional phrases are made up of a preposition and its object. The object of a preposition might be a noun, noun phrase, pronoun, or gerund. Prepositional phrases may function as either an adjective or an adverb:

> Jack picked up the book *in front of him.*

The prepositional phrase *in front of him* acts as an adjective indicating which book Jack picked up.

> The dog ran into the back yard.

The phrase *into the backyard* describes where the dog ran, so it acts as an adverb.

Verb phrases include all of the words in a verb group, even if they are not directly adjacent to each other:

> I *should have woken up* earlier this morning.

> The company **is** now *offering* membership discounts for new enrollers.

This sentence's verb phrase is *is offering.* Even though they are separated by the word *now*, they function together as a single verb phrase.

Structures of Sentences

All sentences contain the same basic elements: a subject and a verb. The *subject* is who or what the sentence is about; the *verb* describes the subject's action or condition. However, these elements, subjects and verbs, can be combined in different ways. The following graphic describes the different types of sentence structures.

Sentence Structure	Independent Clauses	Dependent Clauses
Simple	1	0
Compound	2 or more	0
Complex	1	1 or more
Compound-Complex	2 or more	1 or more

A *simple sentence* expresses a complete thought and consists of one subject and verb combination:

> The children ate pizza.

The subject is *children*. The verb is *ate*.

Either the subject or the verb may be *compound*—that is, it could have more than one element:

> *The children and their parents* ate pizza.

> The children *ate pizza and watched a movie.*

All of these are still simple sentences. Despite having either compound subjects or compound verbs, each sentence still has only one subject and verb combination.

Compound sentences combine two or more simple sentences to form one sentence that has multiple subject-verb combinations:

> *The children ate pizza,* and *their parents watched a movie.*

This structure is comprised of two independent clauses: (1) *the children ate pizza* and (2) *their parents watched a movie.* Compound sentences join different subject-verb combinations using a comma and a coordinating conjunction.

> I called my mom, *but* she didn't answer the phone.

> The weather was stormy, *so* we canceled our trip to the beach.

A *complex sentence* consists of an independent clause and one or more dependent clauses. Dependent clauses join a sentence using *subordinating conjunctions*. Some examples of subordinating conjunctions are *although, unless, as soon as, since, while, when, because, if,* and *before.*

> I missed class yesterday *because* my mother was ill.

> *Before* traveling to a new country, you need to exchange your money to the local currency.

The order of clauses determines their punctuation. If the dependent clause comes first, it should be separated from the independent clause with a comma. However, if the complex sentence consists of an independent clause followed by a dependent clause, then a comma is not always necessary.

A *compound-complex sentence* can be created by joining two or more independent clauses with at least one dependent clause:

> After the earthquake struck, thousands of homes were destroyed, and many families were left without a place to live.

The first independent clause in the compound structure includes a dependent clause—*after the earthquake struck.* Thus, the structure is both complex and compound.

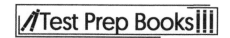

Understanding Methods Used to Appeal to a Specific Audience

Rhetorical Appeals

In an argument or persuasive text, an author will strive to sway readers to an opinion or conclusion. To be effective, an author must consider his or her intended audience. Although an author may write text for a general audience, he or she will use methods of appeal or persuasion to convince that audience. Aristotle asserted that there were three methods or modes by which a person could be persuaded. These are referred to as *rhetorical appeals*.

The three main types of rhetorical appeals are shown in the following graphic.

Ethos, also referred to as an *ethical appeal*, is an appeal to the audience's perception of the writer as credible (or not), based on their examination of their ethics and who the writer is, his/her experience or incorporation of relevant information, or his/her argument. For example, authors may present testimonials to bolster their arguments. The reader who critically examines the veracity of the testimonials and the credibility of those giving the testimony will be able to determine if the author's use of testimony is valid to his or her argument. In turn, this will help the reader determine if the author's thesis is valid. An author's careful and appropriate use of technical language can create an overall knowledgeable effect and, in turn, act as a convincing vehicle when it comes to credibility. Overuse of technical language, however, may create confusion in readers and obscure an author's overall intent.

Pathos, also referred to as a *pathetic* or *emotional appeal*, is an appeal to the audience's sense of identity, self-interest, or emotions. A critical reader will notice when the author is appealing to pathos through anecdotes and descriptions that elicit an emotion such as anger or pity. Readers should also beware of factual information that uses generalization to appeal to the emotions. While it's tempting to believe an author is the source of truth in his or her text, an author who presents factual information as universally true, consistent throughout time, and common to all groups is using *generalization*. Authors

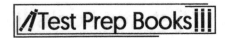

who exclusively use generalizations without specific facts and credible sourcing are attempting to sway readers solely through emotion.

Logos, also referred to as a *logical appeal*, is an appeal to the audience's ability to see and understand the logic in a claim offered by the writer. A critical reader has to be able to evaluate an author's arguments for validity of reasoning and for sufficiency when it comes to argument.

Understanding Development of a Written Argument

Evaluating an Author's Purpose

A reader must be able to evaluate the argument or point the author is trying to make and determine if it is adequately supported. The first step is to determine the main idea. The main idea is what the author wants to say about a specific topic. The next step is to locate the supporting details. An author uses supporting details to illustrate the main idea. These are the details that provide evidence or examples to help make a point. Supporting details often appear in the form of quotations, paraphrasing, or analysis. Test takers should then examine the text to make sure the author connects details and analysis to the main point. These steps are crucial to understanding the text and evaluating how well the author presents his or her argument and evidence. The following graphic demonstrates the connection between the main idea and the supporting details.

Evaluating Evidence

It is important to evaluate the author's supporting details to be sure that they are credible, provide evidence of the author's point, and directly support the main idea. Critical readers examine the facts used to support an author's argument and check those facts against other sources to be sure the facts are correct. They also check the validity of the sources used to be sure those sources are credible, academic, and/or peer- reviewed. A strong argument uses valid, measurable facts to support ideas.

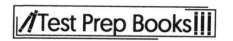

Identifying False Statements

A reader must also be able to identify any *logical fallacies*—logically-flawed statements—that an author may make as those fallacies impact the validity and veracity of the author's claims.

Some of the more common fallacies are shown in the following chart.

Fallacy	Definition
Slippery Slope	A fallacy that is built on the idea that a particular action will lead to a series of events with negative results
Red Herring	The use of an observation or distraction to remove attention from the actual issue
Straw Man	An exaggeration or misrepresentation of an argument so that it is easier to refute
Post Hoc Ergo Propter Hoc	A fallacy that assumes an event to be the consequence of an earlier event merely because it came after it
Bandwagon	A fallacy that assumes because the majority of people feel or believe a certain way then it must be the right way
Ad Hominem	The use of a personal attack on the person or persons associated with a certain argument rather than focusing on the actual argument itself

Readers who are aware of the types of fallacious reasoning are able to weigh the credibility of the author's statements in terms of effective argument. Rhetorical text that contains a myriad of fallacious statements should be considered ineffectual and suspect.

Assessing Reading, Writing, Speaking, and Listening
Identifying Research-Based Approaches to Formative and Summative Assessment

It is almost as important to provide feedback and evaluate a student's skill level as it is to teach. Most classes utilize both formative and summative assessments as a grading template. Although assessment and grading are not the same thing, assessments are often used to award a grade. A *formative assessment* monitors the student's progress in learning and allows continuous feedback throughout the course in the form of homework and in-class assignments, such as quizzes, writing workshops, conferences, or inquiry-based writing prompts. These assessments typically make up a lower percent of the overall grade. Alternatively, a *summative assessment* compares a student's progress in learning against some sort of standard, such as against the progress of other students or by the number of

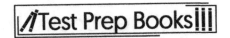

correct answers. These assessments usually make up a higher percent of the overall grade and come in the form of midterm or final exams, papers, or major projects.

One evidence-based method used to assess a student's progress is a rubric. A *rubric* is an evaluation tool that explicitly states the expectations of the assignment and breaks it down into different components. Each component has a clear description and relationship to the assignment as a whole. For writing, rubrics may be *holistic*, judging the overall quality of the writing, or they can be *analytic*, in which different aspects of the writing are evaluated, e.g., structure, style, word choices, and punctuation.

Rubrics can be used in all aspects of a curriculum, including reading comprehension, oral presentations, speeches, performances, papers, projects, and listening comprehension. They are usually formative in nature, but can be summative depending on the purpose. Rubrics allow instructors to provide specific feedback and allow students to understand the expectations for an assignment.

An example of an analytic rubric is displayed below:

Name _____   Date _____

Essay Rubric	4 Mastery	3 Satisfactory	2 Needs Improvement	1 Poor
Writing Quality	-Excellent usage of voice and style -Outstanding organizational skills -Wealth of relevant information	-Style and voice of essay was interesting -Mostly organized -Useful amount of information	-Inconsistent style and voice -Lacked clear organization -Small amount of useful information	-No noticeable style or voice -Virtually no organization -No relevant information
Grammar Conventions	-Essentially no mistakes in grammar -Correct spelling throughout	-Minor amount of grammar and spelling mistakes	-Many errors in grammar conventions and spelling	-Too many grammatical errors to understand the meaning of the piece

Another research-proven strategy is *conferencing*, in which students participate in a group discussion that usually involves the teacher. Students learn best when they can share their thoughts on what they've read or written and receive feedback from their peers and instructors. For writing, conferencing is frequently done in the revision stage. Through discussion, students are also able to enhance their listening and speaking skills. Conferences can be done in a one-on-one setting, typically between a student and instructor, or in a small group of students with guidance from the instructor. They are useful in that they provide an atmosphere of respect where a student can share his or her work and thoughts without fear of judgment. They increase motivation and allow students to explore a variety of

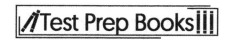

topics and discussions. Conferences also allow the instructor to provide immediate feedback or prompt students for deeper explanations of their ideas.

The most successful conferences have these characteristics:

- Have a set structure

- Focus on only a few points—too many are confusing or distracting

- Are solution based

- Allow students to both discuss their thoughts/works and receive/provide feedback for others

- Encourage the use of appropriate vocabulary

- Provide motivation and personal satisfaction or pleasure from reading and writing

- Allow a time where questions can be asked and immediately answered

Rubrics and conferencing are both methods that provide useful *feedback*, one of the most important elements in the progress of a student's learning. Feedback is essentially corrective instruction delivered in writing, either verbally or non-verbally. Research has shown that the following techniques are the most effective when giving feedback:

Being specific
For a student to know exactly how he or she is doing, feedback should be directed towards specific components of a student's writing, listening, or speaking skills, not a holistic overview. For example, writing "Excellent!" on a student's paper or homework is not useful information as it's unclear what was done well. A paper should provide useful comments throughout the body of the work, for example, "Wording is confusing here," or "Great use of adjectives." However, instructor comments should not overwhelm the student's writing; they should be used to focus their attention on specific areas of success or improvement. This encourages the student to keep doing what he or she is doing well and work on what needs improvement without being overwhelmed.

Being sensitive
Giving feedback is precarious in nature as it entirely depends upon the emotional and mental states of the receiver. Some students do well with "tough love," while others may be discouraged and disheartened to see a slew of comments on their paper. Teachers should pay attention to how a student reacts to feedback. As a general rule, feedback should focus more on the positives so as not to damage self-esteem, while teaching students new techniques for self-correction, instead of simply criticizing what they've done. Also, it's important to try and be aware of the types of feedback each student responds the most effectively to, for example, providing oral feedback for students who don't read well.

Being Prompt
Feedback should be presented sooner rather than later, so that students will not have time to repeat mistakes they are unaware of that may become habitual. Studies have shown that students who are given immediate feedback display a greater increase in performance than those who were given feedback later in the term. As soon as the action has happened, it is important give the appropriate praise or critique so that the student associates the feedback with the action.

Being Explicit

It is important to explain the purpose of the feedback before it is given so that a student does not feel controlled, too closely examined, or competitive. This can cause the learner to feel self-conscious and discourage him or her from performing his or her best. The importance of feedback and how it is meant to improve on a personal skill set should be explained to the student.

Being Focused

Teachers should try and keep the feedback in alignment with the goal the student is expected to achieve. Too much feedback, especially if it is unrelated to the goal, can be overwhelming and distracting from the purpose of the assignment or paper.

Here are some other tips to consider when giving feedback:

Teachers should be aware of their body language and facial expressions when giving feedback—a frown or grimace can be very discouraging, even if the written feedback was mostly positive.

It's conducive to concentrate on one thing at a time. If a student submits a paper with a lot of errors, for example, it may be helpful to identify a prevalent pattern of error and work through strategies to correct it so that student does not feel overwhelmed.

Using effective rubrics can make all the difference—letting students know exactly what is expected will provide them with a basis on which to model their techniques and skills.

Students should be educated on giving feedback. This can be demonstrated by example and through instruction how to give feedback in a positive, constructive way and correct any behavior that trends toward disrespect or excessive competition. Students should also provide feedback to the teacher as well.

Teachers should not give the same comments to every student, but make them personal.

When offering criticism, teachers should always offer tips for how the student can improve.

It's important to avoid personal comments, e.g., "You're so smart!" or "Math isn't your best subject." Rather, the comments should focus on the writing: e.g., "The organization of this paper is clear."

Students shouldn't be compared to each other, e.g., "Look how perfectly Victor composed this sentence!" This can galvanize the students into competing with one another.

Evaluating the Effectiveness of Research-Based Approaches to Formative and Summative Assessment

Most research has already been done to evaluate the effectiveness of certain strategies of formative and summative assessments. Because there are innumerable approaches to the art of teaching, the only real way one can evaluate a strategy's effectiveness is to monitor how the students improve over time with any given approach. If one strategy does not seem to show much improvement, then a different one should be used. Because each student has individual needs, a teacher may need to utilize several different techniques tailored to the needs of each student.

To monitor student process, the following approaches should be considered:

- Asking questions in the classroom during and after a lecture
- Cultivating a classroom environment that encourages student questions
- Circulating around the classroom and engaging in one-on-one conferences during in-class assignments
- Giving periodic quizzes
- Leaving sufficient time for questions at the end of a lecture
- Assigning and collecting homework and returning the corrected material immediately
- Giving midterms and final exams
- Conducting regular reviews of student progress through the above methods and adjusting teaching strategies accordingly

Another strategy to assess student knowledge and identify areas in need of development is to create a K-W-L chart in preparation for a lesson that introduces a new topic. First, students are prompted for what they already know (K). Then, they are asked to consider what they want to know (W). The instructor may then choose to adjust the lesson by spending less time on areas that students are already proficient in and by spending more time on areas that students want to know more about. Finally, after the lesson, students can be asked to reflect on what they learned (L). A K-W-L chart lets students know that they are active participants in their own learning.

Practice Questions

1. Which of the following sentences has an error in capitalization?
    a. The East Coast has experienced very unpredictable weather this year.
    b. My Uncle owns a home in Florida, where he lives in the winter.
    c. I am taking English Composition II on campus this fall.
    d. There are several nice beaches we can visit on our trip to the Jersey Shore this summer.

2. Julia Robinson, an avid photographer in her spare time, was able to capture stunning shots of the local wildlife on her last business trip to Australia.
Which of the following is an adjective in the preceding sentence?
    a. Time
    b. Capture
    c. Avid
    d. Photographer

3. Which of the following sentences uses correct punctuation?
    a. Carole is not currently working; her focus is on her children at the moment.
    b. Carole is not currently working and her focus is on her children at the moment.
    c. Carole is not currently working, her focus is on her children at the moment.
    d. Carole is not currently working her focus is on her children at the moment.

4. Which of these examples is a compound sentence?
    a. Alex and Shane spent the morning coloring and later took a walk down to the park.
    b. After coloring all morning, Alex and Shane spent the afternoon at the park.
    c. Alex and Shane spent the morning coloring, and then they took a walk down to the park.
    d. After coloring all morning and spending part of the day at the park, Alex and Shane took a nap.

5. Which of these examples shows incorrect use of subject-verb agreement?
    a. Neither of the cars are parked on the street.
    b. Both of my kids are going to camp this summer.
    c. Any of your friends are welcome to join us on the trip in November.
    d. Each of the clothing options is appropriate for the job interview.

Answer Explanations

1. B: In Choice B the word *Uncle* should not be capitalized, because it is not functioning as a proper noun. If the word named a specific uncle, such as *Uncle Jerry*, then it would be considered a proper noun and should be capitalized. Choice *A* correctly capitalizes the proper noun *East Coast*, and does not capitalize *winter*, which functions as a common noun in the sentence. Choice *C* correctly capitalizes the name of a specific college course, which is considered a proper noun. Choice *D* correctly capitalizes the proper noun *Jersey Shore*.

2. C: In Choice C, *avid* is functioning as an adjective that modifies the word photographer. *Avid* describes the photographer Julia Robinson's style. The words *time* and *photographer* are functioning as nouns, and the word *capture* is functioning as a verb in the sentence. Other words functioning as adjectives in the sentence include, *local*, *business*, and *spare*, as they all describe the nouns they precede.

3. A: Choice *A* is correctly punctuated because it uses a semicolon to join two independent clauses that are related in meaning. Each of these clauses could function as an independent sentence. Choice *B* is incorrect because the conjunction is not preceded by a comma. A comma and conjunction should be used together to join independent clauses. Choice *C* is incorrect because a comma should only be used to join independent sentences when it also includes a coordinating conjunction such as *and* or *so*. Choice *D* does not use punctuation to join the independent clauses, so it is considered a fused (same as a run-on) sentence.

4. C: Choice *C* is a compound sentence because it joins two independent clauses with a comma and the coordinating conjunction *and*. The sentences in Choices B and D include one independent clause and one dependent clause, so they are complex sentences, not compound sentences. The sentence in Choice A has both a compound subject, *Alex and Shane*, and a compound verb, *spent and took*, but the entire sentence itself is one independent clause.

5. A: Choice *A* uses incorrect subject-verb agreement because the indefinite pronoun *neither* is singular and must use the singular verb form *is*. The pronoun *both* is plural and uses the plural verb form of *are*. The pronoun *any* can be either singular or plural. In this example, it is used as a plural, so the plural verb form *are* is used. The pronoun *each* is singular and uses the singular verb form *is*.

Literature, Reading Processes, and Skills for Reading Literary and Nonliterary Texts

Reading Processes

Critical Thinking Skills

Teachers should educate and encourage students to view reading as an active process of discovering meaning in texts. Reading should not be passive. Readers should question what they read and apply their background knowledge to enhance their understanding and appreciation of written work. Teachers should bear in mind that the meaning derived from a given text for a student may depend on his or her background and experiences.

It's important to read any piece of writing critically. The goal is to discover the point and purpose of what the author is writing about through analysis. It's also crucial to establish the point or stance the author has taken on the topic of the piece. After determining the author's perspective, readers can then more effectively develop their own viewpoints on the subject of the piece.

It is important to distinguish between *fact and opinion* when reading a piece of writing. A fact is information that can be proven true. If information can be disproved, it is not a fact. For example, water freezes at or below thirty-two degrees Fahrenheit. An argument stating that water freezes at seventy degrees Fahrenheit cannot be supported by data and is therefore not a fact. Facts tend to be associated with science, mathematics, and statistics. Opinions are information open to debate. Opinions are often tied to subjective concepts like equality, morals, and rights. They can also be controversial.

Authors often use words like *think, feel, believe,* or *in my opinion* when expressing opinion, but these words won't always appear in an opinion piece, especially if it is formally written. An author's opinion may be backed up by facts, which gives it more credibility, but that opinion should not be taken as fact. A critical reader should be suspect of an author's opinion, especially if it is only supported by other opinions.

Fact	Opinion
There are nine innings in a game of baseball.	Baseball games run too long.
James Garfield was assassinated on July 2, 1881.	James Garfield was a good president.
McDonalds has stores in 118 countries.	McDonalds has the best hamburgers.

Critical readers examine the facts used to support an author's argument. They check the facts against other sources to be sure those facts are correct. They also check the validity of the sources used to be sure those sources are credible, academic, and/or peer- reviewed. Consider that when an author uses another person's opinion to support his or her argument, even if it is an expert's opinion, it is still only an opinion and should not be taken as fact. A strong argument uses valid, measurable facts to support ideas. Even then, the reader may disagree with the argument as it may be rooted in his or her personal beliefs.

An authoritative argument may use the facts to sway the reader. In the example of global warming, many experts differ in their opinions of what alternative fuels can be used to aid in offsetting it. Because

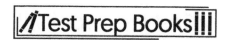

of this, a writer may choose to only use the information and expert opinion that supports his or her viewpoint.

If the argument is that wind energy is the best solution, the author will use facts that support this idea. That same author may leave out relevant facts on solar energy. The way the author uses facts can influence the reader, so it's important to consider the facts being used, how those facts are being presented, and what information might be left out.

Critical readers should also look for errors in the argument such as logical fallacies and bias. A *logical fallacy* is a flaw in the logic used to make the argument. Logical fallacies include slippery slope, straw man, and begging the question. Authors can also reflect *bias* if they ignore an opposing viewpoint or present their side in an unbalanced way. A strong argument considers the opposition and finds a way to refute it. Critical readers should look for an unfair or one-sided presentation of the argument and be skeptical, as a bias may be present. Even if this bias is unintentional, if it exists in the writing, the reader should be wary of the validity of the argument.

Readers should also look for the use of *stereotypes,* which refer to specific groups. Stereotypes are often negative connotations about a person or place and should always be avoided. When a critical reader finds stereotypes in a piece of writing, they should immediately be critical of the argument and consider the validity of anything the author presents. Stereotypes reveal a flaw in the writer's thinking and may suggest a lack of knowledge or understanding about the subject.

Responding to a Passage

Teachers should encourage students to respond to the texts they read and to share their responses with peers. There are a few ways for readers to engage actively with the text, such as making inferences and predictions. An *inference* refers to a point that is implied (as opposed to directly-stated) by the evidence presented:

> Bradley packed up all of the items from his desk in a box and said goodbye to his coworkers for the last time.

From this sentence, though it is not directly stated, readers can infer that Bradley is leaving his job. It's necessary to use inference in order to draw conclusions about the meaning of a passage. Authors make implications through character dialogue, thoughts, effects on others, actions, and looks. Like in life, readers must assemble all the clues to form a complete picture.

When making an inference about a passage, it's important to rely only on the information that is provided in the text itself. This helps readers ensure that their conclusions are valid.

Readers will also find themselves making predictions when reading a passage or paragraph. *Predictions* are guesses about what's going to happen next. Readers can use prior knowledge to help make accurate predictions. Prior knowledge is best utilized when readers make links between the current text, previously read texts, and life experiences. Some texts use suspense and foreshadowing to captivate readers:

A cat darted across the street just as the car came careening around the curve.

One unfortunate prediction might be that the car will hit the cat. Of course, predictions aren't always accurate, so it's important to read carefully to the end of the text to determine the accuracy of predictions.

Identifying Characteristics of Passage Types

Writing can be classified under four passage types: narrative, expository, descriptive (sometimes called technical), and persuasive. Though these types are not mutually exclusive, one form tends to dominate the rest. By recognizing the *type* of passage you're reading, you gain insight into *how* you should read. If you're reading a narrative, you can assume the author intends to entertain, which means you may skim the text without losing meaning. A technical document might require a close read, because skimming the passage might cause the reader to miss salient details.

1. *Narrative* writing, at its core, is the art of storytelling. For a narrative to exist, certain elements must be present. First, it must have characters While many characters are human, characters could be defined as anything that thinks, acts, and talks like a human. For example, many recent movies, such as *Lord of the Rings* and *The Chronicles of Narnia*, include animals, fantastical creatures, and even trees that behave like humans. Second, it must have a plot or sequence of events. Typically, those events follow a standard plot diagram, but recent trends start *in medias res* or in the middle (near the climax). In this instance, foreshadowing and flashbacks often fill in plot details. Finally, along with characters and a plot, there must also be conflict. Conflict is usually divided into two types: internal and external. Internal conflict indicates the character is in turmoil and is presented through the character's thoughts. External conflicts are visible. Types of external conflict include a person versus nature, another person, or society.

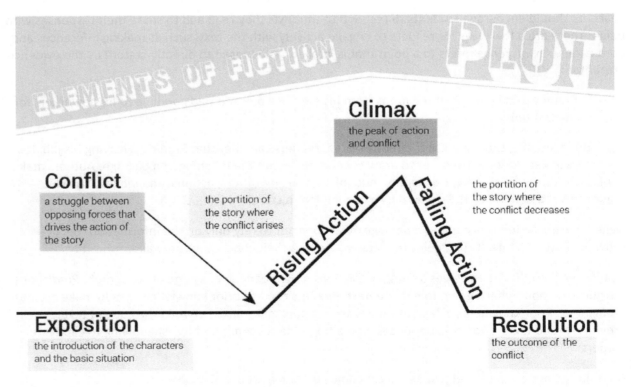

2. *Expository writing is detached and to the point. Since expository* writing is designed to instruct or inform, it usually involves directions and steps written in second person ("you" voice) and lacks any

persuasive or narrative elements. Sequence words such as *first*, *second*, and *third*, or *in the first place*, *secondly*, and *lastly* are often given to add fluency and cohesion. Common examples of expository writing include instructor's lessons, cookbook recipes, and repair manuals.

3. Due to its empirical nature, *technical* writing is filled with steps, charts, graphs, data, and statistics. The goal of technical writing is to advance understanding in a field through the scientific method. Experts such as teachers, doctors, or mechanics use words unique to the profession in which they operate. These words, which often incorporate acronyms, are called *jargon*. Technical writing is a type of expository writing but is not meant to be understood by the general public. Instead, technical writers assume readers have received a formal education in a particular field of study and need no explanation as to what the jargon means. Imagine a doctor trying to understand a diagnostic reading for a car or a mechanic trying to interpret lab results. Only professionals with proper training will fully comprehend the text.

4. *Persuasive* writing is designed to change opinions and attitudes. The topic, stance, and arguments are found in the thesis, positioned near the end of the introduction. Later supporting paragraphs offer relevant quotations, paraphrases, and summaries from primary or secondary sources, which are then interpreted, analyzed, and evaluated. The goal of persuasive writers is not to stack quotes, but to develop original ideas by using sources as a starting point. Good persuasive writing makes powerful arguments with valid sources and thoughtful analysis. Poor persuasive writing is riddled with bias and logical fallacies. Sometimes logical and illogical arguments are sandwiched together in the same piece. Therefore, readers should display skepticism when reading persuasive arguments.

Identifying Reading Strategies

A *reading strategy* is the way a reader interacts with text in order to understand its meaning. It is a skill set that a reader brings to the reading. It employs a reader's ability to use prior knowledge when addressing literature and utilizes a set of methods in order to analyze text. A reading strategy is not simply tackling a text passage as it appears. It involves a more complex system of planning and thought during the reading experience. Current research indicates readers who utilize strategies and a variety of critical reading skills are better thinkers who glean more interpretive information from their reading. Consequently, they are more successful in their overall comprehension.

Pre-reading Strategies

Pre-reading strategies are important, yet often overlooked. Non-critical readers will often begin reading without taking the time to review factors that will help them understand the text. Skipping pre-reading strategies may result in a reader having to re-address a text passage more times than is necessary. Some pre-reading strategies include the following:

- Previewing the text for clues
- Skimming the text for content
- Scanning for unfamiliar words in context
- Formulating questions on sight
- Making predictions
- Recognizing needed prior knowledge

Before reading a text passage, a reader can enhance his or her ability to comprehend material by *previewing the text for clues*. This may mean making careful note of any titles, headings, graphics, notes, introductions, important summaries, and conclusions. It can involve a reader making physical notes regarding these elements or highlighting anything he or she thinks is important before reading. Often, a reader will be able to gain information just from these elements alone. Of course, close reading is required in order to fill in the details. A reader needs to be able to ask what he or she is reading about and what a passage is trying to say. The answers to these general questions can often be answered in previewing the text itself.

It's helpful to use pre-reading clues to determine the main idea and organization. First, any titles, sub-headings, chapter headings should be read, and the test taker should make note of the author's credentials if any are listed. It's important to deduce what these clues may indicate as it pertains to the focus of the text and how it's organized.

During pre-reading, readers should also take special note of how text features contribute to the central idea or thesis of the passage. Is there an index? Is there a glossary? What headings, footnotes, or other visuals are included and how do they relate to the details within the passage? Again, this is where any pre-reading notes come in handy, since a test taker should be able to relate supporting details to these textual features.

Next, a reader should *skim* the text for general ideas and content. This technique does not involve close reading; rather, it involves looking for important words within the passage itself. These words may have something to do with the author's theme. They may have to do with structure—for example, words such as *first, next, therefore*, and *last*. Skimming helps a reader understand the overall structure of a passage and, in turn, this helps him or her understand the author's theme or message.

From there, a reader should quickly *scan* the text for any unfamiliar words. When reading a print text, highlighting these words or making other marginal notation is helpful when going back to read text critically. A reader should look at the words surrounding any unfamiliar ones to see what contextual clues unfamiliar words carry. Being able to define unfamiliar terms through contextual meaning is a critical skill in reading comprehension.

A reader should also *formulate any questions* he or she might have before conducting close reading. Questions such as "What is the author trying to tell me?" or "Is the author trying to persuade my thinking?" are important to a reader's ability to engage critically with the text. Questions will focus a reader's attention on what is important in terms of idea and what is supporting detail.

Along with formulating questions, it is helpful to make predictions of what the answers to these questions and others will be. *Making predictions* involves using information from the text and personal experiences to make a thoughtful guess as to what will happen in the story and what outcomes can be expected.

Last, a reader should recognize that authors assume readers bring a prior knowledge set to the reading experience. Not all readers have the same experience, but authors seek to communicate with their readers. In turn, readers should strive to interact with the author of a particular passage by asking themselves what the passage demands they know during reading. This is also known as making a text-to-self connection. If a passage is informational in nature, a reader should ask "What do I know about this topic from other experiences I've had or other works I've read?" If a reader can relate to the content, he or she will better understand it.

All of the above pre-reading strategies will help the reader prepare for a closer reading experience. They will engage a reader in active interaction with the text by helping to focus the reader's full attention on the details that he or she will encounter during the next round or two of critical, closer reading.

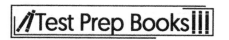

Strategies During Reading

After pre-reading, a test taker can employ a variety of other reading strategies while conducting one or more closer readings. These strategies include the following:

- Clarifying during a close read
- Questioning during a close read
- Organizing the main ideas and supporting details
- Summarizing the text effectively

A reader needs to be able to *clarify* what he or she is reading. This strategy demands a reader think about how and what he or she is reading. This thinking should occur during and after the act of reading. For example, a reader may encounter one or more unfamiliar ideas during reading, then be asked to apply thoughts about those unfamiliar concepts after reading when answering test questions.

Questioning during a critical read is closely related to clarifying. A reader must be able to ask questions in general about what he or she is reading and questions regarding the author's supporting ideas. Questioning also involves a reader's ability to self-question. When closely reading a passage, it's not enough to simply try and understand the author. A reader must consider critical thinking questions to ensure he or she is comprehending intent. It's advisable, when conducting a close read, to write out margin notes and questions during the experience. These questions can be addressed later in the thinking process after reading and during the phase where a reader addresses the test questions. A reader who is successful in reading comprehension will iteratively question what he or she reads, search text for clarification, then answer any questions that arise.

A reader should *organize* main ideas and supporting details cognitively as he or she reads, as it will help the reader understand the larger structure at work. The use of quick annotations or marks to indicate what the main idea is and how the details function to support it can be helpful. Understanding the structure of a text passage is sometimes critical to answering questions about an author's approach, theme, messages, and supporting detail. This strategy is most effective when reading informational or nonfiction text. Texts that try to convince readers of a particular idea, that present a theory, or that try to explain difficult concepts are easier to understand when a reader can identify the overarching structure at work.

Post-reading Strategies

After completing a text, a reader should be able to *summarize* the author's theme and supporting details in order to fully understand the passage. Being able to effectively restate the author's message, sub-themes, and pertinent, supporting ideas will help a reader gain an advantage when addressing standardized test questions.

A reader should also evaluate the strength of the predictions that were made in the pre-reading stage. Using textual evidence, predictions should be compared to the actual events in the story to see if the two were similar or not. Employing all of these strategies will lead to fuller, more insightful reading comprehension.

Understanding the Use of Affixes, Context, and Syntax

Affixes

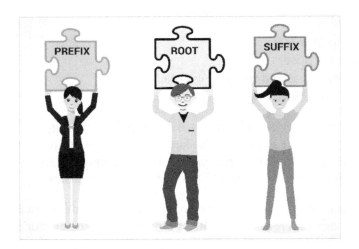

Individual words are constructed from building blocks of meaning. An *affix* is an element that is added to a root or stem word that can change the word's meaning.

For example, the stem word *fix* is a verb meaning *to repair*. When the ending *–able* is added, it becomes the adjective *fixable*, meaning "capable of being repaired." Adding *un–* to the beginning changes the word to *unfixable*, meaning "incapable of being repaired." In this way, affixes attach to the word stem to create a new word and a new meaning. Knowledge of affixes can assist in deciphering the meaning of unfamiliar words.

Affixes are also related to inflection. *Inflection* is the modification of a base word to express a different grammatical or syntactical function. For example, countable nouns such as *car* and *airport* become plural with the addition of *–s* at the end: *cars* and *airports*.

Verb tense is also expressed through inflection. *Regular verbs*—those that follow a standard inflection pattern—can be changed to past tense using the affixes *–ed*, *–d*, or *–ied*, as in *cooked* and *studied*. Verbs can also be modified for continuous tenses by using *–ing*, as in *working* or *exploring*. Thus, affixes are used not only to express meaning but also to reflect a word's grammatical purpose.

A *prefix* is an affix attached to the beginning of a word. The meanings of English prefixes mainly come from Greek and Latin origins. The chart below contains a few of the most commonly used English prefixes.

Prefix	Meaning	Example
a-	not	amoral, asymptomatic
anti-	against	antidote, antifreeze
auto-	self	automobile, automatic
circum-	around	circumference, circumspect
co-, com-, con-	together	coworker, companion
contra-	against	contradict, contrary
de-	negation or reversal	deflate, deodorant
extra-	outside, beyond	extraterrestrial, extracurricular
in-, im-, il-, ir-	not	impossible, irregular
inter-	between	international, intervene
intra-	within	intramural, intranet
mis-	wrongly	mistake, misunderstand
mono-	one	monolith, monopoly
non-	not	nonpartisan, nonsense
pre-	before	preview, prediction
re-	again	review, renew
semi-	half	semicircle, semicolon
sub-	under	subway, submarine
super-	above	superhuman, superintendent
trans-	across, beyond, through	trans-Siberian, transform
un-	not	unwelcome, unfriendly

While the addition of a prefix alters the meaning of the base word, the addition of a *suffix* may also affect a word's part of speech. For example, adding a suffix can change the noun *material* into the verb *materialize* and back to a noun again in *materialization*.

Suffix	Part of Speech	Meaning	Example
-able, -ible	adjective	having the ability to	honorable, flexible
-acy, -cy	noun	state or quality	intimacy, dependency
-al, -ical	adjective	having the quality of	historical, tribal
-en	verb	to cause to become	strengthen, embolden
-er, -ier	adjective	comparative	happier, longer
-est, -iest	adjective	superlative	sunniest, hottest
-ess	noun	female	waitress, actress
-ful	adjective	full of, characterized by	beautiful, thankful
-fy, -ify	verb	to cause, to come to be	liquefy, intensify
-ism	noun	doctrine, belief, action	Communism, Buddhism
-ive, -ative, -itive	adjective	having the quality of	creative, innovative
-ize	verb	to convert into, to subject to	Americanize, dramatize
-less	adjective	without, missing	emotionless, hopeless
-ly	adverb	in the manner of	quickly, energetically
-ness	noun	quality or state	goodness, darkness
-ous, -ious, -eous	adjective	having the quality of	spontaneous, pious
-ship	noun	status or condition	partnership, ownership
-tion	noun	action or state	renovation, promotion
-y	adjective	characterized by	smoky, dreamy

Through knowledge of prefixes and suffixes, a student's vocabulary can be instantly expanded with an understanding of *etymology*—the origin of words. This, in turn, can be used to add sentence structure variety to academic writing.

Context Clues

Familiarity with common prefixes, suffixes, and root words assists tremendously in unraveling the meaning of an unfamiliar word and making an educated guess as to its meaning. However, some words do not contain many easily-identifiable clues that point to their meaning. In this case, rather than looking at the elements within the word, it is useful to consider elements around the word—i.e., its context. *Context* refers to the other words and information within the sentence or surrounding sentences that indicate the unknown word's probable meaning. The following sentences provide context for the potentially-unfamiliar word *quixotic*:

> Rebecca had never been one to settle into a predictable, ordinary life. Her quixotic personality led her to leave behind a job with a prestigious law firm in Manhattan and move halfway around the world to pursue her dream of becoming a sushi chef in Tokyo.

A reader unfamiliar with the word *quixotic* doesn't have many clues to use in terms of affixes or root meaning. The suffix *–ic* indicates that the word is an adjective, but that is it. In this case, then, a reader would need to look at surrounding information to obtain some clues about the word. Other adjectives in the passage include *predictable* and *ordinary*, things that Rebecca was definitely not, as indicated by

"Rebecca had never been one to settle." Thus, a first clue might be that *quixotic* means the opposite of predictable.

The second sentence doesn't offer any other modifier of *personality* other than *quixotic*, but it does include a story that reveals further information about her personality. She had a stable, respectable job, but she decided to give it up to follow her dream. Combining these two ideas together, then— unpredictable and dream-seeking—gives the reader a general idea of what *quixotic* probably means. In fact, the root of the word is the character Don Quixote, a romantic dreamer who goes on an impulsive adventure.

While context clues are useful for making an approximate definition for newly-encountered words, these types of clues also come in handy when encountering common words that have multiple meanings. The word *reservation* is used differently in each the following sentences:

A. That restaurant is booked solid for the next month; it's impossible to make a reservation unless you know somebody.

B. The hospital plans to open a branch office inside the reservation to better serve Native American patients who cannot easily travel to the main hospital fifty miles away.

C. Janet Clark is a dependable, knowledgeable worker, and I recommend her for the position of team leader without reservation.

All three sentences use the word to express different meanings. In fact, most words in English have more than one meaning—sometimes meanings that are completely different from one another. Thus, context can provide clues as to which meaning is appropriate in a given situation. A quick search in the dictionary reveals several possible meanings for *reservation*:

- An exception or qualification
- A tract of public land set aside, such as for the use of American Indian tribes
- An arrangement for accommodations, such as in a hotel, on a plane, or at a restaurant

Sentence A mentions a restaurant, making the third definition the correct one in this case. In sentence B, some context clues include Native Americans, as well as the implication that a reservation is a place— "inside the reservation," both of which indicate that the second definition should be used here. Finally, sentence C uses *without reservation* to mean "completely" or "without exception," so the first definition can be applied here.

Using context clues in this way can be especially useful for words that have multiple, widely varying meanings. If a word has more than one definition and two of those definitions are the opposite of each other, it is known as an *auto-antonym*—a word that can also be its own antonym. In the case of auto-antonyms, context clues are crucial to determine which definition to employ in a given sentence. For example, the word *sanction* can either mean "to approve or allow" or "a penalty." Approving and penalizing have opposite meanings, so *sanction* is an example of an auto-antonym. The following sentences reflect the distinction in meaning:

A. In response to North Korea's latest nuclear weapons test, world leaders have called for harsher sanctions to punish the country for its actions.

B. The general has sanctioned a withdrawal of troops from the area.

A context clue can be found in sentence A, which mentions "to punish." A punishment is similar to a penalty, so sentence A is using the word *sanction* according to this definition.

Other examples of auto-antonyms include *oversight*—"to supervise something" or "a missed detail"), *resign*—"to quit" or "to sign again, as a contract," and *screen*—"to show" or "to conceal." For these types of words, recognizing context clues is an important way to avoid misinterpreting the sentence's meaning.

Syntax

Syntax refers to the arrangement of words, phrases, and clauses to form a sentence. Knowledge of syntax can also give insight into a word's meaning. The section above considered several examples using the word *reservation* and applied context clues to determine the word's appropriate meaning in each sentence. Here is an example of how the placement of a word can impact its meaning and grammatical function:

A. The development team has reserved the conference room for today.

B. Her quiet and reserved nature is sometimes misinterpreted as unfriendliness when people first meet her.

In addition to using *reserved* to mean different things, each sentence also uses the word to serve a different grammatical function. In sentence A, *reserved* is part of the verb phrase *has reserved*, indicating the meaning "to set aside for a particular use." In sentence B, *reserved* acts as a modifier within the noun phrase "her quiet and reserved nature." Because the word is being used as an adjective to describe a personality characteristic, it calls up a different definition of the word—"restrained or lacking familiarity with others." As this example shows, the function of a word within the overall sentence structure can allude to its meaning. It is also useful to refer to the earlier chart about suffixes and parts of speech as another clue into what grammatical function a word is serving in a sentence.

Analyzing Nuances of Word Meaning and Figures of Speech

By now, it should be apparent that language is not as simple as one word directly correlated to one meaning. Rather, one word can express a vast array of diverse meanings, and similar meanings can be expressed through different words. However, there are very few words that express exactly the same meaning. For this reason, it is important to be able to pick up on the nuances of word meaning.

Many words contain two levels of meaning: connotation and denotation as discussed previously in the informational texts and rhetoric section. A word's *denotation* is its most literal meaning—the definition that can readily be found in the dictionary. A word's *connotation* includes all of its emotional and cultural associations.

In literary writing, authors rely heavily on connotative meaning to create mood and characterization. The following are two descriptions of a rainstorm:

A. The rain slammed against the windowpane and the wind howled through the fireplace. A pair of hulking oaks next to the house cast eerie shadows as their branches trembled in the wind.

B. The rain pattered against the windowpane and the wind whistled through the fireplace. A pair of stately oaks next to the house cast curious shadows as their branches swayed in the wind.

Description A paints a creepy picture for readers with strongly emotional words like *slammed*, connoting force and violence. *Howled* connotes pain or wildness, and *eerie* and *trembled* connote fear. Overall, the connotative language in this description serves to inspire fear and anxiety.

However, as can be seen in description B, swapping out a few key words for those with different connotations completely changes the feeling of the passage. *Slammed* is replaced with the more cheerful *pattered*, and *hulking* has been swapped out for *stately*. Both words imply something large, but *hulking* is more intimidating whereas *stately* is more respectable. *Curious* and *swayed* seem more playful than the language used in the earlier description. Although both descriptions represent roughly the same situation, the nuances of the emotional language used throughout the passages create a very different sense for readers.

Selective choice of connotative language can also be extremely impactful in other forms of writing, such as editorials or persuasive texts. Through connotative language, writers reveal their biases and opinions while trying to inspire feelings and actions in readers:

- Parents won't stop complaining about standardized tests.

- Parents continue to raise concerns about standardized tests.

Readers should be able to identify the nuance in meaning between these two sentences. The first one carries a more negative feeling, implying that parents are being bothersome or whiny. Readers of the second sentence, though, might come away with the feeling that parents are concerned and involved in their children's education. Again, the aggregate of even subtle cues can combine to give a specific emotional impression to readers, so from an early age, students should be aware of how language can be used to influence readers' opinions.

Another form of non-literal expression can be found in *figures of speech*. As with connotative language, figures of speech tend to be shared within a cultural group and may be difficult to pick up on for learners outside of that group. In some cases, a figure of speech may be based on the literal denotation of the words it contains, but in other cases, a figure of speech is far removed from its literal meaning. A case in point is *irony*, where what is said is the exact opposite of what is meant:

> The new tax plan is poorly planned, based on faulty economic data, and unable to address the financial struggles of middle class families. Yet legislators remain committed to passing this brilliant proposal.

When the writer refers to the proposal as brilliant, the opposite is implied—the plan is "faulty" and "poorly planned." By using irony, the writer means that the proposal is anything but brilliant by using the word in a non-literal sense.

Another figure of speech is *hyperbole*—extreme exaggeration or overstatement. Statements like, "I love you to the moon and back" or "Let's be friends for a million years" utilize hyperbole to convey a greater depth of emotion, without literally committing oneself to space travel or a life of immortality.

Figures of speech may sometimes use one word in place of another. *Synecdoche*, for example, uses a part of something to refer to its whole. The expression "Don't hurt a hair on her head!" implies protecting more than just an individual hair, but rather her entire body. "The art teacher is training a class of Picassos" uses Picasso, one individual notable artist, to stand in for the entire category of talented artists. Another figure of speech using word replacement is *metonymy*, where a word is replaced with something closely associated to it. For example, news reports may use the word "Washington" to refer to the American government or "the crown" to refer to the British monarch.

Roles of Phonological Awareness, Phonics, and Word Recognition Skills in Literacy Development

It is imperative that educators understand the five basic components of reading education. If there is any deficit in any one of these following components, a child is likely to experience reading difficulty:

- Phonemic Awareness
- Phonics
- Fluency
- Vocabulary
- Comprehension

Phonemic Awareness

A phoneme is the smallest unit of sound in a given language and is one aspect under the umbrella of skills associated with phonological awareness. A child demonstrates phonemic awareness when identifying rhymes, recognizing alliterations, and isolating specific sounds inside a word or a set of words. Students who demonstrate basic phonemic awareness will eventually also be able to independently and appropriately blend together a variety of phonemes.

Some classroom strategies to strengthen phonemic awareness may include:

- Introduction to nursery rhymes and word play
- Speech discrimination techniques to train the ear to hear more accurately
- Repeated instruction connecting sounds to letters and blending sounds
- Use of visual images coupled with corresponding sounds and words
- Teaching speech sounds through direct instruction
- Comparing known to unfamiliar words
- Practicing pronunciation of newly introduced letters, letter combinations, and words
- Practicing word decoding
- Differentiating similar sounding words

Phonological and Phonemic Awareness Instruction

Age-appropriate and developmentally appropriate instruction for phonological and phonemic awareness is key to helping students strengthen their reading and writing skills. Phonological and phonemic awareness, or PPA, instruction works to enhance correct speech, improve understanding and application of accurate letter-to-sound correspondence, and strengthen spelling skills. Since skill-building involving phonemes is not a natural process but needs to be taught, PPA instruction is especially important for students who have limited access and exposure to reading materials and who lack familial encouragement to read. Strategies that educators can implement include leading word and sound games, focusing on phoneme skill-building activities, and ensuring all activities focus on the fun, playful nature of words and sounds instead of rote memorization and drilling techniques.

Phonics

Phonics is the ability to apply letter-sound relationships and letter patterns in order to accurately pronounce written words. Students with strong phonics skills are able to recognize familiar written

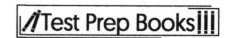

words with relative ease and quickly decipher or "decode" unfamiliar words. As one of the foundational skills for reading readiness, phonics essentially enables young readers to translate printed words into recognizable speech. If students lack proficiency in phonics, their ability to read fluently and to increase vocabulary will be limited, which consequently leads to reading comprehension difficulties.

Emergent readers benefit from explicit word decoding instruction that focuses on letter-sound relationships. This includes practicing sounding out words and identifying exceptions to the letter-sound relationships. A multi-sensory approach to word decoding instruction has also been found to be beneficial. By addressing a wide variety of learning styles and providing visual and hands-on instruction, educators help to bridge the gap between guided word decoding and it as an automatic process.

The Role of Fluency in Supporting Comprehension

Fluency

When students are able to read fluently, they read with accuracy, a steady and consistent speed, and an appropriate expression. A fluent reader can seamlessly connect word recognition to comprehension, whether reading silently or aloud. In other words, reading fluency is an automatic recognition and accurate interpretation of text. Without the ability to read fluently, a child's reading comprehension will be limited. Each time a child has to interrupt his or her reading to decode an unfamiliar word, comprehension is impaired.

There are a number of factors that contribute to the success of reading fluency. It is important that students have many opportunities to read. Access to a variety of reading genres at appropriate reading levels and effective reading fluency instruction also play important roles in how successful students will become as fluent readers. The key is to have students repeat the same passage several times in order to become familiar with the words in the text and increase their overall speed and accuracy. Poems are an effective choice when teaching fluency, since they are usually concise and offer rhyming words in an entertaining, rhythmic pattern. Some other instructional strategies to consider include:

- Modeling reading fluency with expression
- Tape-assisted reading
- Echo reading
- Partner reading
- Small group and choral reading

Comprehension

Comprehension is defined as the level of understanding of content that a child demonstrates during and after the reading of a given text. Comprehension begins well before a child is able to read. Adults and educators can foster comprehension by reading aloud to students and helping them respond to the content and relate it to their prior knowledge. Throughout the reading process, the child asks and answers relevant questions confirming her or his comprehension and is able to successfully summarize the text upon completion.

Since reading comprehension encompasses several cognitive processes, including the awareness and understanding of phonemes, phonics, and the ability to construct meaning from text, educators should employ reading comprehension strategies prior to, during, and after reading. Reading comprehension is a lifelong process. As the genres of written text change and written language becomes more complex, it is essential that educators continually reinforce reading comprehension strategies throughout a student's educational career.

Some instructional strategies to consider are:

- Pre-teaching new vocabulary
- Monitoring for understanding
- Answering and generating questions
- Summarizing

Basic Components of Vocabulary and Strategies to Help Students Determine the Meaning of Unknown Words

Vocabulary

Vocabulary consists of the bank of words that students can understand and apply fluently in order to communicate effectively. A strong vocabulary and word recognition base enables students to access prior knowledge and experiences in order to make connections in written texts. A strong vocabulary also allows students to express ideas, learn new concepts, and decode the meanings of unfamiliar words by using context clues. Conversely, if a child's vocabulary knowledge is limited and does not steadily increase, reading comprehension will be negatively affected. If students become frustrated with their lack of understanding of written texts, they will likely choose to only read texts at their comfort level or refuse to read altogether. With direct instruction, educators introduce specific words to pre-teach before reading, or examine word roots, prefixes, and suffixes. Through indirect instruction, educators ensure that students are regularly exposed to new words. This engages students in high-quality conversations and social interactions and provides access to a wide variety of challenging and enjoyable reading material.

Morphology

The study of morphology generally deals with the structure and formation of words. A phoneme is the smallest unit of sound that does not necessarily carry meaning. Essentially, phonemes are combined to form words, and words are combined to form sentences. Morphology looks at the smallest meaningful part of a word, known as a morpheme. In contrast to a phoneme, a morpheme must carry a sound and a meaning. Free morphemes are those that can stand alone, carrying both sound and meaning, as in the following words: girl, boy, man, and lady. Just as the name suggests, bound morphemes are bound to other morphemes in order to carry meaning. Examples of bound morphemes include: ish, ness, ly, and dis.

Semantics

Semantics is the branch of linguistics that addresses meanings. Morphemes, words, phrases, and sentences all carry distinct meanings. The way these individual parts are arranged can have a significant effect on meaning. In order to construct language, students must be able to use semantics to arrange and rearrange words to achieve the particular meaning they are striving for. Activities that teach semantics revolve around teaching the arrangement of word parts (morphology) and root words, and then the teaching of vocabulary. Moving from vocabulary words into studying sentences and sentence structure leads students to learn how to use context clues to determine meaning and to understand anomalies such as metaphors, idioms, and allusions. There are five types of semantic relationships that are critical to understand:

Hyponyms refer to a relationship between words where general words have multiple more-specific words (hyponyms) that fall into the same category (e.g., horse: mare, stallion, foal, Appaloosa, Clydesdale).

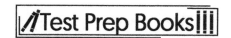

Meronyms refer to a relationship between words where a whole word has multiple parts (meronyms) that comprise it (e.g., horse: tail, mane, hooves, ears).

Synonyms refer to words that have the same meaning as another word (e.g., instructor/teacher/educator, canine/dog, feline/cat, herbivore/vegetarian).

Antonyms refer to words that have the opposite meaning as another word (e.g., true/false, up/down, in/out, right/wrong).

Homonyms refer to words that are spelled the same (homographs) or sound the same (homophones) but mean different things (e.g., there/their/they're, two/too/to, principal/principle, plain/plane, (kitchen) sink/ sink (down as in water)).

Syntax

With its origins from the Greek word, "syntaxis," which means arrangement, *syntax* is the study of phrase and sentence formation. The study of syntax focuses on the ways in which specific words can be combined to create coherent meaning. For example: the simple rearrangement of the words, "I can run," is different from the question, "Can I run?" which is also different from the meaningless "Run I can."

The following methods can be used to teach syntax:

Proper Syntax Modeling: Students don't need to be corrected for improper syntax. Instead, they should be shown ways to rephrase what they said with proper syntax. If a student says, "Run I can," then the teacher should say, "Oh, you can run how fast?" This puts syntax in place with conversational skills.

Open-Ended Sentences: Students can complete open-ended sentences with proper syntax both orally and in written format, or they can correct sentences that have improper syntax so that they make sense.

Listening for Syntax: Syntax is auditory. Students can often hear a syntax error before they can see it in writing. Teachers should have students use word cards or word magnets to arrange and rearrange simple sentences and read them aloud to check for syntax.

Repetition: Syntax can be practiced by using songs, poems, and rhymes for repetitive automation.

Pragmatics

Pragmatics is the study of what words mean in certain situations. It helps to understand the intentions and interpretations of intentions through words used in human interaction. Different listeners and different situations call for different language and intonations of language. When people engage in a conversation, it is usually to convey a certain message, and the message (even using the same words) can change depending on the setting and the audience. The more fluent the speaker, the more success she or he will have in conveying the intended message.

The following methods can be used to teach pragmatics:

When students state something incorrectly, a response can be given to what they intended to say in the first place. For instance, if a student says, "That's how it didn't happen." Then the teacher might say, "Of course, that's not how it happened." Instead of putting students on defense by being corrected, this method puts them at ease and helps them learn.

Role-playing conversations with different people in different situations can help teach pragmatics. For example, pretend playing can be used where a situation remains the same but the audience changes, or the audience stays the same but the situations change. This can be followed with a discussion about how language and intonations change too.

Different ways to convey a message can be used, such as asking vs. persuading, or giving direct vs. indirect requests and polite vs. impolite messages.

Various non-verbal signals can be used to see how they change pragmatics. For example, students can be encouraged to use mismatched words and facial expressions, such as angry words while smiling or happy words while pretending to cry.

Strategies to Help Read New and/or Difficult Words

Students who are developing reading fluency and comprehension skills can become frustrated when presented with unfamiliar words in a given text. With direct phonics instruction, educators can teach students to decode words and then use context clues to define the words while reading. If students have a strong enough understanding of language structures, including nouns and verbs, educators can ask them to consider what part of speech the unknown word might be based on and where it might fit into the sentence. Other useful strategies involve self-monitoring, in which students are asked to think as they read and ask themselves if what they have just read makes sense. Focusing on visual clues, such as drawings and photographs, may give students valuable insight into deciphering unknown words. Looking for the word in another section of the text to see how it relates to the overall meaning could give a clue to the new vocabulary word. Spelling the word out loud or looking for word chunks, prefixes, and suffixes, as well as demonstrating how to segment the unknown word into its individual syllables, may also be effective strategies to employ.

One of the most valuable strategies, however, for helping students to read and understand new words is pre-teaching. In this strategy, educators select what they evaluate to be the unfamiliar words in the text and then introduce them to the class before reading. Educators using this method should be careful not to simply ask the students to read the text and then spell the new words correctly. They should also provide clear definitions and give the students the opportunity to read these words in various sentences to decipher word meaning. This method can dramatically reduce how often students stop reading in order to reflect on unknown words. Educators are often unsure as to whether to correct every mispronounced word a child makes when reading. If the mispronounced word still makes sense, it is sometimes better to allow the child to continue to read, since the more the child stops, the more the child's reading comprehension and fluency are negatively affected.

Drawing Conclusions and Comprehending Texts

When drawing conclusions about texts or passages, readers should do two main things: 1) Use the information that they already know and 2) Use the information they have learned from the text or passage. Authors write with an intended purpose, and it is the reader's responsibility to understand and form logical conclusions of authors' ideas. It is important to remember that the reader's conclusions should be supported by information directly from the text. Readers cannot simply form conclusions based off of only information they already know.

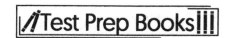

There are several ways readers can draw conclusions from authors' ideas, such as note taking, text evidence, text credibility, writing a response to text, directly stated information versus implications, outlining, summarizing, and paraphrasing. Each will be reviewed independently.

Note Taking

When readers take notes throughout texts or passages, they are jotting down important facts or points that the author makes. Note taking is a useful record of information that helps readers understand the text or passage and respond to it. When taking notes, readers should keep lines brief and filled with pertinent information so that they are not rereading a large amount of text, but rather just key points, elements, or words. After readers have completed a text or passage, they can refer to their notes to help them form a conclusion about the author's ideas in the text or passage.

Text Evidence

Text evidence is the information readers find in a text or passage that supports the main idea or point(s) in a story. In turn, text evidence can help readers draw conclusions about the text or passage. The information should be taken directly from the text or passage and placed in quotation marks. Text evidence provides readers with information to support ideas about the text so that they do not rely simply on their own thoughts. Details should be precise, descriptive, and factual. Statistics are a great piece of text evidence because they provide readers with exact numbers and not just a generalization. For example, instead of saying "Asia has a larger population than Europe," authors could provide detailed information such as, "In Asia there are over 4 billion people, whereas in Europe there are a little over 750 million." More definitive information provides better evidence to readers to help support their conclusions about texts or passages.

Text Credibility

Credible sources are important when drawing conclusions because readers need to be able to trust what they are reading. Authors should always use credible sources to help gain the trust of their readers. A text is *credible* when it is believable and the author is objective and unbiased. If readers do not trust an author's words, they may simply dismiss the text completely. For example, if an author writes a persuasive essay, he or she is outwardly trying to sway readers' opinions to align with his or her own. Readers may agree or disagree with the author, which may, in turn, lead them to believe that the author is credible or not credible. Also, readers should keep in mind the source of the text. If readers review a journal about astronomy, would a more reliable source be a NASA employee or a medical doctor? Overall, text credibility is important when drawing conclusions, because readers want reliable sources that support the decisions they have made about the author's ideas.

Writing a Response to Text

Once readers have determined their opinions and validated the credibility of a text, they can then reflect on the text. Writing a response to a text is one way readers can reflect on the given text or passage. When readers write responses to a text, it is important for them to rely on the evidence within the text to support their opinions or thoughts. Supporting evidence such as facts, details, statistics, and quotes directly from the text are key pieces of information readers should reflect upon or use when writing a response to text.

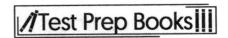

Directly Stated Information Versus Implications

Engaged readers should constantly self-question while reviewing texts to help them form conclusions. Self-questioning is when readers review a paragraph, page, passage, or chapter and ask themselves, "Did I understand what I read?," "What was the main event in this section?," "Where is this taking place?," and so on. Authors can provide clues or pieces of evidence throughout a text or passage to guide readers toward a conclusion. This is why active and engaged readers should read the text or passage in its entirety before forming a definitive conclusion. If readers do not gather all the pieces of evidence needed, then they may jump to an illogical conclusion.

At times, authors directly state conclusions while others simply imply them. Of course, it is easier if authors outwardly provide conclusions to readers because it does not leave any information open to interpretation. On the other hand, implications are things that authors do not directly state but can be assumed based off of information they provided. If authors only imply what may have happened, readers can form a menagerie of ideas for conclusions. For example, look at the following statement: "Once we heard the sirens, we hunkered down in the storm shelter." In this statement, the author does not directly state that there was a tornado, but clues such as "sirens" and "storm shelter" provide insight to the readers to help form that conclusion.

Outlining

An outline is a system used to organize writing. When reading texts, outlining is important because it helps readers organize important information in a logical pattern using roman numerals. Usually, outlines start with the main idea(s) and then branch out into subgroups or subsidiary thoughts of subjects. Not only do outlines provide a visual tool for readers to reflect on how events, characters, settings, or other key parts of the text or passage relate to one another, but they can also lead readers to a stronger conclusion. The sample below demonstrates what a general outline looks like.

I. Main Topic 1
   a. Subtopic 1
   b. Subtopic 2
      1. Detail 1
      2. Detail 2
II. Main Topic 2
   a. Subtopic 1
   b. Subtopic 2
      1. Detail 1
      2. Detail 2

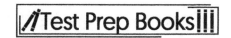

Summarizing

At the end of a text or passage, it is important to summarize what the readers read. Summarizing is a strategy in which readers determine what is important throughout the text or passage, shorten those ideas, and rewrite or retell it in their own words. A summary should identify the main idea of the text or passage. Important details or supportive evidence should also be accurately reported in the summary. If writers provide irrelevant details in the summary, it may cloud the greater meaning of the summary in the text. When summarizing, writers should not include their opinions, quotes, or what they thought the author should have said. A clear summary provides clarity of the text or passage to the readers. Let's review the checklist of items writers should include in their summary.

Summary Checklist
   Title of the story
   Someone: Who is or are the main character(s)?
   Wanted: What did the character(s) want?
   But: What was the problem?
   So: How did the character(s) solve the problem?
   Then: How did the story end? What was the resolution?

Paraphrasing

Another strategy readers can use to help them fully comprehend a text or passage is paraphrasing. Paraphrasing is when readers take the author's words and put them into their own words. When readers and writers paraphrase, they should avoid copying the text—that is plagiarism. It is also important to include as many details as possible when restating the facts. Not only will this help readers and writers recall information, but by putting the information into their own words, they demonstrate whether or not they fully comprehend the text or passage. Look at the example below showing an original text and how to paraphrase it.

Original Text: Fenway Park is home to the beloved Boston Red Sox. The stadium opened on April 20, 1912. The stadium currently seats over 37,000 fans, many of whom travel from all over the country to experience the iconic team and nostalgia of Fenway Park.

Paraphrased: On April 20, 1912, Fenway Park opened. Home to the Boston Red Sox, the stadium now seats over 37,000 fans. Many spectators travel to watch the Red Sox and experience the spirit of Fenway Park.

Paraphrasing, summarizing, and quoting can often cross paths with one another. Review the chart below showing the similarities and differences between the three strategies.

Paraphrasing	Summarizing	Quoting
Uses own words	Puts main ideas into own words	Uses words that are identical to text
References original source	References original source	Requires quotation marks
Uses own sentences	Shows important ideas of source	Uses author's own words and ideas

Demonstrating Common Research-Based Strategies for Reading Instruction

The TexES tests will assess educational candidates' familiarity with common research-based strategies for reading instruction. This will require potential teachers to be knowledgeable in current practices as well as able to evaluate the effectiveness of those practices as applicable to reading tasks and apply them to reading instruction challenges.

As this is a widely varied topic across educational levels, student abilities, and many reading comprehension skills, the potential test taker is advised to read further on the subject. Many online resources are available, but some additional works to consider include:

McGregor, Tanny. *Comprehension Connections: Bridges to Strategic Reading*. Portsmouth, New Hampshire: Heinemann, 2007.

Miller, Brett, Cutting, Laurie E., McCardle, Peggy. *Unraveling Reading Comprehension*. Baltimore, Maryland: Paul H. Brooks Publishing Co., Inc. 2013.

Tovani, Cris. *I Read it, but I Don't Get it: Comprehension Strategies for Adolescent Readers*. Portland, ME: Stenhouse Publishing, 2000.

Wilhelm, Jeffrey D. *Improving Comprehension with Think-Aloud Strategies*. New York, New York: Scholastic Inc., 2001.

A potential educator needs to be aware that teaching reading comprehension involves developing skills beyond mere word recognition. It involves being able to teach critical thinking skills and being able to teach students how to process unfamiliar material based on prior knowledge. It involves getting students involved in what they read, based on their interests, and their ability to relate to the material. It involves encouraging students to ask questions and explore.

In demonstrating one's ability to use common research-based strategies for reading instruction, a potential test taker should be able to show his or her awareness of theory regarding how to activate students' prior knowledge, how to model meta-cognitive practices, and how to employ multiple reading strategies for a variety of situations for the most comprehensive student experience.

Activating Prior Knowledge

Activating students' prior knowledge—sometimes referred to as *schemas*—means being able to get students to ascertain what they already know, so they can apply it to their reading. A common strategy to use prior to reading is a K-W-L chart, a graphic organizer which has students determine what they already know about a topic, what they want to know, and what they learned after reading. Having students complete the K section before reading is a tangible way to activate their schemas.

It is important students make connections and relate reading passages to their own experiences—referred to as *text to self*, to their world knowledge— referred to as *text to world*, and to other texts—referred to as *text to text*. The ability to make these connections helps students better understand what they have read.

Potential teachers should be able to model asking questions during the reading experience and model the finding of those answers, based on prior knowledge. Having students read, then write about the connections they make to the text will increase reading comprehension skills. Of course, teaching students to activate and use their schema as it applies to their reading is a skill that should be taught over time. Encourage students to ask how text passages relate to what they already know within their own lives, how those passages relate to what they already know about the world, and how those passages relate to other things they've read. Doing so will result in more critical thinkers and, in turn, more critical readers.

Metacognitive Practices

Metacognitive strategies ask the student to decode text passages. In part, they require the student to preview text, be able to recognize unfamiliar words, then use context clues to define them for greater understanding. In addition, meta-cognitive strategies in the classroom employ skills such as being able to decode imagery, being able to predict, and being able to summarize. If a student can define unfamiliar vocabulary, make sense of an author's use of imagery, preview text prior to reading, predict outcomes during reading, and summarize the material, he or she is achieving effective reading comprehension. When approaching reading instruction, the teacher who encourages students to use phrases such as *I'm noticing*, *I'm thinking*, and *I'm wondering* is teaching a meta-cognitive type strategy.

Active Reading

It has been shown that the teacher who employs multiple reading strategies in a variety of reading situations has the most success in fostering critical thinkers. Teachers should strive to make reading an active, observable process. *Active reading* involves reading with a purpose and determination to not only understand, but evaluate text using critical reading skills. Critical reading skills need to be fostered in a way that allows students to read and retain information and then gain interactive feedback experience with peers and with an instructor. Employing multiple reading strategies, either through assigned, independent reading with follow up or through a shared experience, aids in active reading.

The following are some of the reading strategies that should be utilized:

- Modeling prediction
- Modeling inference
- Asking students to connect text to self, the world, and to other text
- Asking students to visualize what they read (playing the "video" in their head)
- Asking students to partner in their reading experiences
- Helping students determine the importance of ideas in what they read

- Modeling the critical thinking process
- Modeling analyzation
- Modeling summarization

Interpreting Textual Evidence in Informational Text

Literal and Figurative Meanings

It is important when evaluating informational texts to consider the use of both *literal and figurative meanings*. The words and phrases an author chooses to include in a text must be evaluated. How does the word choice affect the meaning and tone? By recognizing the use of literal and figurative language, a reader can more readily ascertain the message or purpose of a text. Literal word choice is the easiest to analyze as it represents the usual and intended way a word or phrase is used. It is also more common in informational texts because it is used to state facts and definitions. While figurative language is typically associated with fiction and poetry, it can be found in informational texts as well. The reader must determine not only what is meant by the figurative language in context, but also how the author intended it to shape the overall text.

Inference in Informational Text

Inference refers to the reader's ability to understand the unwritten text, i.e., "read between the lines" in terms of an author's intent or message. The strategy asks that a reader not take everything he or she reads at face value but instead, add his or her own interpretation of what the author seems to be trying to convey. A reader's ability to make inferences relies on his or her ability to think clearly and logically about the text. It does not ask that the reader make wild speculation or guess about the material but demands that he or she be able to come to a sound conclusion about the material.

An author's use of less literal words and phrases requires readers to make more inference when they read. Since inference involves *deduction*—deriving conclusions from ideas assumed to be true—there's more room for interpretation. Still, critical readers who employ inference, if careful in their thinking, can still arrive at the logical, sound conclusions the author intends.

Textual Evidence in Informational Text

Once a reader has determined an author's thesis or main idea, he or she will need to understand how textual evidence supports interpretation of that thesis or main idea. Test takers will be asked direct questions regarding an author's main idea and may be asked to identify evidence that would support those ideas. This will require test takers to comprehend literal and figurative meanings within the text passage, be able to draw inferences from provided information, and be able to separate important evidence from minor supporting detail. It's often helpful to skim test questions and answer options prior to critically reading informational text; however, test takers should avoid the temptation to solely look for the correct answers. Just trying to find the "right answer" may cause test takers to miss important supporting textual evidence. Making mental note of test questions is only helpful as a guide when reading.

After identifying an author's thesis or main idea, a test taker should look at the supporting details that the author provides to back up his or her assertions, identifying those additional pieces of information that help expand the thesis. From there, test takers should examine the additional information and related details for credibility, the author's use of outside sources, and be able to point to direct evidence that supports the author's claims. It's also imperative that test takers be able to identify what is strong support and what is merely additional information that is nice to know but not necessary. Being able to make this differentiation will help test takers effectively answer questions regarding an author's use of supporting evidence within informational text.

Prior Knowledge When Reading

To read actively, students should use prior knowledge to make accurate predictions. Effective teachers guide students to make links between the current text, previously read texts, and life experiences. Some texts use suspense and foreshadowing to captivate readers. For example, an intriguing aspect of murder mysteries is that the reader is never sure of the culprit until the author reveals the individual's identity. Authors often build suspense and add depth and meaning to a work by leaving clues to provide hints or predict future events in the story; this is called foreshadowing. While some instances of foreshadowing are subtle, others are quite obvious.

Another way to read actively is to identify examples of inference within text. Authors employ literary devices such as tone, characterization, and theme to engage the audience by showing details of the story instead of merely telling them. For example, if an author said *Bob is selfish*, there's little left to infer. If the author said, *Bob cheated on his test, ignored his mom's calls, and parked illegally*, the reader can infer Bob is selfish. Authors also make implications through character dialogue, thoughts, effects on others, actions, and looks. Like in life, readers must assemble all the clues to form a complete picture.

Active readers should also draw conclusions. When doing so, the reader should ask the following questions: What is this piece about? What does the author believe? Does this piece have merit? Do I believe the author? Would this piece support my argument? The reader should first determine the author's intent. Identify the author's viewpoint and connect relevant evidence to support it. Readers may then move to the most important step: deciding whether to agree and determining whether they are correct. Always read cautiously and critically. Interact with text, and record reactions in the margins. These active reading skills help determine not only what the author thinks, but what you as the reader thinks.

Reading Non-Literary Texts

Non-Fiction Literature

Non-fiction literature is text that is true and accurate in detail. Nonfiction can cover virtually any topic in the natural world. Nonfiction writers conduct research and carefully organize facts before writing. Nonfiction has the following subgenres:

Informational Text — This is text written to impart information to the reader. It may have literary elements such as charts, graphs, indexes, glossaries, or bibliographies.

Persuasive Text —This is text that is meant to sway the reader to have a particular opinion or take a particular action.

Biographies and Autobiographies — This is text that tells intimate details of someone's life. If an author writes the text about someone else, it is a biography. If the author writes it about himself or herself, it is an autobiography.

Communicative text — This is text used to communicate with another person. This includes such texts as emails, formal and informal letters, and tweets. This content often consists of two-sided dialogue between people.

Primary sources are best defined as records or items that serve as evidence of periods of history. To be considered primary, the source documents or objects must have been created during the time period in which they reference. Examples include diaries, newspaper articles, speeches, government documents, photographs, and historical artifacts. In today's digital age, primary sources, which were once in print, often are embedded in secondary sources. Secondary sources, such as websites, history books, databases, or reviews, contain analysis or commentary on primary sources. Secondary sources borrow information from primary sources through the process of quoting, summarizing, or paraphrasing.

Today's students often complete research online through electronic sources. Electronic sources offer advantages over print, and can be accessed on virtually any computer, while libraries or other research centers are limited to fixed locations and specific catalogs. Electronic sources are also efficient and yield massive amounts of data in seconds. The user can tailor a search based on key words, publication years, and article length. Lastly, many databases provide the user with instant citations, saving the user the trouble of manually assembling sources.

Though electronic sources yield powerful results, researchers must use caution. While there are many reputable and reliable sources on the internet, just as many are unreliable or biased sources. It's up to the researcher to examine and verify the reliability of sources. *Wikipedia*, for example, may or may not be accurate, depending on the contributor. Many databases, such as *EBSCO* or *SIRS*, offer peer reviewed articles, meaning the publications have been reviewed for the quality of their content.

Promoting Students' Comprehension of Informational Text and Literature

Promoting Literacy Development
It is widely accepted that the more classroom opportunities a student has for listening, speaking, reading, and writing, the more these skills will strengthen. Educators, who frequently read to emergent readers using exaggerated pauses, inflections, tones, and pronunciation, report encouraging signs of progress in student literacy development and independent reading skills.

Directed Reading-Thinking Activities
Prior to the introduction of a challenging text, educators may spend time with the class predicting what the text might be about. By paying attention to the features of the book or text, students can begin to formulate ideas about the overall content. Educators may try to extend this discussion, prompting students to consider what the setting of the book or written piece might be, what events might take place, and what types of characters they might encounter. When an educator focuses on prediction skills prior to reading, students begin to strengthen their ability to connect literature to real life.

After reading, educators may begin another class discussion, prompting students to consider whether their predictions were accurate and why or why not this was so. For instance, an educator may point out that a student's own life experiences may have prompted her to predict a certain outcome. When students relate literature to their own lives in this way, reading becomes a more enjoyable and meaningful activity. Post-reading activities may also involve small groups of students acting out various scenes or retelling the story in their own words, which also helps the educator to assess students' overall comprehension. Post-reading activities should include discussions regarding various literary elements such as cause and effect or the author's points of view.

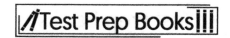

Monitoring Comprehension

Self-monitoring one's comprehension is a valuable lifelong skill for students to learn. Teaching self-monitoring takes advantage of students' natural ability to recognize when they understand the reading and when they do not. Students will need to learn to:

Identify exactly the part of the text where the difficulty occurs
Identify the specific problem and restate the difficult text in their own words
Reread previous portions of the text to gain clues about the problematic piece
Scan future portions of the text for information that helps resolve the question

Metacognition

Skilled readers have learned to think about thinking. This is called metacognition. Using metacognitive strategies is a skill that gives students control over their learning while they read and may involve the use strategies such as:

- Identifying purpose for reading the selection
- Previewing the text
- Matching their reading speed to the challenge level of the selection
- Asking themselves comprehension questions
- Resolving comprehension problems independently or with help
- Checking themselves for understanding after reading the selection

KWL Activities

Good reading teachers know how to help students activate their prior knowledge and draw from personal curiosity to set them up for the learning task. Students can create a KWL (Know/Want to know/Learned) chart to get ready for any unit of instruction. Teachers guide students to identify what they already know about a given topic. They then help them generate questions about the topic. After the instruction takes place, teachers help students analyze what they have learned.

Comprehension of Informational Text

Informational text is written material that has the primary function of imparting information about a topic. It is often written by someone with expertise in the topic and directed at an audience that has less knowledge of the topic. Informational texts are written in a different fashion from storytelling or narrative texts. Typically, this type of text has several organizational and structural differences from narrative text. In informational texts, there are features such as charts, graphs, photographs, headings and subheadings, glossaries, indexes, bibliographies, or other guidance features. With the aid of technology, embedded hyperlinks and video content are also sometimes included. Informational material may be written to compare and contrast, be explanatory, link cause and effect, provide opinion, persuade the reader, or serve a number of other purposes. Finally, informational texts typically use a different style of language than narrative texts, which instead, focus more on storytelling. Historically, informational texts were not introduced until students were ready to read to learn versus still learning to read. However, research is now suggesting that informational text can be developmentally appropriate for students at a much younger age.

One very effective strategy for increasing comprehension of informational text is *reciprocal teaching*. Reciprocal teaching is a method of small group teaching that relies on students assuming different roles to practice four reading strategies particularly helpful for readers of informational texts. Predicting, summarizing, questioning, and clarifying will lead students to understand and apply what they read.

Skilled readers have acquired a set of techniques that make informational reading effective for them. They begin by previewing text selections and making educated guesses as to what the content will include. They then identify the purpose for reading the text and can explain why the content will be important to know. They are able to filter the reading selection to screen out the trivial points and focus on the most important facts. Using critical thinking skills, they monitor their own understanding of the information by asking themselves questions about what they have read. They use multiple methods to determine the meaning of unknown vocabulary. Finally, they can concisely and succinctly form an overall summary of what they have learned from the text.

Predicting

Predicting requires thinking ahead and, after reading, verifying whether predictions were correct. This method engages students with the text and gets them to pay attention to details that tell them whether their predictions might be coming true. The goal is to help students learn to base their predictions on clues from the text. They should not only state what they predict but also be able to comment on the specifics of the text that lead them to make those predictions.

Summarizing

Through summarizing, students learn to identify the main ideas and differentiate them from the less important information in the text. It helps them remember what they read and retell the central concepts in their own words. As students learn to break down larger chunks of information into more concise sentences, they use analytical thinking skills and hone their critical reading capabilities.

Questioning Techniques

Questioning has immeasurable value in the reading process. Answering questions about a text gives purpose for reading to students and focuses them on reading to learn information. Similarly, generating questions about a text for others to answer enables a student to analyze what is important to learn in the text and glean summarizing skills. Keeping Bloom's Taxonomy in mind, teachers can scaffold students toward increased critical thinking capabilities.

Bloom's Taxonomy shows the hierarchy of learning progressing through the following stages:

1. Remembering
2. Understanding
3. Applying
4. Analyzing
5. Evaluating
6. Creating

Clarifying

This is the post-reading phase where students learn to clear up any misunderstandings and unanswered questions. Strategies for clarifying include defining any unknown words, rereading at a slower pace, reviewing previous segments of the text, referring to their summaries, and skimming future portions of the text.

Understanding Organizational Patterns and Structures

Organizational Structure within Informational Text

Informational text is specifically designed to relate factual information, and although it is open to a reader's interpretation and application of the facts, the structure of the presentation is carefully designed to lead the reader to a particular conclusion or central idea. When reading informational text, it is important that readers are able to understand its organizational structure as the structure often directly relates to an author's intent to inform and/or persuade the reader.

The first step in identifying the text's structure is to determine the thesis or main idea. The thesis statement and organization of a work are closely intertwined. *A thesis statement* indicates the writer's purpose and may include the scope and direction of the text. It may be presented at the beginning of a text or at the end, and it may be explicit or implicit.

Once a reader has a grasp of the thesis or main idea of the text, he or she can better determine its organizational structure. Test takers are advised to read informational text passages more than once in order to comprehend the material fully. It is also helpful to examine any text features present in the text including the table of contents, index, glossary, headings, footnotes, and visuals. The analysis of these features and the information presented within them, can offer additional clues about the central idea and structure of a text. The following questions should be asked when considering structure:

- How does the author assemble the parts to make an effective whole argument?

- Is the passage linear in nature and if so, what is the timeline or thread of logic?

- What is the presented order of events, facts, or arguments? Are these effective in contributing to the author's thesis?

- How can the passage be divided into sections? How are they related to each other and to the main idea or thesis?

- What key terms are used to indicate the organization?

Next, test takers should skim the passage, noting the first line or two of each body paragraph—the *topic sentences*—and the conclusion. Key *transitional terms*, such as *on the other hand*, *also*, *because*, *however*, *therefore*, *most importantly*, and *first*, within the text can also signal organizational structure. Based on these clues, readers should then be able to identify what type of organizational structure is being used. The following organizational structures are most common:

- *Problem/solution*—organized by an analysis/overview of a problem, followed by potential solution(s)

- *Cause/effect*—organized by the effects resulting from a cause or the cause(s) of a particular effect

- *Spatial order*—organized by points that suggest location or direction—e.g., top to bottom, right to left, outside to inside

- *Chronological/sequence order*—organized by points presented to indicate a passage of time or through purposeful steps/stages

- *Comparison/Contrast*—organized by points that indicate similarities and/or differences between two things or concepts

- *Order of importance*—organized by priority of points, often most significant to least significant or vice versa

Identifying Rhetorical Strategies

Rhetoric refers to an author's use of particular strategies, appeals, and devices to persuade an intended audience. The more effective the use of rhetoric, the more likely the audience will be persuaded.

Determining an Author's Point of View

A *rhetorical strategy*—also referred to as a *rhetorical mode*—is the structural way an author chooses to present his/her argument. Though the terms noted below are similar to the organizational structures noted earlier, these strategies do not imply that the entire text follows the approach. For example, a cause and effect organizational structure is solely that, nothing more. A persuasive text may use cause and effect as a strategy to convey a singular point. Thus, an argument may include several of the strategies as the author strives to convince his or her audience to take action or accept a different point of view. It's important that readers are able to identify an author's thesis and position on the topic in order to be able to identify the careful construction through which the author speaks to the reader. The following are some of the more common rhetorical strategies:

- Cause and effect—establishing a logical correlation or causation between two ideas
- Classification/division—the grouping of similar items together or division of something into parts
- Comparison/contrast—the distinguishing of similarities/differences to expand on an idea
- Definition—used to clarify abstract ideas, unfamiliar concepts, or to distinguish one idea from another
- Description—use of vivid imagery, active verbs, and clear adjectives to explain ideas
- Exemplification—the use of examples to explain an idea
- Narration—anecdotes or personal experience to present or expand on a concept
- Problem/Solution—presentation of a problem or problems, followed by proposed solution(s)

Rhetorical Strategies and Devices

A *rhetorical device* is the phrasing and presentation of an idea that reinforces and emphasizes a point in an argument. A rhetorical device is often quite memorable. One of the more famous uses of a rhetorical device is in John F. Kennedy's 1961 inaugural address: "Ask not what your country can do for you, ask what you can do for your country." The contrast of ideas presented in the phrasing is an example of the rhetorical device of antimetabole. Some other common examples are provided below, but test takers should be aware that this is not a complete list.

Device	Definition	Example
Allusion	A reference to a famous person, event, or significant literary text as a form of significant comparison	"We are apt to shut our eyes against a painful truth, and listen to the song of that siren till she transforms us into beasts." Patrick Henry
Anaphora	The repetition of the same words at the beginning of successive words, phrases, or clauses, designed to emphasize an idea	"We shall not flag or fail. We shall go on to the end. We shall fight in France, we shall fight on the seas and oceans, we shall fight with growing confidence … we shall fight in the fields and in the streets, we shall fight in the hills. We shall never surrender." Winston Churchill
Understatement	A statement meant to portray a situation as less important than it actually is to create an ironic effect	"The war in the Pacific has not necessarily developed in Japan's favor." Emperor Hirohito, surrendering Japan in World War II
Parallelism	A syntactical similarity in a structure or series of structures used for impact of an idea, making it memorable	"A penny saved is a penny earned." Ben Franklin
Rhetorical question	A question posed that is not answered by the writer though there is a desired response, most often designed to emphasize a point	"Can anyone look at our reduced standing in the world today and say, 'Let's have four more years of this?'" Ronald Reagan

Identifying Information in an Index or Table of Contents

An index is an alphabetical listing of topics, such as people, works, or concepts that appear at the end of expository materials like textbooks, cookbooks, and repair manuals. When these key words are used in paragraphs, they sometimes appear in bold writing to indicate their importance and let the reader know that they're found in the index as well.

Index listings often discard articles like *a*, *an*, and *the*. Additionally, authors will be listed by their last names, not first. Topics may be further divided into subtopics. If you start by looking for the most basic topics first, you can quickly acquire information. For example, when looking for a cookie recipe in a cookbook, first find the word *cookie* in the index and then examine the indented list of cookie-related topics located directly beneath the original heading.

Some textbooks have multiple indexes arranged by different subjects. If, for instance, you're dealing with a weighty literature textbook, you might find one index that lists authors and another devoted to concepts. The lengthier the book, the more likely you are to find this format.

While an index is typically found at the end of a book, a table of contents is found at the beginning to help readers quickly locate information. A table of contents is arranged differently, however, because it provides a chronological listing of each chapter and a corresponding page number. Each entry may also include a description, summary statement, or objective.

When students first receive a textbook, they should take time to preview the table of contents to create a framework for mentally organizing information. By classifying the contents, the reader creates mental schemas and becomes more likely to retain the information longer.

Analyzing Headings and Subheadings

Headings and subheadings are used in writing to organize discussions and allow the reader to find information quickly. Headings show a complete change in thought. Subheadings, which fall below headings, show different aspects of the same topic. For instance, if you saw the title *Government* and the heading *Forms of Government*, you might see the subheadings *Monarchy*, *Oligarchy*, *Democracy*, *Socialism*, and *Totalitarianism*.

As well as providing organization and structure, headings and subheadings also put more white space on a page, which places less strain on the reader's eyes. It's a good idea to skim a document and get familiar with headings and subheadings. Write down the title, headings, and subheadings before you begin reading to provide structure to your notes and thoughts.

Analyzing and Using Text Features

Text features are used to bring clarity or to affect the meaning of it. Bolding, italics, and underlining are all used to make words stand out.

Bolded words are often key concepts and can usually be found in summary statements at the end of chapters and in indexes.

Italics can be used to identify words of another language or to add extra emphasis to a word or phrase. Writers will sometime place words in italics when the word is being referred to as the word itself. Quotation marks or italics can be used for this, as long as there is consistency .

Italics are also used to represent a character's thoughts.

Entering Jessica's room, Jessica's mom stepped over a pile of laundry, a stack of magazines, and a pile of dishes. *My messy daughter*, she thought, shaking her head.

In addition, formatting—such as indentation or bullet points—helps to clearly present content. Writers can come up with their own uses for text features based on what they feel is best. It's important to catch on to the purpose of the text features that the writer uses.

Analyzing and Evaluating Text Structure

Depending on what the author is attempting to accomplish, certain formats or text structures work better than others. For example, a sequence structure might work for narration but not when identifying similarities and differences between dissimilar concepts. Similarly, a comparison-contrast structure is not useful for narration. It's the author's job to put the right information in the correct format.

Readers should be familiar with the five main literary structures:

1. *Sequence* structure (sometimes referred to as the order structure) is when the order of events proceed in a predictable order. In many cases, this means the text goes through the plot elements: exposition, rising action, climax, falling action, and resolution. Readers are introduced to characters, setting, and conflict in the exposition. In the rising action, there's an increase in tension and suspense. The climax is the height of tension and the point of no return. Tension decreases during the falling action. In the resolution, any conflicts presented in the exposition are solved, and the story concludes. An informative text that is structured sequentially will often go in order from one step to the next.

2. In the *problem-solution* structure, authors identify a potential problem and suggest a solution. This form of writing is usually divided into two paragraphs and can be found in informational texts. For example, cell phone, cable, and satellite providers use this structure in manuals to help customers troubleshoot or identify problems with services or products.

3. When authors want to discuss similarities and differences between separate concepts, they arrange thoughts in a *comparison-contrast* paragraph structure. Venn diagrams are an effective graphic organizer for comparison-contrast structures because they feature two overlapping circles that can be used to organize similarities and differences. A comparison-contrast essay organizes one paragraph based on similarities and another based on differences. A comparison-contrast essay can also be arranged with the similarities and differences of individual traits addressed within individual paragraphs. Words such as *however*, *but*, and *nevertheless* help signal a contrast in ideas.

4. *Descriptive* writing structure is designed to appeal to your senses. Much like an artist who constructs a painting, good descriptive writing builds an image in the reader's mind by appealing to the five senses: sight, hearing, taste, touch, and smell. However, overly descriptive writing can become tedious; sparse descriptions can make settings and characters seem flat. Good authors strike a balance by applying descriptions only to passages, characters, and settings that are integral to the plot.

5. Passages that use the *cause and effect* structure are simply asking *why* by demonstrating some type of connection between ideas. Words such as *if*, *since*, *because*, *then*, or *consequently* indicate relationship. By switching the order of a complex sentence, the writer can rearrange the emphasis on different clauses. Saying *If Sheryl is late, we'll miss the dance* is different from saying *We'll miss the dance if Sheryl is late*. One emphasizes Sheryl's tardiness while the other emphasizes missing the dance. Paragraphs can also be arranged in a cause and effect format. Since the format—before and after—is sequential, it is useful when authors wish to discuss the impact of choices. Researchers often apply this paragraph structure to the scientific method.

Identifying Information from a Graph

Texts may have graphical representations to help illustrate and visually support assertions made. For example, graphs can be used to express samples or segments of a population or demonstrate growth or decay. Three of the most popular graphical formats include line graphs, bar graphs, and pie charts.

Line graphs rely on a horizontal X-axis and a vertical Y-axis to establish baseline values. Dots are plotted where the horizontal and vertical axes intersect, and those dots are connected with lines. Compared to bar graphs or pie charts, line graphs are more useful for looking at the past and present and predicting future outcomes. For instance, a potential investor would look for stocks that demonstrated steady growth over many decades when examining the stock market. Note that severe spikes up and down indicate instability, while line graphs that display a slow but steady increase may indicate good returns.

Here's an example of a bar graph:

Bar graphs are usually displayed on a vertical Y-axis. The bars themselves can be two- or three-dimensional, depending on the designer's tastes. Unlike a line graph, which shows the fluctuation of only one variable, the X-axis on a bar graph is excellent for making comparisons, because it shows differences between several variables. For instance, if a consumer wanted to buy a new tablet, she could narrow the selection down to a few choices by using a bar graph to plot the prices side by side. The tallest bar would be the most expensive tablet, the shortest bar would be the cheapest.

A pie chart is divided into wedges that represent a numerical piece of the whole. Pie charts are useful for demonstrating how different categories add up to 100 percent. However, pie charts are not useful in comparing dissimilar items. High schools tend to use pie charts to track where students end up after graduation. Each wedge, for instance, might be labeled *vocational school, two-year college, four-year college, workforce,* or *unemployed*. By calculating the size of each wedge, schools can offer classes in the same ratios as where students will end up after high school. Pie charts are also useful for tracking finances. Items such as car payments, insurance, rent, credit cards, and entertainment would each get their own wedge proportional to the amount spent in a given time period. If one wedge is inordinately bigger than the rest, or if a wedge is expendable, it might be time to create a new financial strategy.

Identifying Scale Readings

Most measuring instruments have scales to allow someone to determine precise measurement. Many of these instruments are becoming digitized, such as their screens' output measurements; for example, weighing scales and tire-pressure gauges often have digital screens. However, it's still important to know how to read scales. Many rulers have scales for inches on one side and scales for centimeters on the other side. On the inches' side, the longest black lines indicate the inch marks, and the slightly shorter lines indicate the half-inch marks. Progressively shorter black lines indicate the quarter-inch, eighth-inch, and sometimes even sixteenth-inch marks.

Using Legends and Map Keys

Legends and map keys are placed on maps to identify what the symbols on the map represent. Generally, map symbols stand for things like railroads, national or state highways, and public parks. Legends and maps keys can generally be found in the bottom right corner of a map. They are necessary to avoid the needless repetition of the same information because of the large amounts of information condensed onto a map. In addition, there may be a compass rose that shows the directions of north, south, east, and west. Most maps are oriented such that the top of the map is north.

Maps also have scales, which are a type of legend or key that show relative distances between fixed points. If you were on a highway and nearly out of gas, a map's scale would help you determine if you could make it to the next town before running out of fuel.

Evaluating Product Information to Determine the Most Economical Buy

When evaluating product information, be on the lookout for bolded and italicized words and numbers, which indicate the information is especially important. Also be on the lookout for repeated or similar information, which indicates importance. If you're trying to find the best deal, it might be useful to do a side-by-side comparison. Using software, like Microsoft Excel, can help you organize and compare costs systematically.

In addition, being a savvy shopper in today's market means not only having a decent grasp of math, but also understanding how retailers use established techniques to encourage consumers to spend more. Look for units of measurement—pounds, ounces, liters, grams, etc.—then divide the amount by the cost. By comparing this way, you may find products on sale cost more than ones that are not.

You should also take into consideration any tax or shipping costs. Obviously, the more an item costs, the more tax or shipping tends to cost too. Most brick and mortar establishments, like Target, Walmart, and Sears, are required to charge tax based on location, but some internet sites, like Amazon, Overstock, and eBay, will offer no tax or free shipping as an incentive. Comparisons between local stores and internet sites can aid in finding the best deal.

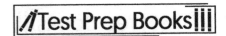

Identifying Information from a Telephone Book

The yellow pages in printed telephone books offer an alphabetical listing of businesses and services. Along with basic contact information—address, phone number, and business information—some will pay more to include an advertisement. Though more flashy and engaging than basic contact information, ads are not necessarily indicative of better service. Similar to the yellow pages, the white pages offer an alphabetical listing of people's names, addresses, and phone numbers. The blue pages provide an alphabetical listing of government agencies and numbers. Most of the information previously only available in telephone books can now be found online.

Identifying Information from a Listing of Items

When similar items are sold, they are often placed in tables or charts for the consumer's convenience. Either scanning horizontally across a row or vertically down a column (or a combination of both) provides the opportunity for a quick comparison. Basic math plays a part in the decision making, but consumers should also consider warranties, product reputations, and hidden costs, such as tax or shipping.

For example, consider menus. Meals are individually labeled or multiple items are grouped under one heading, such as appetizers or main dishes. Substitutions may or may not have an added cost. Drinks might be ordered separately or included with the meal. Some restaurants offer free refills while others charge for each glass. If in doubt, ask your server. Regardless of the order, sales tax or a tip is seldom included. If gratuity is included, it's usually due to the size of your party and is noted on the menu. A 15-20 percent tip is customary in the United States.

For movie listings, however, prices may fluctuate based on age (teenager versus senior citizen) and time (early-bird showing versus evening). Movie listings are typically oriented vertically, either on a marquis, a display, or an easel. The current movies are usually listed with each of their show times.

Identifying the Appropriate Source for Locating Information

With a wealth of information at your fingertips in this digital age, it's important to know not only the type of information you're looking for, but also in what medium you're most likely to find it. Information needs to be specific and reliable. For example, if you're repairing a car, an encyclopedia would be mostly useless. While an encyclopedia might include information about cars, an owner's manual will contain the specific information needed for repairs. Information must also be reliable or credible so that it can be trusted. A well-known newspaper may have reliable information, but a peer-reviewed journal article will have likely gone through a more rigorous check for validity. Determining bias can be helpful in determining credibility. If the information source (person, organization, or company) has something to gain from the reader forming a certain view on a topic, it's likely the information is skewed. For example, if you are trying to find the unemployment rate, the Bureau of Labor Statistics is a more credible source than a politician's speech.

Resource Materials and Digital Tools

Teachers are learning to adapt their writing instruction to integrate today's technology standards and to enhance engagement in the writing process. The key is to still build a strong foundation of the fundamentals of writing while using current technology. Gone are the days when writing relied solely on handwritten pieces and when the tools of the trade were pencils, paper, hardback dictionaries, and encyclopedias. Online resources are now the backbone of the writing experience. It is now possible to integrate photo, video, and other interactive components into a completed project to provide a well-rounded engagement with media. In order to have an education conducive to college and career readiness and success, students need online research and digital media writing skills.

There are many compelling reasons to teach students to be digitally aware and prudent users of technology when it comes to their writing. With current digital technology, the writing process has become a much more collaborative experience. In higher education and in career settings, collaborative skills are essential. Publishing and presenting are now simplified such that completed work is often read by a wide variety of audiences. Writing can be instantly shared with parents, peers, educators, and the general public, including experts in the field. Students are more apt to take an interest in the writing process when they know that others are reading their writing. Feedback is also simplified because so many platforms allow comments from readers. Teachers can be interactive with the students throughout the process, allowing formative assessment and integration of personalized instruction. Technology is simply a new vehicle for human connection and interactivity.

A student may be exposed to a plethora of technology, but this does not mean that she or he necessarily knows how to use it for learning. The teacher is still responsible for guiding, monitoring, and scaffolding the students toward learning objectives. It is critical that educators teach students how to locate credible information and to reliably cite their sources using bibliographies. Platforms and apps for online learning are varied and plentiful. Here are some ideas for how to use technology for writing instruction in the classroom:

Use a projector with a tablet to display notes and classwork for the group to see. This increases instructional time because notes are already available rather than having to be written in real-time. This also provides the ability to save, email, and post classwork and notes for students and parents to access on their own time. A student can work at his or her own pace and still keep up with instruction. Student screens can be displayed for peer-led teaching and sharing of class work.

More technology in class means less paperwork. Digital drop-boxes can be used for students to turn in assignments. Teachers can save paper, keep track of student revisions of work, and give feedback electronically.

Digital media can be used to differentiate instruction for multiple learning styles and multiple skill levels. Instead of using standardized textbook learning for everyone, teachers can create and collect resources for individualizing course content.

Inquiry- and problem-based learning is easier with increased collaborative capabilities provided by digital tools.

Digital textbooks and e-readers can replace hardback versions of text that are prone to damage and loss. Students can instantly access definitions for new words, as well as annotate and highlight useful information without ruining a hardbound book.

Library databases can be used to locate reliable research information and resources. There are digital tools for tracking citation information, allowing annotations for internet content, and for storing internet content.

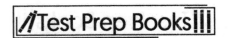

Mobile devices may be used in the classroom to encourage reading and writing when students use them to text, post, blog, and tweet.

PowerPoint and other presentation software can be used to model writing for students and to provide a platform for presenting their work.

Students can create a classroom blog, review various blog sites, and use blogs as they would diaries or journals. They can even write from the perspective of the character in a book or a famous historical person.

Web quests can be used to help guide students on research projects. They can get relevant information on specific topics and decide what pieces to include in their writing.

Students can write about technology as a topic. They can "teach" someone how to use various forms of technology, specific learning platforms, or apps.

Students can create webpages, make a class webpage, and then use it to help with home-school communication.

Online feedback and grading systems can be used. There are many to choose from. This may allow students to see the grading rubric and ask questions or receive suggestions from the teacher.

Students and teachers can use email to exchange ideas with other schools or experts on certain topics that are being studied in the classroom.

Game show-style reviews can be created for units of study to use on computers or on an overhead projector.

A wiki website can be created that allows students to collaborate, expand on each other's work, and do peer editing and revision.

Publishing tools can be used to publish student work on the web or in class newspapers or social media sites.

Sequences of Events in Informational Texts

Analyzing and explaining a set of ideas or events calls for students to follow the logic of an author's text. It's necessary to be able to follow a plot or different concepts presented in an informational text in order to understand its meaning. To reinforce this concept, teachers can have students identify the main idea and supporting points. Successfully doing this demonstrates an understanding of the framework of an argument or the plot of a narrative, for example. It can also help students to recognize patterns in the way an author organizes a text. Students should also be able to make meaningful connections between these ideas.

Evaluating Consumer, Workplace, and Public Documents

It is important for students to be able to read consumer, workplace, and public documents and understand them without prior knowledge of their content. Structure and content can provide clues to meaning. Knowing how to analyze these texts will help students when they encounter them in everyday life. Some examples of these types of documents are insurance forms, a job application, or a service contract. These documents may contain terminology that readers are unfamiliar with. Teachers can help students to decipher meaning through analysis of the structure and purpose of these documents. They can also help students evaluate key terms and the use of text features like graphics and headers.

Interpreting Informational Texts in their Contexts

Context refers to all the cultural, social, political associations of a text. The way an author was raised and the environment in which they have lived can influence how he or she writes. When a reader knows more about the norms of a culture, such as what is an appropriate greeting among strangers (a hug, a handshake, a nod, etc.), it can allow a deeper understanding when such an event occurs in a text. It's important to take these kinds of associations into consideration when determining things like the author's intended audience and purpose. Teachers can help students to understand context by pointing out the cultural, social, and political aspects of a text, which may be unfamiliar to students, and educating them as to their meaning. An informational text's primary purpose is to convey information about the world. Examples of informational texts are speeches like Abraham Lincoln's *Gettysburg Address* or Martin Luther King's *I Have a Dream* speech or a scientific text like Euclid's *Elements*. The overall goal of these texts is to inform readers, and not to entertain or tell the story of a character.

Literary Elements, Genres, and Movements

Understanding the Characteristics of Literary Genres

Classifying literature involves an understanding of the concept of genre. A *genre* is a category of literature that possesses similarities in style and in characteristics. Based on form and structure, there are four basic genres.

Fictional Prose

Fictional prose consists of fictional works written in standard form with a natural flow of speech and without poetic structure. Fictional prose primarily utilizes grammatically complete sentences and a paragraph structure to convey its message.

Drama

Drama is fiction that is written to be performed in a variety of media, intended to be performed for an audience, and structured for that purpose. It might be composed using poetry or prose, often straddling the elements of both in what actors are expected to present. Action and dialogue are the tools used in drama to tell the story.

Poetry

Poetry is fiction in verse that has a unique focus on the rhythm of language and focuses on intensity of feeling. It is not an entire story, though it may tell one; it is compact in form and in function. Poetry can be considered as a poet's brief word picture for a reader. Poetic structure is primarily composed of lines and stanzas. Together, poetic structure and devices are the methods that poets use to lead readers to feeling an effect and, ultimately, to the interpretive message.

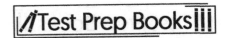

Literary Nonfiction

Literary nonfiction is prose writing that is based on current or past real events or real people and includes straightforward accounts as well as those that offer opinions on facts or factual events. The TExES exam distinguishes between *literary nonfiction*—a form of writing that incorporates literary styles and techniques to create factually-based narratives—and informational texts, which will be addressed in the next section.

Identifying Characteristics of Major Forms Within Each Genre

Fictional Prose

Fiction written in prose can be further broken down into **fiction genres**—types of fiction. Some of the more common genres of fiction are as follows:

- **Classical fiction**: a work of fiction considered timeless in its message or theme, remaining noteworthy and meaningful over decades or centuries—e.g., Charlotte Brontë's *Jane Eyre*, Mark Twain's *Adventures of Huckleberry Finn*

- **Fables**: short fiction that generally features animals, fantastic creatures, or other forces within nature that assume human-like characters and has a moral lesson for the reader—e.g., *Aesop's Fables*

- **Fairy tales**: children's stories with magical characters in imaginary, enchanted lands, usually depicting a struggle between good and evil, a sub-genre of folklore—e.g., Hans Christian Anderson's *The Little Mermaid*, *Cinderella* by the Brothers Grimm

- **Fantasy**: fiction with magic or supernatural elements that cannot occur in the real world, sometimes involving medieval elements in language, usually includes some form of sorcery or witchcraft and sometimes set on a different world—e.g., J.R.R. Tolkien's *The Hobbit*, J.K. Rowling's *Harry Potter and the Sorcerer's Stone*, George R.R. Martin's *A Game of Thrones*

- **Folklore**: types of fiction passed down from oral tradition, stories indigenous to a particular region or culture, with a local flavor in tone, designed to help humans cope with their condition in life and validate cultural traditions, beliefs, and customs—e.g., William Laughead's *Paul Bunyan and The Blue Ox*, the Buddhist story of "The Banyan Deer"

- **Mythology**: closely related to folklore but more widespread, features mystical, otherworldly characters and addresses the basic question of why and how humans exist, relies heavily on allegory and features gods or heroes captured in some sort of struggle—e.g., Greek myths, Genesis I and II in the Bible, Arthurian legends

- **Science fiction**: fiction that uses the principle of extrapolation—loosely defined as a form of prediction—to imagine future realities and problems of the human experience—e.g., Robert Heinlein's *Stranger in a Strange Land*, Ayn Rand's *Anthem*, Isaac Asimov's *I, Robot*, Philip K. Dick's *Do Androids Dream of Electric Sheep?*

- **Short stories**: short works of prose fiction with fully-developed themes and characters, focused on mood, generally developed with a single plot, with a short period of time for settings—e.g., Edgar Allan Poe's "Fall of the House of Usher," Shirley Jackson's "The Lottery," Isaac Bashevis Singer's "Gimpel the Fool"

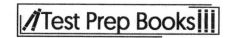

Drama

Drama refers to a form of literature written for the purpose of performance for an audience. Like prose fiction, drama has several genres. The following are the most common ones:

- **Comedy**: a humorous play designed to amuse and entertain, often with an emphasis on the common person's experience, generally resolved in a positive way—e.g., Richard Sheridan's *School for Scandal*, Shakespeare's *Taming of the Shrew*, Neil Simon's *The Odd Couple*

- **History**: a play based on recorded history where the fate of a nation or kingdom is at the core of the conflict—e.g., Christopher Marlowe's *Edward II*, Shakespeare's *King Richard III*, Arthur Miller's *The Crucible*

- **Tragedy**: a serious play that often involves the downfall of the protagonist. In modern tragedies, the protagonist is not necessarily in a position of power or authority—e.g., Jean Racine's *Phèdre*, Arthur Miller's *Death of a Salesman*, John Steinbeck's *Of Mice and Men*

- **Melodrama**: a play that emphasizes heightened emotion and sensationalism, generally with stereotypical characters in exaggerated or realistic situations and with moral polarization—e.g., Jean-Jacques Rousseau's *Pygmalion*

- **Tragi-comedy**: a play that has elements of both tragedy—a character experiencing a tragic loss—and comedy—the resolution is often positive with no clear distinctive mood for either—e.g., Shakespeare's *The Merchant of Venice*, Anton Chekhov's *The Cherry Orchard*

Poetry

The genre of **poetry** refers to literary works that focus on the expression of feelings and ideas through the use of structure and linguistic rhythm to create a desired effect.

Different poetic structures and devices are used to create the various major forms of poetry. Some of the most common forms are discussed in the following chart.

Type	Poetic Structure	Example
Ballad	A poem or song passed down orally which tells a story and in English tradition usually uses an ABAB or ABCB rhyme scheme	William Butler Yeats' "The Ballad of Father O'Hart"
Epic	A long poem from ancient oral tradition which narrates the story of a legendary or heroic protagonist	Homer's *The Odyssey* Virgil's *The Aeneid*
Haiku	A Japanese poem of three unrhymed lines with five, seven, and five syllables (in English) with nature as a common subject matter	Matsuo Bashō "An old silent pond . . . A frog jumps into the pond, splash! Silence again."
Limerick	A five-line poem written in an AABBA rhyme scheme, with a witty focus	From Edward Lear's *Book of Nonsense*: "There was a Young Person of Smyrna Whose grandmother threatened to burn her . . ."
Ode	A formal lyric poem that addresses and praises a person, place, thing, or idea	Edna St. Vincent Millay's "Ode to Silence"
Sonnet	A fourteen-line poem written in iambic pentameter	Shakespeare's Sonnets 18 and 130

Literary Nonfiction

Nonfiction works are best characterized by their subject matter, which must be factual and real, describing true life experiences. There are several common types of literary non-fiction.

Biography

A *biography* is a work written about a real person (historical or currently living). It involves factual accounts of the person's life, often in a re-telling of those events based on available, researched factual information. The re-telling and dialogue, especially if related within quotes, must be accurate and reflect reliable sources. A biography reflects the time and place in which the person lived, with the goal of creating an understanding of the person and his/her human experience. Examples of well-known biographies include *The Life of Samuel Johnson* by James Boswell and *Steve Jobs* by Walter Isaacson.

Autobiography

An *autobiography* is a factual account of a person's life written by that person. It may contain some or all of the same elements as a biography, but the author is the subject matter. An autobiography will be told in first person narrative. Examples of well-known autobiographies in literature include *Night* by Elie Wiesel and *Margaret Thatcher: The Autobiography* by Margaret Thatcher.

Memoir

A *memoir* is a historical account of a person's life and experiences written by one who has personal, intimate knowledge of the information. The line between memoir, autobiography, and biography is

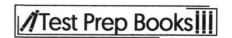

often muddled, but generally speaking, a memoir covers a specific timeline of events as opposed to the other forms of nonfiction. A memoir is less all-encompassing. It is also less formal in tone and tends to focus on the emotional aspect of the presented timeline of events. Some examples of memoirs in literature include *Angela's Ashes* by Frank McCourt and *All Creatures Great and Small* by James Herriot.

Journalism

Some forms of *journalism* can fall into the category of literary non-fiction—e.g., travel writing, nature writing, sports writing, the interview, and sometimes, the essay. Some examples include Elizabeth Kolbert's "The Lost World, in the Annals of Extinction series for *The New Yorker* and Gary Smith's "Ali and His Entourage" for *Sports Illustrated*.

Understanding Literary Interpretation

Literary interpretation is an interpretation and analysis of a literary work, based on the textual evidence in the work. It is often subjective as critical readers may discern different meanings in the details. A TExES test taker needs to be prepared for questions that will test how well he or she can read a passage, make an analysis, and then provide evidence to support that analysis.

Literal and Figurative Meanings

When analyzing and interpreting fiction, readers must be active participants in the experience. Some authors make their messages clearer than others, but the onus is on the reader to add layers to what is read through interpretation. In literary interpretation, the goal is not to offer an opinion as to the inherent value of the work. Rather, the goal is to determine what the text means by analyzing the *literal and figurative meanings* of the text through critical reading.

Critical reading is close reading that elicits questions as the reader progresses. Many authors of fiction use literary elements and devices to further theme and to speak to their audience. These elements often utilize language that has an alternate or figurative meaning in addition to their actual or literal meaning. Readers should be asking questions about these and other important details as a passage is analyzed. What unfamiliar words are there? What is their contextual definition? How do they contribute to the overall feel of the work? How do they contribute to the mood and general message? Literal and figurative meanings are discussed further in the informational texts and rhetoric section.

Drawing Inferences

An *inference* refers to a point that is implied (as opposed to directly-stated) by the evidence presented. It's necessary to use inference in order to draw conclusions about the meaning of a passage. Authors make implications through character dialogue, thoughts, effects on others, actions, and looks.

When making an inference about a passage, it's important to rely only on the information that is provided in the text itself. This helps readers ensure that their conclusions are valid. Drawing inferences is also discussed in the informational texts and rhetoric section.

Textual Evidence

It's helpful to read a passage a few times, noting details that seem important to the piece. Textual evidence within the details helps readers draw a conclusion about a passage. *Textual evidence* refers to information—facts and examples that support the main idea. Textual evidence will likely come from outside sources and can be in the form of quoted or paraphrased material. In order to draw a conclusion from evidence, it's important to examine the credibility and validity of that evidence as well as how (and if) it relates to the main idea. Effective use of textual evidence should connect to the main idea and support a specific point. Textual evidence is examined further in the informational texts and rhetoric section.

Identifying Literary Elements

There is no one, final definition of what literary elements are. They can be considered features or characteristics of fiction, but they are really more of a way that readers can unpack a text for the purpose of analysis and understanding the meaning. The elements contribute to a reader's literary interpretation of a passage as to how they function to convey the central message of a work. The most common literary elements used for analysis are the presented below.

Point of View

The *point of view* is the position the narrator takes when telling the story in prose. If a narrator is incorporated in a drama, the point of view may vary; in poetry, point of view refers to the position the speaker in a poem takes.

First Person

The first person point of view is when the writer uses the word "I" in the text. Poetry often uses first person, e.g., William Wordsworth's "I Wandered Lonely as a Cloud." Two examples of prose written in first person are Suzanne Collins' *The Hunger Games* and Anthony Burgess's *A Clockwork Orange*.

Second Person

The second person point of view is when the writer uses the pronoun "you." It is not widely used in prose fiction, but as a technique, it has been used by writers such as William Faulkner in *Absalom, Absalom!* and Albert Camus in *The Fall*. It is more common in poetry—e.g., Pablo Neruda's "If You Forget Me."

Third Person

Third person point of view is when the writer utilizes pronouns such as him, her, or them. It may be the most utilized point of view in prose as it provides flexibility to an author and is the one with which readers are most familiar. There are two main types of third person used in fiction. *Third person omniscient* uses a narrator that is all-knowing, relating the story by conveying and interpreting thoughts/feelings of all characters. In *third person limited,* the narrator relates the story through the perspective of one character's thoughts/feelings, usually the main character.

Plot

The *plot* is what happens in the story. Plots may be singular, containing one problem, or they may be very complex, with many sub-plots. All plots have exposition, a conflict, a climax, and a resolution. The *conflict* drives the plot and is something that the reader expects to be resolved. The plot carries those events along until there is a resolution to the conflict.

Tone

The *tone* of a story reflects the author's attitude and opinion about the subject matter of the story or text. Tone can be expressed through word choice, imagery, figurative language, syntax, and other details. The emotion or mood the reader experiences relates back to the tone of the story. Some examples of possible tones are humorous, somber, sentimental, and ironic.

Setting

The *setting* is the time, place, or set of surroundings in which the story occurs. It includes time or time span, place(s), climates, geography—man-made or natural—or cultural environments. Emily Dickinson's poem "Because I could not stop for Death" has a simple setting—the narrator's symbolic ride with Death through town towards the local graveyard. Conversely, Leo Tolstoy's *War and Peace* encompasses numerous settings within settings in the areas affected by the Napoleonic Wars, spanning 1805 to 1812.

Characters

Characters are the story's figures that assume primary, secondary, or minor roles. *Central* or *major* characters are those integral to the story—the plot cannot be resolved without them. A central character can be a *protagonist* or hero. There may be more than one protagonist, and he/she doesn't always have to possess good characteristics. A character can also be an *antagonist*—the force against a protagonist.

Dynamic characters change over the course of the plot time. *Static* characters do not change. A *symbolic* character is one that represents an author's idea about society in general—e.g., Napoleon in Orwell's *Animal Farm*. *Stock* characters are those that appear across genres and embrace stereotypes—e.g., the cowboy of the Wild West or the blonde bombshell in a detective novel. A *flat* character is one that does not present a lot of complexity or depth, while a *rounded* character does. Sometimes, the *narrator* of a story or the *speaker* in a poem can be a character—e.g., Nick Carraway in F. Scott Fitzgerald's *The Great Gatsby* or the speaker in Robert Browning's "My Last Duchess." The narrator might also function as a character in prose, though not be part of the story—e.g., Charles Dickens' narrator of *A Christmas Carol*.

Analyzing the Foundational U.S. Documents

Teachers must familiarize themselves with foundational U.S. documents such as The Declaration of Independence, The U.S. Constitution, and The Bill of Rights to engage students with the past. Each should be evaluated for their place in history as well as their significance today. Careful evaluation of these documents can aid teachers in interpreting their meaning and significance. This will help teach students to understand the overall purpose of each document and any language that may be unfamiliar. Documents should be evaluated for author, purpose, context, and audience.

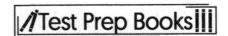

The following documents have been briefly evaluated in this manner:

Document	Author	Purpose	Context	Audience
U.S. Constitution	James Madison and other Founding Fathers	Create government, divide power between states and federal government, protect personal liberty	Written in 1787 at the Constitutional Convention in Philadelphia	All citizens of the United States
The Declaration of Independence	Thomas Jefferson and other Founding Fathers	The U.S. wanted to declare independence from Britain	Written in July 1776 for the Continental Congress	The King of England, US citizens, other foreign nations

Identifying Literary Contexts

Understanding that works of literature emerged either because of a particular context—or perhaps despite a context—is key to analyzing them effectively.

Historical Context

The *historical context* of a piece of literature can refer to the time period, setting, or conditions of living at the time it was written as well as the context of the work. For example, Hawthorne's *The Scarlet Letter* was published in 1850, though the setting of the story is 1642-1649. Historically, then, when Hawthorne wrote his novel, the United States found itself at odds as the beginnings of a potential Civil War were in view. Thus, the historical context is potentially significant as it pertains to the ideas of traditions and values, which Hawthorne addresses in his story of Hester Prynne in the era of Puritanism.

Cultural Context

The *cultural context* of a piece of literature refers to cultural factors, such as the beliefs, religions, and customs that surround and are in a work of literature. The Puritan's beliefs, religion, and customs in Hawthorne's novel would be significant as they are at the core of the plot—the reason Hester wears the A and why Arthur kills himself. The customs of people in the Antebellum Period, though not quite as restrictive, were still somewhat similar. This would impact how the audience of the time received the novel.

Literary Context

*Literary contex*t refers to the consideration of the genre, potentially at the time the work was written. In 1850, Realism and Romanticism were the driving forces in literature in the U.S., with depictions of life as it was at the time in which the work was written or the time it was written *about* as well as some works celebrating the beauty of nature. Thus, an audience in Hawthorne's time would have been well satisfied with the elements of both offered in the text. They would have been looking for details about everyday things and people (Realism), but they also would appreciate his approach to description of nature and the focus on the individual (American Romanticism). The contexts would be significant as they would pertain to evaluating the work against those criteria.

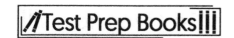

Here are some questions to use when considering context:

> When was the text written?
> What was society like at the time the text was written, or what was it like, given the work's identified time period?
> Who or what influenced the writer?
> What political or social influences might there have been?
> What influences may there have been in the genre that may have affected the writer?

Additionally, test takers should familiarize themselves with literary periods such as Old and Middle English, American Colonial, American Renaissance, American Naturalistic, and British and American Modernist and Post-Modernist movements. Most students of literature will have had extensive exposure to these literary periods in history, and while it is not necessary to recognize every major literary work on sight and associate that work to its corresponding movement or cultural context, the test taker should be familiar enough with the historical and cultural significance of each test passage in order to be able to address test questions correctly.

The following brief description of some literary contexts and their associated literary examples follows. It is not an all-inclusive list. The test taker should read each description, then follow up with independent study to clarify each movement, its context, its most familiar authors, and their works.

Metaphysical Poetry

Metaphysical poetry is the descriptor applied to 17th century poets whose poetry emphasized the lyrical quality of their work. These works contain highly creative poetic conceits or metaphoric comparisons between two highly dissimilar things or ideas. Metaphysical poetry is characterized by highly prosaic language and complicated, often layered, metaphor.

Poems such as John Donne's "The Flea," Andrew Marvell's "To His Coy Mistress," George Herbert's "The Collar," Henry Vaughan's "The World," and Richard Crashaw's "A Song" are associated with this type of poetry.

British Romanticism

British Romanticism was a cultural and literary movement within Europe that developed at the end of the 18th century and extended into the 19th century. It occurred partly in response to aristocratic, political, and social norms and partly in response to the Industrial Revolution of the day. Characterized by intense emotion, major literary works of British Romanticism embrace the idea of aestheticism and the beauty of nature. Literary works exalted folk customs and historical art and encouraged spontaneity of artistic endeavor. The movement embraced the heroic ideal and the concept that heroes would raise the quality of society.

Authors who are classified as British Romantics include Samuel Taylor Coleridge, John Keats, George Byron, Mary Shelley, Percy Bysshe Shelley, and William Blake. Well-known works include Samuel Taylor Coleridge's "Kubla Khan," John Keats' "Ode on a Grecian Urn," George Byron's "Childe Harold's Pilgrimage," Mary Shelley's *Frankenstein*, Percy Bysshe Shelley's "Ode to the West Wind," and William Blake's "The Tyger."

American Romanticism

American Romanticism occurred within the American literary scene beginning early in the 19th century. While many aspects were similar to British Romanticism, it is further characterized as having gothic aspects and the idea that individualism was to be encouraged. It also embraced the concept of the *noble savage*—the idea that indigenous culture uncorrupted by civilization is better than advanced society.

Well-known authors and works include Nathanial Hawthorne's *The House of the Seven Gables*, Edgar Allan Poe's "The Raven" and "The Cask of Amontillado," Emily Dickinson's "I Felt a Funeral in My Brain" and James Fenimore Cooper's *The Last of the Mohicans*.

Transcendentalism

Transcendentalism was a movement that applied to a way of thinking that developed within the United States, specifically New England, around 1836. While this way of thinking originally employed philosophical aspects, transcendentalism spread to all forms of art, literature, and even to the ways people chose to live. It was born out of a reaction to traditional rationalism and purported concepts such as a higher divinity, feminism, humanitarianism, and communal living. Transcendentalism valued intuition, self-reliance, and the idea that human nature was inherently good.

Well-known authors include Ralph Waldo Emerson, Henry David Thoreau, Louisa May Alcott, and Ellen Sturgis Hooper. Works include Ralph Waldo Emerson's "Self-Reliance" and "Uriel," Henry David Thoreau's *Walden* and *Civil Disobedience*, Louisa May Alcott's *Little Women*, and Ellen Sturgis Hooper's "I Slept, and Dreamed that Life was Beauty."

The Harlem Renaissance

The Harlem Renaissance is the descriptor given to the cultural, artistic, and social boom that developed in Harlem, New York, at the beginning of the 20th century, spanning the 1920s and 1930s. Originally termed *The New Negro Movement*, it emphasized African-American urban cultural expression and migration across the United States. It had strong roots in African-American Christianity, discourse, and intellectualism. The Harlem Renaissance heavily influenced the development of music and fashion as well. Its singular characteristic was to embrace Pan-American culturalisms; however, strong themes of the slavery experience and African-American folk traditions also emerged. A hallmark of the Harlem Renaissance was that it laid the foundation for the future Civil Rights Movement in the United States.

Well-known authors and works include Zora Neale Hurston's *Their Eyes Were Watching God*, Richard Wright's *Native Son*, Langston Hughes' "I, Too," and James Weldon Johnson's "God's Trombones: Seven Negro Sermons in Verse" and *The Book of American Negro Poetry*.

Identifying Major Literary Works and Authors

The TExES test assumes test takers will have a familiarity with a wide range of American, British, World, and Young Adult literary works. In most cases, the test taker will be presented with a quoted literary passage and be required to answer one or more questions about it. This may involve having to identify the literary work presented from a list of options.

The ability of the test taker to demonstrate familiarity of major literary works is key in success when taking TExES exams. The following chart offers some examples of major works in addition to those listed elsewhere in this guide, but the list not exhaustive.

American
Fictional Prose
   Harriet Beecher Stowe | *Uncle Tom's Cabin*
   Ernest Hemingway | *For Whom the Bell Tolls*

Jack London | *The Call of the Wild*
Toni Morrison | *Beloved*
N. Scott Momaday | *The Way to Rainy Mountain*
J.D. Salinger | *Catcher in the Rye*
John Steinbeck | *Grapes of Wrath*
Alice Walker | *The Color Purple*

Drama
Edward Albee | *Who's Afraid of Virginia Woolf?*
Lorraine Hansberry | *A Raisin in the Sun*
Amiri Baraka | *Dutchman*
Eugene O'Neill | *Long Day's Journey into Night*
Sam Shephard | *Buried Child*
Thornton Wilder I *Our Town*
Tennessee Williams | *A Streetcar Named Desire*

Poetry
Anne Bradstreet | "In Reference to her Children, 23 June 1659"
Emily Dickinson | "Because I could not stop for Death"
Sylvia Plath | "Mirror"
Langston Hughes | "Harlem"
Edgar Allen Poe | "The Raven"
Phillis Wheatley | "On Being Brought from Africa to America"
Walt Whitman | "Song of Myself"

Literary Non-fiction
Maya Angelou | *I Know Why the Caged Bird Sings*
Truman Capote | In Cold Blood
Frederick Douglass | *My Bondage and My Freedom*
Archie Fire Lame Deer | The Gift of Power: The Life and Teachings of a Lakota Medicine Man
Helen Keller | *The Story of My Life*
Dave Pelzer | *A Child Called "It"*

British
Fictional Prose
John Bunyan | *The Pilgrim's Progress*
Joseph Conrad | *Heart of Darkness*
Charles Dickens | *Tale of Two Cities*
George Eliot | *Middlemarch*
George Orwell | *1984*
Mary Shelley | *Frankenstein*

Drama
Samuel Beckett | *Waiting for Godot*
Caryl Churchill | *Top Girls*
William Congreve | *The Way of the World*
Michael Frayn | *Noises Off*

William Shakespeare | *Macbeth*
Oscar Wilde | *The Importance of Being Earnest*

Poetry

Elizabeth Barrett Browning | "How Do I Love Thee? (Sonnet 43)"
Robert Burns | "A Red, Red Rose"
Samuel Taylor Coleridge | "Rime of the Ancient Mariner"
T.S. Eliot | "Love Song of J. Alfred Prufrock"
John Milton | "Paradise Lost"

Literary Non-fiction

Vera Brittain | *Testament of Youth*
T. E. Lawrence | *Seven Pillars of Wisdom*
Doris Lessing | *Going Home*
Brian Blessed | *Absolute Pandemonium: The Autobiography*
Virginia Woolf | *A Room of One's Own*

World
Fictional Prose

Anonymous | *The Epic of Gilgamesh*
Chinua Achebe | *Things Fall Apart*
Margaret Atwood | *The Handmaid's Tale*
Pearl S. Buck | *The Good Earth*
Miguel de Cervantes | *Don Quixote*
Fyodor Dostoyevsky | *Crime and Punishment*
Gabriel Garcia Marquez | *One Hundred Years of Solitude*
James Joyce | *Ulysses*
Nikos Kazantzakis | *Zorba the Greek*
Boris Pasternak | *Dr. Zhivago*
Amy Tan | *The Joy Luck Club*
Voltaire | *Candide*

Drama

Bertolt Brecht | *Mother Courage and her Children*
Anton Chekhov | *The Seagull*
Lady Gregory | *Workhouse Ward*
Henrik Ibsen | *A Doll's House*
Luigi Pirandello | *Six Characters in Search of an Author*
Molière | *Tartuffe*
Sophocles | *Antigone*
August Strindberg | *Miss Julie*
Vyasa | *The Bhagavad Gita*
Johann Wolfgang von Goethe | *Faust*

Poetry

Anonymous | *Beowulf*
Anonymous | *The Ramayana*
Dante Alighieri | *The Divine Comedy*

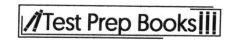

Federico García Lorca | *Gypsy Ballads*
Omar Khayyám | *The Rubaiyat*
Kahlil Gibran | *The Prophet*
Andrew Barton "Banjo" Paterson | *"Waltzing Matilda"*
Taslima Nasrin | *"Character"*
Kostis Palamas | *"Ancient Eternal And Immortal Spirit"*
Maria Elena Cruz Varela | *"Kaleidoscope"*
King David | The 23rd Psalm, the Judeo-Christian Bible

Literary Non-fiction

Pavel Basinsky | *Flight from Paradise*
Jung Chang | *Wild Swans*
Confucius | *The Analects of Confucius*
Viktor Frankl | *Man's Search for Meaning*
Mahatma Gandhi | *India of my Dreams*
Nelson Mandela | *Long Walk to Freedom*
Fatema Mernissi | *Beyond the Veil*
Jonathan Swift | *"A Modest Proposal"*

Young Adult
Fictional Prose

Jodi Lynn Anderson | *Tiger Lily*
Lois Lowry | *The Giver*
Scott O'Dell | *Island of the Blue Dolphins*
Katherine Paterson Jacob | *Have I Loved*
Antoine de Saint-Exupéry | *The Little Prince*
Ellen Raskin | *The Westing Game*
P. L. Travers | *Mary Poppins*
Marcus Zusak | *The Book Thief*

Drama

Peter Dee | *Voices from the High School*
William Gibson | *The Miracle Worker*

Poetry

Sandra Cisneros | *"Eleven"*
Eamon Grennan | *"Cat Scat"*
Tom Junod | *"My Mother Couldn't Cook"*
Tupac Shakur | *"The Rose that Grew from Concrete"*

Literary Non-fiction

Sherman Alexie | *The Absolutely True Diary of a Part-Time Indian*
Anne Frank | *The Diary of Anne Frank*
Philip Hoose | *The Boys who Challenged Hitler*
Cynthia Levinson | *We've Got a Job*
Malala Yousafzai and Christina Lamb | *I am Malala*

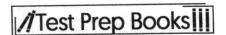

Reading and Engaging with Literature

Responding to Literature

Just as there are a variety of literary texts, so too are there a variety of responses to such texts. Educators should encourage students to engage with and respond to literature in ways that feel appropriate and meaningful to them as well as model different types of responses to texts. Experiential responses invoke a student's prior knowledge or experience, helping demonstrate a text-to-text or text-to-life connection. For example, in such a response, students might compare and contrast a text's main character with themselves or with a character from another book. Plot, theme, or events can also be evaluated this way, with students looking for parallels in their own lives or in other things they've learned about. Aesthetic responses tap into a student's emotional response to a text and can demonstrate his or her feelings or perspective on the literature. Aesthetic texts themselves often promote a sensory experience for the reader, and the writer may choose words in a specific way based on their sound or other artistic element. Likewise, aesthetic responses are often somewhat creative and artistic. Pragmatic responses are more strictly informative, explanatory, analytical, or argumentative and are less focused on the emotional response or personal connection to a text.

Teachers should encourage a variety of forms of responses to literature, relying on different modes of language arts and tapping into other disciplines as well. For example, students can discuss or present oral reflections to texts, they can be tasked with written assignments, or they may choose to respond in a more artistic fashion through painting, music, or a dramatic performance.

Encouraging Students to Read a Variety of Literature and Engage in Reading

There are many ways that educators can motivate students to read literature and explore the variety of literary works in their leisure time. Building an engaging classroom library is a great starting place. Teachers can highlight books from different cultural backgrounds, time periods, literary genres, and themes, rotating the "featured" works to encourage well-rounded literary interest. They can prominently display particular books on a rotating basis and have a section to display peer suggestions as well. Teachers can also collaborate with the local library so that students can easily learn about the resources, programs, and available services at the library and how to obtain access. This is a good opportunity to work with librarians to facilitate students' research needs as well. Hosting extracurricular book clubs with or without parent involvement can also engage students and encourage reading and the importance of literature in the household. Monthly selections can be pulled from a variety of genres and an evening meeting can be a celebration to discuss the book and mingle with peers and their family members.

Setting aside independent reading time during class time is also a way to convey the message that reading is valued and should be a daily practice. Students can use this time to pick selections from the classroom or school library. Similarly, teachers can pick a piece of literature for daily or weekly read alouds. This practice can also serve as a launching pad for critical discussions and vocabulary lessons. Inviting local authors can also be inspiring for readers and writers alike.

To help motivate students to pick a variety of literary works, teachers can give students "mystery books" and wrap a particular book for each student for free reading time. This removes the judgment aspect of selecting a book and often ends up being an enticing way for students to connect with a different kind of book because it was specially chosen just for them.

Finally, having students record short video reviews of their favorite books and posting them on a class webpage is a fun way for students to learn and share with one another about books they find appealing.

Promoting Analysis of Literature

It is also helpful for educators to encourage students to evaluate literature through a variety of lenses. For example, students can be critical readers by thinking about how a piece of literature fits within its social and historical context. The setting can be compared to other literary works as well as current real-life political, global, or social environments. With this critical reader lens, students should also think about the plot and characters and evaluate their merit, their relevancy within the story's context, and the author's ability to convey the elements of the story in an engaging, effective, and reasonable way. Educators should focus on guiding students to evaluate the literary devices employed by a text's author and how such elements contribute to the text's meaning and effectiveness.

Through another lens, readers can analyze a story in its meaning and relatability to the human experience or the reader's own personal experiences. Many pieces of literature, even if seemingly diverse or far-removed from the reader's life, have events, themes, or characters that a reader can relate to based on their own experiences or the experience of humanity at large. Teachers of students in grades 7–12 are in a unique position to help students who are facing significant changes in their own lives. Teachers can use literature to help students identify with their own increasing awareness and understanding of themselves and others in the world. Literature can be a powerful vehicle for self-understanding as well as for exploring the human experience of others in situations vastly different than one's own. For this reason, it is even more beneficial for students to engage with a wide variety of literary texts to promote an understanding and appreciation for different times, cultures, attitudes, and experiences.

Practice Questions

Questions 1 and 2 are based on the following passage:

Dear Brand-X Employees:

Over the past ten years, Brand-X has been happy to provide free daycare to Brand-X employees. Based on the dedication, long workdays, and professionalism shown daily, it's the least Brand-X management can do. Brand-X wouldn't be where it is today without the hard work of countless, unsung heroes and is truly blessed to have such an amazing staff.

Unfortunately, Brand-X is subject to the same economic forces as any other company. We regret to inform you that, beginning March 15th, Brand-X has decided to discontinue the childcare program. This was a difficult decision to make, one that was arrived at only with the greatest of deliberation. Many other options were discussed, and this seemed to be the only one that allowed Brand-X to still stay competitive while not reducing staff.

Fortunately, all other programs—employee rewards, vacation and sick days, retirement options, volunteer days—have not been impacted. In addition, on Friday we'll be hosting a free lunch buffet. Employees are welcome to wear jeans.

Hope to see you there,

Brand-X Management

1. Which of the following words best describe the tone in the first, second, and third paragraphs?
   a. Relieved; conciliatory; ominous
   b. Conciliatory; ominous; relieved
   c. Proud; apologetic; placating
   d. Placating; apologetic; proud

2. "Unfortunately, Brand-X is subject to the same economic forces as any other company." This line was most likely provided to do what?
   a. Emphasize that Brand-X is no worse than other companies.
   b. Redirect blame from Brand-X to outside forces.
   c. Encourage staff to look for work elsewhere.
   d. Intimidate staff into cooperating.

Questions 3–5 are based upon the following passage:

Insects as a whole are preeminently creatures of the land and the air. This is shown not only by the possession of wings by a vast majority of the class, but by the mode of breathing to which reference has already been made, a system of branching air-tubes carrying atmospheric air with its combustion-supporting oxygen to all the insect's tissues. The air gains access to these tubes through a number of paired air-holes or spiracles, arranged segmentally in series.

It is of great interest to find that, nevertheless, a number of insects spend much of their time under water. This is true of not a few in the perfect winged state, as for example aquatic beetles and water-bugs ('boatmen' and 'scorpions') which have some way of protecting their spiracles when submerged, and, possessing usually the power of flight, can pass on occasion from pond or stream to upper air. But it is advisable in connection with our present subject to dwell especially on some insects that remain continually under water till they are ready to undergo their final moult and attain the winged state, which they pass entirely in the air. The preparatory instars of such insects are aquatic; the adult instar is aerial. All may-flies, dragon-flies, and caddis-flies, many beetles and two-winged flies, and a few moths thus divide their life-story between the water and the air. For the present we confine attention to the Stone-flies, the May-flies, and the Dragon-flies, three well-known orders of insects respectively called by systematists the Plecoptera, the Ephemeroptera and the Odonata.

In the case of many insects that have aquatic larvae, the latter are provided with some arrangement for enabling them to reach atmospheric air through the surface-film of the water. But the larva of a stone-fly, a dragon-fly, or a may-fly is adapted more completely than these for aquatic life; it can, by means of gills of some kind, breathe the air dissolved in water.

Excerpt adapted from The Life-Story of Insects, by Geo H. Carpenter

3. Which statement best details the central idea in this passage?
   a. It introduces certain insects that transition from water to air.
   b. It delves into entomology, especially where gills are concerned.
   c. It defines what constitutes as insects' breathing.
   d. It invites readers to have a hand in the preservation of insects.

4. What is the purpose of the first paragraph in relation to the second paragraph?
   a. The first paragraph serves as a cause, and the second paragraph serves as an effect.
   b. The first paragraph serves as a contrast to the second.
   c. The first paragraph is a description for the argument in the second paragraph.
   d. The first and second paragraphs are merely presented in a sequence.

5. Which of the statements reflect information that one could reasonably infer based on the author's tone?
   a. The author's tone is persuasive and attempts to call the audience to action.
   b. The author's tone is passionate due to excitement over the subject and personal narrative.
   c. The author's tone is informative and exhibits interest in the subject of the study.
   d. The author's tone is somber, depicting some anger at the state of insect larvae.

Answer Explanations

1. C: Brand-X Management uses a proven technique to deliver bad news: sandwich it between good. The first paragraph extolls the virtue of its employees: "Brand-X wouldn't be where it is today without the hard work of countless, unsung heroes and is truly blessed to have such an amazing staff." The management of Brand-X is proud of its employees. The second paragraph delivers the bad news. Along with the announcement of the termination of the childcare program, Brand-X management provides several reasons why, such as they're "subject to the same economic forces as any other company" and their decision "allowed Brand-X to still stay competitive while not reducing staff." The passage implies that they didn't want to—they had to. The tone of the second paragraph is apologetic. The third paragraph ends on a positive note. Management reminds staff that other services—employee rewards, vacation and sick days, retirement options, volunteer days—have not been impacted, and on Friday employees will have a luncheon and be allowed to wear jeans. This passage is there to not only remind employees why it's still beneficial to work there, but also to provide evidence that Brand-X wants its employees to be happy by hosting luncheons and letting employees wear jeans. It's designed to reduce their hostilities about cancelling the program, or, in other words, placate or appease them.

2. B: "Unfortunately, Brand-X is subject to the same economic forces as any other company." This line was most likely provided to redirect blame from Brand-X to outside forces. Throughout the second paragraph, Brand-X consistently defends its decision to cancel the childcare program. Based on the context of the paragraph, it's continually implied that management was left with no choice. While it might be true that Brand-X is no worse than other companies (others are forced to do the same), this statement supports the idea that it's beyond their control, a message reiterated throughout the paragraph. Nowhere in the paragraph does Brand-X encourage employees to look for work elsewhere. In fact, management does the opposite by reminding employees why they want to continue working there: employee rewards, vacation and sick days, retirement options, and volunteer days. The tone of the passage is not intimidating. No threats are made, implied or otherwise. For example, when management makes reference to reducing staff, it's described as an undesirable choice, not a viable option.

3. A: It introduces certain insects that transition from water to air. Choice *B* is incorrect because although the passage talks about gills, it is not the central idea of the passage. Choices *C* and *D* are incorrect because the passage does not "define" or "invite," but only serves as an introduction to stoneflies, dragonflies, and mayflies and their transition from water to air.

4. B: The first paragraph serves as a contrast to the second. Notice how the first paragraph goes into detail describing how insects are able to breathe air. The second paragraph acts as a contrast to the first by stating "[i]t is of great interest to find that, nevertheless, a number of insects spend much of their time under water." Watch for transition words such as "nevertheless" to help find what type of passage you're dealing with.

5. C: The author's tone is informative and exhibits interest in the subject of the study. Overall, the author presents us with information on the subject. One moment where personal interest is depicted is when the author states, "It is of great interest to find that, nevertheless, a number of insects spend much of their time under water."

Written Communication

Writing as an Ongoing Process

Understanding Research-Based Approaches to Teaching Components of Writing

Recognizing Research-Based Strategies for Teaching the Writing Process

Current trends in education have recognized the need to cultivate writing skills that prepare students for higher education and professional careers. To this end, writing skills are being integrated into other subjects beyond the language arts classroom. The skills and strategies used in language arts class, then, should be adaptable for other learning tasks. In this way, students can achieve greater proficiency by incorporating writing strategies into every aspect of learning.

To teach writing, it is important that writers know the writing process. Students should be familiar with the five components of the writing process:

1. *Pre-writing*: The drafting, planning, researching, and brainstorming of ideas
2. *Writing*: The part of the project in which the actual, physical writing takes place — *drafting*
3. *Revising*: Adding to, removing, rearranging, or re-writing sections of the piece
4. *Editing*: Analyzing and correcting mistakes in grammar, spelling, punctuation, formatting, and word choice
Publishing: Distributing the finished product to the teacher, employer, or other students

The *writing workshop* is possibly the most common approach to teaching writing. It is an organized approach in which the student is guided by the teacher and usually contains the following components:

- *Short lesson* (~10 min) in which the teacher focuses on a particular aspect of the writing process—e.g., strategies, organization, technique, processes, craft—and gives explicit instructions for the task at hand

- *Independent writing time* (~30 min) in which the student engages in the writing activity and works through the process while receiving help from the teacher, writing in his/her own style on either a chosen topic or one assigned, and engaging with other students

- *Sharing* (~10 min) in which the student shares a piece of his or her work, either in a small group or as a class, and gains insight by listening to the work of other students

Another common strategy is *teacher modeling*, in which the student views the teacher as a writer and is therefore more apt to believe the teacher's instruction on the subject. To be a good writing teacher, the teacher must be a good writer. Therefore, it is important that the teacher practice his or her own writing on a somewhat regular basis through blogging, journaling, or creative writing, in order to keep his or her skills sharp. The following are some strategies for teacher writing:

- *Sharing written work*: This strategy is a good audio and/or visual learning technique. The teacher should frequently share personal writing with students so that the student recognizes the instructor as having authority on the subject. Many teachers also encourage feedback from the students to stimulate critical thinking skills.

- *Writing in front of students*: This strategy is very effective as a visual learning technique as the students watch as the teacher works through the writing process. This could include asking the students to provide a question or topic on which to write and then writing on blackboard or projector.

- *Encouraging real-world writing*: This is a kinesthetic teaching strategy in which the teacher urges students to write as frequently as possible and to share their written work with other students or an authentic audience. Teachers may also find it beneficial to show students their own blogs and other online media to demonstrate exactly how it's done. Students may also choose to model their writing after a published author, imitating his or her style, sentence structure, and word choices to become comfortable with the writing process.

Finally, a good thing for a student to have is a *writer's notebook*, which contains all the student's written work over the course of the curriculum, including warm-up assignments, drafts, brainstorming templates, and completed works. This allows the student to review previous writing assignment, learn from their mistakes, and see concrete evidence for improvement. Depending on the age group, many of the assignments could be performed on a word processor to encourage computer literacy.

Identifying Strategies for Teaching Writing Tasks

There are over thirty research-proven strategies for teaching all components of the writing process through a variety of different tasks, the most comprehensive of which will be covered in this section.

Evidence shows that the most effective strategy for teaching writing is to have the students use the process-writing approach, in which they practice planning, writing, reviewing, editing, and publishing their work. Students should be taught how to write for a specific audience, take personal responsibility for their own work, and participate in the writing process with other students, such as a discussion-like setting where they can brainstorm together. Additionally, specific goals should be assigned, either classroom wide or to fit individual needs, through activities that encourage attention to spelling, grammar, sentence combination, and writing for specific audiences.

- For pre-writing, students should also be exposed to the process of generating and organizing ideas before they set pen to paper, such as being given a specific topic and considering many different aspects associated with that topic using a *brainstorming web* or *mindmap*, visually dividing a project into main topics and subtopics. Teachers can help students by encouraging them to explore what they already know about a subject, topic, or genre. They can then illustrate how to go about researching and gathering information or data by using teacher modeling to access a variety of resources. Another research-based strategy is to require students to analyze and summarize a model text through writing, which encourages them to condense a composition into its main ideas and, in doing so, allows them to understand how these ideas were expressed and organized.

- To teach the actual act of writing, *freewriting* is an effective writing warm-up activity as it requires nothing more than for the student to continually write uninterrupted for an allotted amount of time. One of the most common problems many students encounter is being uncertain what to write or how to begin. Freewriting creates a space in which the student does not have to worry about either of those things—they simply need to write. For this particular strategy, a teacher should avoid assigning a particular topic, genre, or format, nor should the student be encouraged or required to share what they have written so that they may write freely and without fear of judgment. After the allotted time for freewriting is up, students can

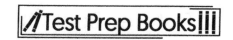

then read back over what they have written and select the most interesting sentences and ideas to expand upon in a more organized piece of writing.

Another form of instruction is *discipline-based inquiry*, which encourages students to analyze writing models in a particular mode to better grasp the characteristics of that style. For example, before assigning students a persuasive writing assignment, an instructor would first give several samples of persuasive passages to students and ask them to read the texts carefully, paying attention to components such as diction—what kind of emotional or connotative language the writer uses to subtly influence readers' opinion, supporting arguments—how the writer integrates objective data to support a subjective argument, and organization—how the writer presents the information and argument. By focusing students' attention on a specific writing mode, the instructor allows students to use their analytical and observation skills to formulate an idea about the prominent characteristics of a particular mode of writing.

In *Self-Regulated Strategy Development* (SRSD), instructors progressively instill independent skills in students by first prompting students for their prior knowledge about a subject, building on that background knowledge, instructing them more deeply in strategies related to the learning objective, and then practicing the strategy enough times so that it becomes an embedded habit in students' learning process.

Finally, encouraging students to write with one another in a collaborative setting is a good way to enhance revision, editing, and publishing skills by learning, discussing, and writing for each other. By giving constructive feedback to their peers, students learn how to recognize and apply standards of effective writing, and they also become more skilled at troubleshooting and making corrections when problems occur in the writing process.

POWER Strategy for Teaching the Writing Process
The POWER strategy helps all students to take ownership of the writing process by prompting them to consciously focus on what they are writing.

The POWER strategy is an acronym for the following:

- Prewriting or Planning
- Organizing
- Writing a first draft
- Evaluating the writing
- Revising and rewriting

Prewriting and Planning
During the Prewriting and Planning phase, students learn to consider their audience and purpose for the writing project. Then they compile information they wish to include in the piece of writing from their background knowledge and/or new sources.

Organizing
Next, students decide on the organizational structure of their writing project. There are many types of organizational structures, but the common ones are: story/narrative, informative, opinion, persuasive, compare and contrast, explanatory, and problem/solution formats. Often graphic organizers are an important part of helping students complete this step of the writing process.

Writing

In this step, students write a complete first draft of their project. Educators may begin by using modeled writing to teach this step in the process. It may be helpful for beginning writers to work in small groups or pairs. Verbalizing their thoughts before writing them is also a helpful technique.

Evaluating

In this stage, students reread their writing and note the segments that are particularly strong or need improvement. Then they participate in peer editing. They ask each other questions about the piece. The peers learn to provide feedback and constructive criticism to help the student improve. Scoring rubrics are a helpful tool in this phase to guide students as they edit each other's work.

Revising and Rewriting

Finally, the student incorporates any changes she or he wishes to make based on the evaluating process. Then students rewrite the piece into a final draft and publish it however it best fits the audience and purpose of the writing.

6+1 Traits Strategy for Teaching Writing

6+1 Traits is a model for teaching writing that uses a common language to explain the standards for what good writing looks like. Students learn to evaluate whether these expectations have been met in their own writing and then edit, revise, and rewrite accordingly. The 6+1 Traits are the characteristics that make writing readable and effective no matter what genre of writing is being used. The 6+1 Traits are as follows:

- Ideas
- Organization
- Voice
- Word choice
- Sentence fluency
- Conventions
- Presentation

The Ideas Trait

This trait is the content of the writing. This is where students learn to select an important topic for their writing. They are taught to narrow down and focus their idea. Then they learn to develop and elaborate on the specific idea. Finally, they investigate and discover the information and details that best convey the idea to others.

The Organization Trait

This trait teaches students how to build the framework for their writing. They choose an organizational strategy or purpose for the writing and build the details upon that structure. There are many purposes for writing, and they all have different frameworks. However, there are commonalities that students can learn to effectively organize their writing so it makes sense to the reader. Students learn to invite the reader into their work with an effective introduction. They are taught how to create thoughtful transitions between ideas and key points in their writing and how to create logical and purposeful sequencing of ideas. Finally, students are taught how to create a powerful conclusion to their piece that summarizes the information but leaves the reader with something to think about. Many students are inclined to jump into their writing without a clear direction for where it is going. The organization trait teaches them to plan and purpose their writing toward excellence.

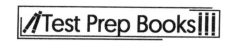

The Voice Trait

This is the trait that gives the writing a sense of individuality and connection to the author. It shows that the writing is meaningful and that the author cares about it. It is what makes the writing uniquely the author's own. It is how the reader begins to know the author and what she or he "sounds like." Students learn to recognize "voice" in some writing samples and find their own "voice" to apply to their work. Students are taught to speak on an emotional level directly to their readers. Students experiment with matching their style to the audience and the purpose of the writing. Students are taught to enjoy taking risks and putting their personal touch into their work.

The Word Choice Trait

This trait gives writing a sense of functional communication through precise language that is rich and enlightening. If the work is narrative, the words create images in the mind's eye; if the work is descriptive, the words clarify and expand thoughts and ideas. If the work is persuasive, the words give new perspective and invite thought. Students learn not only to choose exceptional vocabulary, but also to hone their skills for using ordinary words well. Students are taught to describe things using striking language. They learn to use exact language that is accurate, concise, precise, and lively.

The Sentence Fluency Trait

When sentences are built to fit together and move with one another to create writing that is easy to read aloud, the author has written with fluency. Students learn to eliminate awkward word patterns that otherwise would encumber the reader. Sentences and paragraphs start and stop in precisely the right places so that the writing moves well. Students are taught to establish a flow, develop a rhythm, and give cadence to their work. They edit their sentences to vary the structure and length. Educators can teach fluency through reading aloud beautifully written examples and contrasting them with less fluent work.

The Conventions Trait

Here the focus changes from creation of the piece to preparation for the reader. Instead of revision that the first five traits teach, this trait teaches editing skills. The students learn to make their writing clear and understandable through the use of proper grammar, spelling, capitalization, and punctuation. Students are taught the differences between revision and editing. They learn basic editing marks and symbols. Teachers can assist students to learn conventions through guided editing and regular practice. Expectations for correctness need to be kept developmentally appropriate. If immediate correctness is expected, students may shy away from experimenting and taking risks.

The Presentation Trait

This trait focuses on the final appearance of the work. Presentation is not a concern during the process of the other six traits, nor must perfect presentation be expected for every work a student does. Students are taught to make their work inviting and accessible to the reader of the end product. They learn to show they care about their writing when it is neat and readable. Students are taught about uniform spacing, legible handwriting, appropriate use of fonts and sizes, and how to use bullets, numbers, headings, charts, graphs, and pictures to help make the work visually appealing. Students are taught about the publishing process and are given opportunities to showcase their finished products.

Purposeful Writing

Purposeful writing practices have a significant effect on writing development. Purposeful writing refers to intentional writing practices for the purpose of communicating. Through learning to write well, students can begin to use writing as a method of thinking through issues and solving problems. They become more adept with questioning and investigation. Students learn to accurately convey and critique information. They can more readily express real or imagined experiences to others. Through the varied writing purposes, students learn to focus on what the audience understands, while at other times, they focus on the topic and what information they are trying to impart. Other situations call for focus on their own thinking and feelings. Writing as a whole becomes more effective and accessible as students glean skills for writing with purpose. Some of the writing purposes are as follows:

- Letter writing
- Poetry and Songs
- Creative and Narrative writing
- Informative writing
- Opinion writing
- Persuasive writing
- Compare and Contrast writing
- Explanatory/Expository writing
- Problem and Solution writing

Interpreting and Applying Research to Writing Challenges

Teaching writing to many students can be challenging as they all possess individual needs, individual learning styles, and individual emotional responses to feedback. There is no one way to teach writing that will address the needs of every student, and the techniques may vary between genres, topics, and audiences. However, teachers should keep in mind the five fundamental criteria, which research has shown to be most effective.

The most important way a student learns is by doing—being given as many opportunities to write as possible. Activities such a pre-writing, writing on prompts, peer revision, and writing in groups should be implemented as often as possible in many different types of subjects.

A welcoming, encouraging, and judgment-free atmosphere is the most conducive environment for learning how to write, where students can feel comfortable in engaging in activities, sharing what they have written, brainstorming ideas, providing feedback to peers, and giving/receiving mutual respect.

Feedback should be specific and individualized—teachers must provide sufficient time to students to help them reach their writing goals and improve on their weaknesses, while also being mindful of students' responses to criticism. At the same time, teachers should give students the tools they need to self-evaluate their own writing and identify areas of improvement.

Strategies for teaching writing should be varied and comprehensive. Teachers should be able to adjust their pedagogical techniques to meet individualized needs while still maintaining the fundamental approaches to teaching all elements of the writing process.

Learning is often achieved through writing—not only of the writing process, but of all subjects in general. Keeping a reflective journal of what they have learned at school encourages students to learn the material as they must make sense of it through writing it down. Having a student write on a historical event or a scientific theory provides the same advantage. Writing skills learned in a language arts class can and should be utilized in other subject areas.

While there are many challenges to teaching a range of students, each student can have his or her learning needs met if the teacher utilizes all five of these methods in his or her instructional approaches.

Revisions

Leaving a few minutes at the end to revise and proofread offers an opportunity for writers to polish things up. Putting one's self in the reader's shoes and focusing on what the essay actually says helps writers identify problems—it's a movement from the mindset of writer to the mindset of editor. The goal is to have a clean, clear copy of the essay. The following areas should be considered when proofreading:

- Sentence fragments
- Awkward sentence structure
- Run-on sentences
- Incorrect word choice
- Grammatical agreement errors
- Spelling errors
- Punctuation errors
- Capitalization errors

Organization

Good writing is not merely a random collection of sentences. No matter how well written, sentences must relate and coordinate appropriately with one another. If not, the writing seems random, haphazard, and disorganized. Therefore, good writing must be organized, where each sentence fits a larger context and relates to the sentences around it.

Transition Words

The writer should act as a guide, showing the reader how all the sentences fit together. Consider the seat belt example again:

> Seat belts save more lives than any other automobile safety feature. Many studies show that airbags save lives as well. Not all cars have airbags. Many older cars don't. Air bags aren't entirely reliable. Studies show that in 15% of accidents, airbags don't deploy as designed. Seat belt malfunctions are extremely rare.

There's nothing wrong with any of these sentences individually, but together they're disjointed and difficult to follow. The best way for the writer to communicate information is through the use of transition words. Here are examples of transition words and phrases that tie sentences together, enabling a more natural flow:

To show causality: *as a result, therefore,* and *consequently*
To compare and contrast: *however, but,* and *on the other hand*
To introduce examples: *for instance, namely,* and *including*
To show order of importance: *foremost, primarily, secondly,* and *lastly*

NOTE: This is not a complete list of transitions. There are many more that can be used; however, most fit into these or similar categories. The important point is that the words should clearly show the relationship between sentences, supporting information, and the main idea.

Here is an update to the previous example using transition words. These changes make it easier to read and bring clarity to the writer's points:

> Seat belts save more lives than any other automobile safety feature. Many studies show that airbags save lives as well; however, not all cars have airbags. For instance, some older cars don't. Furthermore, air bags aren't entirely reliable. For example, studies show that in 15% of accidents, airbags don't deploy as designed, but, on the other hand, seat belt malfunctions are extremely rare.

Also be prepared to analyze whether the writer is using the best transition word or phrase for the situation. Take this sentence for example: "As a result, seat belt malfunctions are extremely rare." This sentence doesn't make sense in the context above because the writer is trying to show the contrast between seat belts and airbags, not the causality.

Logical Sequence

Even if the writer includes plenty of information to support their point, the writing is only coherent when the information is in a logical order. First, the writer should introduce the main idea, whether for a paragraph, a section, or the entire piece. Second, they should present evidence to support the main idea by using transitional language. This shows the reader how the information relates to the main idea and to the sentences around it. The writer should then take time to interpret the information, making sure necessary connections are obvious to the reader. Finally, the writer can summarize the information in a closing section.

Though most writing follows this pattern, it isn't a set rule. Sometimes writers change the order for effect. For example, the writer can begin with a surprising piece of supporting information to grab the reader's attention, and then transition to the main idea. Thus, if a passage doesn't follow the logical order, don't immediately assume it's wrong. However, most writing usually settles into a logical sequence after a nontraditional beginning.

Introductions and Conclusions

Examining the writer's strategies for introductions and conclusions puts the reader in the right mindset to interpret the rest of the text. Look for methods the writer might use for introductions such as:

- Stating the main point immediately, followed by outlining how the rest of the piece supports this claim.

- Establishing important, smaller pieces of the main idea first, and then grouping these points into a case for the main idea.

- Opening with a quotation, anecdote, question, seeming paradox, or other piece of interesting information, and then using it to lead to the main point.

Whatever method the writer chooses, the introduction should make their intention clear, establish their voice as a credible one, and encourage a person to continue reading.

Conclusions tend to follow a similar pattern. In them, the writer restates their main idea a final time, often after summarizing the smaller pieces of that idea. If the introduction uses a quote or anecdote to grab the reader's attention, the conclusion often makes reference to it again. Whatever way the writer

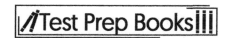

chooses to arrange the conclusion, the final restatement of the main idea should be clear and simple for the reader to interpret. Finally, conclusions shouldn't introduce any new information.

Precision

People often think of precision in terms of math, but precise word choice is another key to successful writing. Since language itself is imprecise, it's important for the writer to find the exact word or words to convey the full, intended meaning of a given situation. For example:

> The number of deaths has gone down since seat belt laws started.

There are several problems with this sentence. First, the word *deaths* is too general. From the context, it's assumed that the writer is referring only to deaths caused by car accidents. However, without clarification, the sentence lacks impact and is probably untrue. The phrase "gone down" might be accurate, but a more precise word could provide more information and greater accuracy. Did the numbers show a slow and steady decrease of highway fatalities or a sudden drop? If the latter is true, the writer is missing a chance to make their point more dramatically. Instead of "gone down" they could substitute *plummeted*, *fallen drastically*, or *rapidly diminished* to bring the information to life. Also, the phrase "seat belt laws" is unclear. Does it refer to laws requiring cars to include seat belts or to laws requiring drivers and passengers to use them? Finally, *started* is not a strong verb. Words like *enacted* or *adopted* are more direct and make the content more real. When put together, these changes create a far more powerful sentence:

> The number of highway fatalities has plummeted since laws requiring seat belt usage were enacted.

However, it's important to note that precise word choice can sometimes be taken too far. If the writer of the sentence above takes precision to an extreme, it might result in the following:

The incidence of high-speed, automobile accident related fatalities has decreased 75% and continued to remain at historical lows since the initial set of federal legislations requiring seat belt use were enacted in 1992.

This sentence is extremely precise, but it takes so long to achieve that precision that it suffers from a lack of clarity. Precise writing is about finding the right balance between information and flow. This is also an issue of conciseness (discussed in the next section).

The last thing to consider with precision is a word choice that's not only unclear or uninteresting, but also confusing or misleading. For example:

The number of highway fatalities has become hugely lower since laws requiring seat belt use were enacted.

In this case, the reader might be confused by the word *hugely*. Huge means large, but here the writer uses *hugely* to describe something small. Though most readers can decipher this, doing so disconnects them from the flow of the writing and makes the writer's point less effective.

Conciseness

"Less is more" is a good rule to follow when writing a sentence. Unfortunately, writers often include extra words and phrases that seem necessary at the time, but add nothing to the main idea. This confuses the reader and creates unnecessary repetition. Writing that lacks conciseness is usually guilty of excessive wordiness and redundant phrases. Here's an example containing both of these issues:

> When legislators decided to begin creating legislation making it mandatory for automobile drivers and passengers to make use of seat belts while in cars, a large number of them made those laws for reasons that were political reasons.

There are several empty or "fluff" words here that take up too much space. These can be eliminated while still maintaining the writer's meaning. For example:

"Decided to begin" could be shortened to "began"
"Making it mandatory for" could be shortened to "requiring"
"Make use of" could be shortened to "use"
"A large number" could be shortened to "many"
In addition, there are several examples of redundancy that can be eliminated:

"Legislators decided to begin creating legislation" and "made those laws"
"Automobile drivers and passengers" and "while in cars"
"Reasons that were political reasons"
These changes are incorporated as follows:

> When legislators began requiring drivers and passengers to use seat belts, many of them did so for political reasons.

There are many general examples of redundant phrases, such as "add an additional," "complete and total," "time schedule," and "transportation vehicle." If asked to identify a redundant phrase on the test, look for words that are close together with the same (or similar) meanings.

Agreement in Number

Subjects and verbs must agree in number. If a sentence has a singular subject, then it must use a singular verb. If there is a plural subject, then it must use a plural verb.

Singular Noun	Singular Verb	Plural Noun	Plural verb
Man	has	men	have
child	plays	children	play
basketball	bounces	basketballs	bounce

Agreement in Person

Verbs must also agree in person. A subject that uses first person must include a verb that is also in first person. The same is true for second and third person subjects and verbs.

	Noun	Verb
First person	I	am
Second person	you	are
Third person	she	is

Common Agreement Errors

Compound Subjects
Compound subjects are when two or more subjects are joined by a coordinating conjunction, such as *and*, *or*, *neither*, or *nor*. Errors in agreement sometimes occur when there is a compound subject:

Incorrect: Mike and I am in a meeting this morning.

Correct: Mike and I are in a meeting this morning.

A compound subject always uses the plural form of the verb to match with the plural subject. In the above example, readers can substitute "Mike and I" for "we" to make it easier to determine the verb: "We *are* in a meeting this morning."

Separation of Subject and Verb
Errors sometimes occur when the subject is separated from the verb by a prepositional phrase or parenthetical element:

Incorrect: The objective of the teachers are to help students learn.

Correct: The objective of the teachers is to help students learn.

The verb must agree with the singular subject *objective*, not the word *teachers*, which is the object of the preposition *of* and does not influence the subject. An easy way to determine if the subject and verb agree is to take out the middle preposition: "The objective *is* to help students learn."

Indefinite Pronouns
Indefinite pronouns refer to people or groups in a general way: *each, anyone, none, all, either, neither,* and *everyone*. Some indefinite pronouns are always singular, such as *each, everyone, someone,* and *everybody*, which affects verb choice:

Incorrect: Each of them are competing in the race.

Correct: Each of them is competing in the race.

While the word *them* can indicate that a plural verb is needed, the subject *each* is singular regardless of what it refers to, requiring the singular verb, *is*.

Other indefinite pronouns can be singular or plural, depending on what they are referring to, such as *anyone, all,* and *some.*

Some of the orders are scheduled to arrive today.

Some refers to *orders*, which is plural, so the plural verb (*are*) is needed.

Some of the cake is left on the dining room table.

Some refers to *cake*, which is singular, so the singular verb (*is*) is needed.

Subjects Joined by Or and Nor

Compound subjects joined by *or* or *nor* rely on the subject nearest to the verb to determine conjugation and agreement:

> Neither Ben nor Jeff was in attendance at the conference.

> Pink or purple is the bride's color choice.

In each example, the subjects are both singular, so the verb should be singular.

If one subject is singular and the other plural, the subject nearest to the verb is the one that needs to agree:

> Either the shirt or pants are hanging on the clothesline.

In this example there is a singular subject (*shirt*) and a plural subject (*pants*), so the verb (*are*) should agree with the subject nearest to it (*pants*).

Collective Nouns

Collective nouns can use a singular or plural verb depending on their function in the sentence. If the collective noun is acting as a unit, then a singular verb is needed. Otherwise, it's necessary to use a plural verb.

> The staff is required to meet every third Friday of the month.

The *staff* is meeting as a collective unit, so a singular verb is needed.

> The staff are getting in their cars to go home.

The staff get into their cars separately, so a plural verb is needed.

Plural Nouns with Singular Meaning

Certain nouns end in *s*, like a plural noun, but have singular meaning, such as *mathematics, news,* and *civics*. These nouns should use a singular verb.

> The news is on at 8:00 tonight.

Nouns that are single things, but have two parts, are considered plural and should use a plural verb, such as *scissors, pants,* and *tweezers*.

> My favorite pants are in the washing machine.

There Is and There Are

There cannot be a subject, so verb agreement should be based on a word that comes after the verb.

> There is a hole in the road.

The subject in this sentence is *hole*, which is singular, so the verb should be singular (*is*).

> There are kids playing kickball in the street.

The subject in this sentence is *kids*, which is plural, so the verb should be plural (*are*).

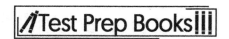

Verb Tense

Shifting verb forms entails conjugation, which is used to indicate tense, voice, or mood.

Verb tense is used to show when the action in the sentence took place. There are several different verb tenses, and it is important to know how and when to use them. Some verb tenses can be achieved by changing the form of the verb, while others require the use of helping verbs (e.g., *is, was,* or *has*).

Present tense shows the action is happening currently or is ongoing:
    I walk to work every morning.

    She is stressed about the deadline.

Past tense shows that the action happened in the past or that the state of being is in the past:
    I walked to work yesterday morning.

    She was stressed about the deadline.

Future tense shows that the action will happen in the future or is a future state of being:
    I will walk to work tomorrow morning.

    She will be stressed about the deadline.

Present perfect tense shows action that began in the past, but continues into the present:
    I have walked to work all week.

    She has been stressed about the deadline.

Past perfect tense shows an action was finished before another took place:
    I had walked all week until I sprained my ankle.

    She had been stressed about the deadline until we talked about it.

Future perfect tense shows an action that will be completed at some point in the future:
    By the time the bus arrives, I will have walked to work already.

Sentence Types

There are four ways in which we can structure sentences: simple, compound, complex, and compound-complex. Sentences can be composed of just one clause or many clauses joined together.

When a sentence is composed of just one clause (an independent clause), we call it a simple sentence. Simple sentences do not necessarily have to be short sentences. They just require one independent clause with a subject and a predicate. For example:

    Thomas marched over to Andrew's house.

    Jonah and Mary constructed a simplified version of the Eiffel Tower with Legos.

When a sentence has two or more independent clauses we call it a compound sentence. The clauses are connected by a comma and a coordinating conjunction—*and, but, or, nor, for*—or by a semicolon. Compound sentences do not have dependent clauses. For example:

> We went to the fireworks stand, and we bought enough fireworks to last all night.

> The children sat on the grass, and then we lit the fireworks one at a time.

When a sentence has just one independent clause and includes one or more dependent clauses, we call it a complex sentence:

> Because she slept well and drank coffee, Sarah was quite productive at work.

> Although Will had coffee, he made mistakes while using the photocopier.

When a sentence has two or more independent clauses and at least one dependent clause, we call it a compound-complex sentence:

> It may come as a surprise, but I found the tickets, and you can go to the show.

> Jade is the girl who dove from the high-dive, and she stunned the audience silent.

Sentence Fragments

Remember that a complete sentence must have both a subject and a verb. Complete sentences consist of at least one independent clause. Incomplete sentences are called sentence fragments. A sentence fragment is a common error in writing. Sentence fragments can be independent clauses that start with subordinating words, such as *but, as, so that,* or *because,* or they could simply be missing a subject or verb.

You can correct a fragment error by adding the fragment to a nearby sentence or by adding or removing words to make it an independent clause. For example:

> Dogs are my favorite animals. Because cats are too independent. (Incorrect; the word because creates a sentence fragment)

> Dogs are my favorite animals because cats are too independent. (Correct; the fragment becomes a dependent clause.)

> Dogs are my favorite animals. Cats are too independent. (Correct; the fragment becomes a simple sentence.)

Run-on Sentences

Another common mistake in writing is the run-on sentence. A run-on is created when two or more independent clauses are joined without the use of a conjunction, a semicolon, a colon, or a dash. We don't want to use commas where periods belong. Here is an example of a run-on sentence:

> Making wedding cakes can take many hours I am very impatient, I want to see them completed right away.

There are a variety of ways to correct a run-on sentence. The method you choose will depend on the context of the sentence and how it fits with neighboring sentences:

Making wedding cakes can take many hours. I am very impatient. I want to see them completed right away. (Use periods to create more than one sentence.)

Making wedding cakes can take many hours; I am very impatient—I want to see them completed right away. (Correct the sentence using a semicolon, colon, or dash.)

Making wedding cakes can take many hours and I am very impatient, so I want to see them completed right away. (Correct the sentence using coordinating conjunctions.)

I am very impatient because I would rather see completed wedding cakes right away than wait for it to take many hours. (Correct the sentence by revising.)

Dangling and Misplaced Modifiers

A modifier is a word or phrase meant to describe or clarify another word in the sentence. When a sentence has a modifier but is missing the word it describes or clarifies, it's an error called a dangling modifier. We can fix the sentence by revising to include the word that is being modified. Consider the following examples with the modifier italicized:

Having walked five miles, this bench will be the place to rest. (Incorrect; this version of the sentence implies that the bench walked the miles, not the person.)

Having walked five miles, Matt will rest on this bench. (Correct; in this version, *having walked five miles* correctly modifies *Matt*, who did the walking.)

Since midnight, my dreams have been pleasant and comforting. (Incorrect; in this version, the adverb clause *since midnight* cannot modify the noun *dreams*.)

Since midnight, I have had pleasant and comforting dreams. (Correct; in this version, *since midnight* modifies the verb *have had*, telling us when the dreams occurred.)

Sometimes the modifier is not located close enough to the word it modifies for the sentence to be clearly understood. In this case, we call the error a misplaced modifier. Here is an example with the modifier italicized and the modified word in underlined.

We gave the hot <u>cocoa</u> to the children *that was filled with marshmallows.* (Incorrect; this sentence implies that the children are what are filled with marshmallows.)

We gave the hot <u>*cocoa* *that was filled with marshmallows*</u> to the children. (Correct; here, the cocoa is filled with marshmallows. The modifier is near the word it modifies.)

Parallelism and Subordination

Parallelism
To be grammatically correct we must use articles, prepositions, infinitives, and introductory words for dependent clauses consistently throughout a sentence. This is called parallelism. We use parallelism

when we are matching parts of speech, phrases, or clauses with another part of the sentence. Being inconsistent creates confusion. Consider the following example.

> *Incorrect:* Be ready for running and to ride a bike during the triathlon.

> *Correct:* Be ready to run and to ride a bike during the triathlon.

> *Correct:* Be ready for running and for riding a bike during the triathlon.

In the incorrect example, the gerund *running* does not match with the infinitive *to ride.* Either both should be infinitives or both should be gerunds.

Subordination

Sometimes we have unequal pieces of information in a sentence where one piece is more important than the other. We need to show that one piece of information is subordinate to the other. We can make the more important piece an independent clause and connect the other piece by making it a dependent clause. Consider this example:

> *Central thought:* Kittens can always find their mother.

> *Subordinate:* Kittens are blind at birth.

> *Complex Sentence:* Despite being blind at birth, kittens can always find their mother.

The sentence "Kittens are blind at birth" is made subordinate to the sentence "Kittens can always find their mother" by placing the word "Despite" at the beginning and removing the subject, thus turning an independent clause ("kittens are blind at birth") into a subordinate phrase ("Despite being blind at birth").

Clauses

Clauses are groups of words within a sentence that have both a subject and a verb. We can distinguish a clause from a phrase because phrases do not have both a subject and a verb. There are several types of clauses; clauses can be independent or dependent and can serve as a noun, an adjective, or an adverb.

An *independent clause* could stand alone as its own sentence if the rest of the sentence were not there. For example:

> *The party is on Tuesday* after the volleyball game is over.

> *I am excited to go to the party* because my best friend will be there.

A *dependent clause*, or subordinating clause, is the part of the sentence that gives supportive information but cannot create a proper sentence by itself. However, it will still have both a subject and a verb; otherwise, it is a phrase. In the example above, *after the volleyball game is over* and *because my best friend will be there* are dependent because they begin with the conjunctions *after* and *because*, and a proper sentence does not begin with a conjunction.

Noun clauses are groups of words that collectively form a noun. Look for the opening words *whether, which, what, that, who, how,* or *why.* For example:

> I had fun cooking what we had for dinner last night.

> I'm going to track down whoever ate my sandwich.

Adjective clauses collectively form an adjective that modifies a noun or pronoun in the sentence. If you can remove the adjective clause and the leftovers create a standalone sentence, then the clause should be set off with commas, parentheses, or dashes. If you can remove the clause it is called nonrestrictive. If it can't be removed without ruining the sentence, then it is called restrictive and does not get set off with commas.

> Jenna, *who hates to get wet,* fell into the pool. (Nonrestrictive)

> The girl *who hates to get wet* fell into the pool. (Restrictive; the clause tells us which girl, and if removed there is confusion)

Adverbial clauses serve as an adverb in the sentence, modifying a verb, adjective, or other adverb. Look for the opening words *after, before, as, as if, although, because, if, since, so, so that, when, where, while,* or *unless.*

> She lost her wallet after she left the theme park.

> Her earring fell through the crack before she could catch it.

Phrases

A phrase is a group of words that go together but do not include both a subject and a verb. We use them to add information, explain something, or make the sentence easier for the reader to understand. Unlike clauses, phrases cannot ever stand alone as their own sentence if the rest of the sentence were not there. They do not form complete thoughts. There are noun phrases, prepositional phrases, verbal phrases, appositive phrases, and absolute phrases. Let's look at each of these.

Noun phrases: A noun phrase is a group of words built around a noun or pronoun that serves as a unit to form a noun in the sentence. Consider the following examples. The phrase is built around the underlined word. The entire phrase can be replaced by a noun or pronoun to test whether or not it is a noun phrase.

> I like the chocolate chip ice cream. (I like it.)

> I know all the shortest routes. (I know them.)

> I met the best supporting actress. (I met her.)

Prepositional phrases: These are phrases that begin with a preposition and end with a noun or pronoun. We use them as a unit to form the adjective or adverb in the sentence. Prepositional phrases that introduce a sentence are called introductory prepositional phrases and are set off with commas.

I found the Frisbee *on the roof peak.* (Adverb; where it was found)

The girl *with the bright red hair* was prom queen. (Adjective; which girl)

Before the sequel, we wanted to watch the first movie. (Introductory phrase)

Verbal phrases: Some phrases look like verbs but do not serve as the verb in the sentence. These are called verbal phrases. There are three types: participial phrases, gerund phrases, and infinitive phrases.

Participial phrases start with a participle and modify nouns or pronouns; therefore, they act as the adjective in the sentence.

Beaten by the sun, we searched for shade to sit in. (Modifies the pronoun *we*)

The hikers, *being eaten by mosquitoes,* longed for repellant. (Modifies the noun *hikers*)

Gerund phrases often look like participles because they end in *-ing*, but they serve as the noun, not the adjective, in the sentence. Like any noun, we can use them as the subject or as the object of a verb or preposition in the sentence.

Eating green salad is the best way to lose weight. (Subject)

Sumo wrestlers are famous for *eating large quantities of food.* (Object)

Infinitive phrases often look like verbs because they start with the word *to,* but they serve as an adjective, adverb, or noun.

To survive the chill is the goal of the Polar Bear Plunge. (Noun)

A hot tub is at the scene *to warm up after the jump.* (Adverb)

The jumpers have hot cocoa *to drink right away.* (Adjective)

Appositive phrases: We can use any of the above types of phrases to rename nouns or pronouns, and we call this an appositive phrase. Appositive phrases usually appear either just before or just after the noun or pronoun they are renaming. Appositive phrases are essential when the noun or pronoun is too general, and they are nonessential when they just add information.

The two famous brothers Orville and Wilbur Wright invented the airplane. (Essential)

Sarah Calysta, *my great grandmother,* is my namesake. (Nonessential)

Absolute phrases: When a participle comes after a noun and forms a phrase that is not otherwise part of the sentence, it's called an absolute phrase. Absolute phrases are not complete thoughts and cannot stand alone because they do not have a subject and a verb. They are not essential to the sentence in that they do not explain or add additional meaning to any other part of the sentence.

The engine roaring, Jada closed her eyes and waited for the plane to take off.

The microphone crackling, the flight attendant announced the delayed arrival.

Peer Conferences

Peer conferences develop student's writing skills when they are structured, and when the guidelines for student reviewers are clear. Teachers can provide a guided peer conference using a specific set of questions for review. Questions can be adjusted to fit the assignment goals. Reviewers can provide responses verbally or in written form. Verbal discussion can help reinforce the revision step in the writing process, and make students aware of how their writing is received by an audience.

Writing Style

A writer's style is the way that he or she presents information through sentence structure, word choice, and even punctuation. Style is influenced by the writing situation and the intended audience. A writer's voice is an element of style that shows the writer's personality. It is what makes the writing unique to the writer. Voice and style can be developed through listening to examples of styles in other's writing. Developing an ear for different writing styles can help students to develop their own style.

Writing Skills

Coherent writing involves the use of clause-joining devices, such as the use of coordinators and punctuation such as semicolons and commas. Ideas should flow logically and fluidly and these skills should develop through writing instruction as well as by reading quality work. Writing skills are influenced by a number of factors. A student's personal experience, for example, can influence his or her voice writing. Socio-economic factors can also influence a student's writing skills and success. Early reading experiences can also be a factor in how writers develops their skills. Students who are regularly read to from a young age tend to have more developed vocabularies and better writing skills, while those that did not receive early literacy experiences are often not be as successful in their writing. These factors must be addressed and considered in the development of writing instruction in order to meet the needs of all students.

Effective Writing

Identifying Modes of Writing

Distinguishing Between Common Modes of Writing

To distinguish between the common modes of writing, it is important to identify the primary purpose of the work. This can be determined by considering what the author is trying to say to the reader. Although there are countless different styles of writing, all written works tend to fall under four primary categories: argumentative/persuasive, informative expository, descriptive, and narrative.

The below table highlights the purpose, distinct characteristics, and examples of each rhetorical mode.

Writing Mode	Purpose	Distinct Characteristics	Examples
Argumentative	To persuade	Opinions, loaded or subjective language, evidence, suggestions of what the reader should do, calls to action	Critical reviews Political journals Letters of recommendation Cover letters Advertising
Informative	To teach or inform	Objective language, definitions, instructions, factual information	Business and scientific reports Textbooks Instruction manuals News articles Personal letters Wills Informative essays Travel guides Study guides
Descriptive	To deliver sensory details to the reader	Heavy use of adjectives and imagery, language that appeals to any of the five senses	Poetry Journal entries Often used in narrative mode
Narrative	To tell a story, share an experience, entertain	Series of events, plot, characters, dialogue, conflict	Novels Short stories Novellas Anecdotes Biographies Epic poems Autobiographies

Identifying Common Types of Writing

The following steps help to identify examples of common types within the modes of writing:

1. Identifying the audience—to whom or for whom the author is writing
2. Determining the author's purpose—why the author is writing the piece
3. Analyzing the word choices and how they are used

To demonstrate, the following passage has been marked to illustrate *the addressee*, the author's purpose, and word choices:

To Whom It May Concern:

I am extraordinarily excited to be applying to the Master of Environmental Science program at Australian National University. I believe the richness in biological and cultural diversity, as well as Australia's close proximity to the Great Barrier Reef, would provide a deeply fulfilling

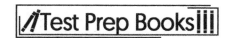

educational experience. *I am writing to express why I believe I would be an <u>excellent</u> addition to the program.*

While in college, I participated in a three-month public health internship in Ecuador, where I spent time both learning about medicine in a third world country and also about the Ecuadorian environment, including the Amazon Jungle and the Galápagos Islands. <u>My favorite experience</u> through the internship, besides swimming with sea lions in San Cristóbal, was helping to neutralize parasitic potable water and collect samples for analysis in Puyo.

Though my undergraduate studies related primarily to the human body, I took several courses in natural science, including a year of chemistry, biology, and physics as well as a course in a calculus. <u>I am confident</u> that my fundamental knowledge in these fields will prepare me for the science courses integral to the Masters of Environmental Science.

Having identified the *addressee*, it is evident that this selection is a letter of some kind. Further inspection into the author's purpose, seen in *bold*, shows that the author is trying to explain why he or she should be accepted into the environmental science program, which automatically places it into the argumentative mode as the writer is trying to persuade the reader to agree and to incite the reader into action by encouraging the program to accept the writer as a candidate. In addition to revealing the purpose, the use of emotional language—extraordinarily, excellent, deeply fulfilling, favorite experience, confident—illustrates that this is a persuasive piece. It also provides evidence for why this person would be an excellent addition to the program, given their experience in Ecuador and with scientific curriculum.

The following passage presents an opportunity to solidify this method of analysis and practice the steps above to determine the mode, as well as the author's purpose and audience.

> The biological effects of laughing have long been an interest of medicine and psychology. Laughing is often speculated to lower blood pressure because it induces feelings of relaxation and elation. Participants in a study were shown a series of videos that elicited laughter, and their blood pressure was taken before and after the viewings. An average decrease in blood pressure was observed, though researchers concluded that the results were not significant.

This selection contains factual information, or data, is devoid of any adjectives or flowery descriptions, and is not trying to convince readers of any particular stance. Though the audience is not directly addressed, the purpose of the passage is to present the results of an experiment to those who would be interested in the biological effects of laughter—most likely a scientific community. Thus, this passage is an example of informative writing.

Below is another passage to help identify examples of the common writing modes, taken from *The Endeavor Journal of Sir Joseph Banks*:

10th May 1769 – THE ENGLISH CREW GET TAHITIAN NAMES

We have now got the Indian name of the Island, Otahite, so therefore for the future I shall call it. As for our own names the Indians find so much dificulty in pronouncing them that we are forcd to indulge them in calling us what they please, or rather what they say when they attempt to pronounce them. I give here the List: Captn Cooke *Toote*, Dr Solander *Torano*, Mr Hicks *Hete*, Mr Gore *Toárro*, Mr Molineux *Boba* from his Christian name Robert, Mr Monkhouse *Mato*, and myself *Tapáne*. In this manner they have names for almost every man in the ship.

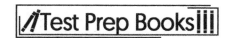

This extract contains no elements of an informative or persuasive intent and does not seem to follow any particular line of narrative. The passage gives a list of the different names that the Indians have given the crew members, as well as the name of an island. Although there is no context for the selection, through the descriptions, it is clear that the author and his comrades are on an island trying to communicate with the native inhabitants. Hence, this passage is a journal that reflects the descriptive mode.

These are only a few of the many examples that can be found in the four primary modes of writing.

Determining the Appropriate Mode of Writing

The author's *primary purpose* is defined as the reason an author chooses to write a selection, and it is often dependent on his or her *audience*. A biologist writing a textbook, for example, does so to communicate scientific knowledge to an audience of people who want to study biology. An audience can be as broad as the entire global population or as specific as women fighting for equal rights in the bicycle repair industry. Whatever the audience, it is important that the author considers its demographics—age, gender, culture, language, education level, etc.

If the author's purpose is to persuade or inform, he or she will consider how much the intended audience knows about the subject. For example, if an author is writing on the importance of recycling to anyone who will listen, he or she will use the informative mode—including background information on recycling—and the argumentative mode—evidence for why it works, while also using simple diction so that it is easy for everyone to understand. If, on the other hand, the writer is proposing new methods for recycling using solar energy, the audience is probably already familiar with standard recycling processes and will require less background information, as well as more technical language inherent to the scientific community.

If the author's purpose is to entertain through a story or a poem, he or she will need to consider whom he/she is trying to entertain. If an author is writing a script for a children's cartoon, the plot, language, conflict, characters, and humor would align with the interests of the age demographic of that audience. On the other hand, if an author is trying to entertain adults, he or she may write content not suitable for children. The author's purpose and audience are generally interdependent.

Understanding the Task, Purpose, and Audience

Identifying the Task, Purpose, and Intended Audience

An author's *writing style*—the way in which words, grammar, punctuation, and sentence fluidity are used—is the most influential element in a piece of writing, and it is dependent on the purpose and the audience for whom it is intended. Together, a writing style and mode of writing form the foundation of a written work, and a good writer will choose the most effective mode and style to convey a message to readers.

Writers should first determine what they are trying to say and then choose the most effective mode of writing to communicate that message. Different writing modes and *word choices* will affect the tone of a piece—that is, its underlying attitude, emotion, or character. The argumentative mode may utilize words that are earnest, angry, passionate, or excited whereas an informative piece may have a sterile, germane, or enthusiastic tone. The tones found in narratives vary greatly, depending on the purpose of the writing. *Tone* will also be affected by the audience—teaching science to children or those who may be uninterested would be most effective with enthusiastic language and exclamation points whereas

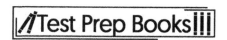

teaching science to college students may take on a more serious and professional tone, with fewer charged words and punctuation choices that are inherent to academia.

Sentence fluidity—whether sentences are long and rhythmic or short and succinct—also affects a piece of writing as it determines the way in which a piece is read. Children or audiences unfamiliar with a subject do better with short, succinct sentence structures as these break difficult concepts up into shorter points. A period, question mark, or exclamation point is literally a signal for the reader to stop and takes more time to process. Thus, longer, more complex sentences are more appropriate for adults or educated audiences as they can fit more information in between processing time.

The amount of *supporting detail* provided is also tailored to the audience. A text that introduces a new subject to its readers will focus more on broad ideas without going into greater detail whereas a text that focuses on a more specific subject is likely to provide greater detail about the ideas discussed.

Writing styles, like modes, are most effective when tailored to their audiences. Having awareness of an audience's demographic is one of the most crucial aspects of properly communicating an argument, a story, or a set of information.

Choosing the Most Appropriate Type of Writing

Before beginning any writing, it is imperative that a writer have a firm grasp on the message he or she wishes to convey and how he or she wants readers to be affected by the writing. For example, does the author want readers to be more informed about the subject? Does the writer want readers to agree with his or her opinion? Does the writer want readers to get caught up in an exciting narrative? The following steps are a guide to determining the appropriate type of writing for a task, purpose, and audience:

1. Identifying the purpose for writing the piece
2. Determining the audience
3. Adapting the writing mode, word choices, tone, and style to fit the audience and the purpose

It is important to distinguish between a work's purpose and its main idea. The essential difference between the two is that the *main idea* is what the author wants to communicate about the topic at hand whereas the *primary purpose* is why the author is writing in the first place. The primary purpose is what will determine the type of writing an author will choose to utilize, not the main idea, though the two are related. For example, if an author writes an article on the mistreatment of animals in factory farms and, at the end, suggests that people should convert to vegetarianism, the main idea is that vegetarianism would reduce the poor treatment of animals. The primary purpose is to convince the reader to stop eating animals. Since the primary purpose is to galvanize an audience into action, the author would choose the argumentative writing mode.

The next step is to consider to whom the author is appealing as this will determine the type of details to be included, the diction to be used, the tone to be employed, and the sentence structure to be used. An audience can be identified by considering the following questions:

- What is the purpose for writing the piece?
- To whom is it being written?
- What is their age range?
- Are they familiar with the material being presented, or are they just being newly introduced to it?

- Where are they from?
- Is the task at hand in a professional or casual setting?
- Is the task at hand for monetary gain?

These are just a few of the numerous considerations to keep in mind, but the main idea is to become as familiar with the audience as possible. Once the audience has been understood, the author can then adapt the writing style to align with the readers' education and interests. The audience is what determines the *rhetorical appeal* the author will use—ethos, pathos, or logos. *Ethos* is a rhetorical appeal to an audience's ethics and/or morals. Ethos is most often used in argumentative and informative writing modes. *Pathos* is an appeal to the audience's emotions and sympathies, and it is found in argumentative, descriptive, and narrative writing modes. *Logos* is an appeal to the audience's logic and reason and is used primarily in informative texts as well as in supporting details for argumentative pieces. Rhetorical appeals are discussed in depth in the informational texts and rhetoric section of the test.

If the author is trying to encourage global conversion to vegetarianism, he or she may choose to use all three rhetorical appeals to reach varying personality types. Those who are less interested in the welfare of animals but are interested in facts and science would relate more to logos. Animal lovers would relate better to an emotional appeal. In general, the most effective works utilize all three appeals.

Finally, after determining the writing mode and rhetorical appeal, the author will consider word choice, sentence structure, and tone, depending on the purpose and audience. The author may choose words that convey sadness or anger when speaking about animal welfare if writing to persuade, or he or she will stick to dispassionate and matter-of-fact tones, if informing the public on the treatment of animals in factory farms. If the author is writing to a younger or less-educated audience, he or she may choose to shorten and simplify sentence structures and word choice. If appealing to an audience with more expert knowledge on a particular subject, writers will more likely employ a style of longer sentences and more complex vocabulary.

Depending on the task, the author may choose to use a first person, second person, or third person point of view. First person and second person perspectives are inherently more casual in tone, including the author and the reader in the rhetoric, while third person perspectives are often seen in more professional settings.

Evaluating the Effectiveness of a Piece of Writing

An effective and engaging piece of writing will cause the reader to forget about the author entirely. Readers will become so engrossed in the subject, argument, or story at hand that they will almost identify with it, readily adopting beliefs proposed by the author or accepting all elements of the story as believable. On the contrary, poorly written works will cause the reader to be hyperaware of the author, doubting the writer's knowledge of a subject or questioning the validity of a narrative. Persuasive or expository works that are poorly researched will have this effect, as well as poorly planned stories with significant plot holes. An author must consider the task, purpose, and audience to sculpt a piece of writing effectively.

When evaluating the effectiveness of a piece, the most important thing to consider is how well the purpose is conveyed to the audience through the mode, use of rhetoric, and writing style.

The purpose must pass through these three aspects for effective delivery to the audience. If any elements are not properly considered, the reader will be overly aware of the author, and the message will be lost. The following is a checklist for evaluating the effectiveness of a piece:

Does the writer choose the appropriate writing mode—argumentative, narrative, descriptive, informative—for his or her purpose?

Does the writing mode employed contain characteristics inherent to that mode?

Does the writer consider the personalities/interests/demographics of the intended audience when choosing rhetorical appeals?

Does the writer use appropriate vocabulary, sentence structure, voice, and tone for the audience demographic?

Does the author properly establish himself/herself as having authority on the subject, if applicable?

Does the piece make sense?

Another thing to consider is the medium in which the piece was written. If the medium is a blog, diary, or personal letter, the author may adopt a more casual stance towards the audience. If the piece of writing is a story in a book, a business letter or report, or a published article in a journal or if the task is to gain money or support or to get published, the author may adopt a more formal stance. Ultimately, the writer will want to be very careful in how he or she addresses the reader.

Finally, the effectiveness of a piece can be evaluated by asking how well the purpose was achieved. For example, if students are assigned to read a persuasive essay, instructors can ask whether the author influences students' opinions. Students may be assigned two differing persuasive texts with opposing perspectives and be asked which writer was more convincing. Students can then evaluate what factors contributed to this—for example, whether one author uses more credible supporting facts, appeals more effectively to readers' emotions, presents more believable personal anecdotes, or offers stronger counterargument refutation. Students can then use these evaluations to strengthen their own writing skills.

Using Clear and Coherent Writing

Identifying Details that Develop a Main Idea

The main idea of a piece is the central topic or theme. To identify the main idea, a reader should consider these questions: "What's the point? What does the author want readers to take away from this text?" Everything within the selection should relate back to the main idea because it is the center of the organizational web of any written work. Particularly in articles and reports, the main idea often appears within the opening paragraphs to orient the reader to what the author wants to say about the subject. A sentence that expresses the main idea is known as a thesis sentence or *thesis statement*.

After the main idea has been introduced, *supporting details* are what develop the main idea—they make up the bulk of the work. Without supporting details, the main idea would simply be a statement, so additional details are needed to give that statement weight and validity. Supporting details can often be identified by recognizing the key words that introduce them. The following example offers several supporting details, with key words underlined:

> Man did not evolve from apes. Though we share a common ancestor, humans and apes originated through very different evolutionary paths. There are several reasons why this is true. The <u>first</u> reason is that, logically, if humans evolved from apes, modern-day apes and humans would not coexist. Evolution occurs when a genetic mutation in a species ensures the survival over the rest of the species, allowing them to pass on their genes and create a new lineage of organisms. <u>Another</u> reason is that hominid fossils only fall into one of two categories—ape-like or human-like—and there are very strong differences between the two. Australopithecines, the hominid fossils originally believed to be ancestral to humans, are ape-like, indicated by their long arms, long and curved fingers, and funnel-shaped chests. Their hand bones suggest that they "knuckle-walked" like modern day chimpanzees and gorillas, something not found in *Homo sapien* fossils. <u>Finally</u>, there is no fossilized evidence to suggest a transition between the ape-like ancestor and the *Homo sapien*, indicating that a sudden mutation may have been responsible. These and many other reasons are indicative that humans and ape-like creatures are evolutionarily different.

The underlined words—*first, another,* and *finally*—are the key words that identify the supporting details. These details can be summarized as follows:

- Humans and apes could not coexist.
- Human-like and ape-like fossils are very different.
- No transition is seen between humans and ape-like ancestors.

The supporting details all relate to the central idea that "Man did not evolve from apes," which is the first sentence of the paragraph.

Even though supporting details are more specific than the main idea, they should nevertheless all be directly related to the main idea. Without sufficient supporting details, the writer's main idea will be too weak to be effective.

Organizing a Text Clearly and Coherently

There are five basic elements inherent in effective writing, and each will be discussed throughout the various subheadings of this section.

Main idea: The driving message of the writing, clearly stated or implied

Clear organization: The effective and purposeful arrangement of the content to support the main idea

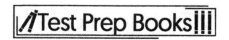

Supporting details/evidence: Content that gives appropriate depth and weight to the main idea of the story, argument, or information

Diction/tone: The type of language, vocabulary, and word choice used to express the main idea, purposefully aligned to the audience and purpose

Adherence to conventions of English: Correct spelling, grammar, punctuation, and sentence structure, allowing for clear communication of ideas

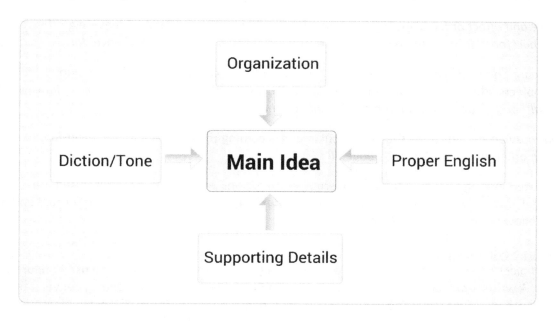

Using Varied and Effective Transitions

Transitions are the glue that holds the writing together. They function to purposefully incorporate new topics and supporting details in a smooth and coherent way. Usually, transitions are found at the beginnings of sentences, but they can also be located in the middle as a way to link clauses together. There are two types of clauses: independent and dependent as discussed in the language use and vocabulary section.

Transition words connect clauses within and between sentences for smoother writing. "I dislike apples. They taste like garbage." is choppier than "I dislike apples because they taste like garbage." Transitions demonstrate the relationship between ideas, allow for more complex sentence structures, and can alert the reader to which type of organizational format the author is using. For example, the above selection on human evolution uses the words *first, another,* and *finally* to indicate that the writer will be listing the reasons why humans and apes are evolutionarily different.

Transition words can be categorized based on the relationships they create between ideas:

General order: signaling elaboration of an idea to emphasize a point—e.g., *for example, for instance, to demonstrate, including, such as, in other words, that is, in fact, also, furthermore, likewise, and, truly, so, surely, certainly, obviously, doubtless*

Chronological order: referencing the time frame in which main event or idea occurs—e.g., *before, after, first, while, soon, shortly thereafter, meanwhile*

Numerical order/order of importance: indicating that related ideas, supporting details, or events will be described in a sequence, possibly in order of importance—e.g., *first, second, also, finally, another, in addition, equally important, less importantly, most significantly, the main reason, last but not least*

Spatial order: referring to the space and location of something or where things are located in relation to each other—e.g., *inside, outside, above, below, within, close, under, over, far, next to, adjacent to*

Cause and effect order: signaling a causal relationship between events or ideas—e.g., *thus, therefore, since, resulted in, for this reason, as a result, consequently, hence, for, so*

Compare and contrast order: identifying the similarities and differences between two or more objects, ideas, or lines of thought—e.g., *like, as, similarly, equally, just as, unlike, however, but, although, conversely, on the other hand, on the contrary*

Summary order: indicating that a particular idea is coming to a close—e.g., *in conclusion, to sum up, in other words, ultimately, above all*

Sophisticated writing also aims to avoid overuse of transitions and ensure that those used are meaningful. Using a variety of transitions makes the writing appear more lively and informed and helps readers follow the progression of ideas.

Justifying Stylistic Choices

Stylistic choices refer to elements such as a writer's diction, sentence structure, and use of figurative language. A writer's *diction* is his or her word choice and may be elevated, academic, conversational, humorous, or any other style. The choice of diction depends on the purpose of a piece of writing. A textbook or a research paper is likely to use academic diction whereas a blog post will use more conversational expressions.

Sentence structure also affects an author's writing style. Will he or she use short, staccato sentences or longer sentences with complex structure? Effective writing tends to incorporate both styles to increase reader interest or to punctuate ideas.

Figurative language includes the use of simile, metaphor, hyperbole, or allusion, to name but a few examples. Creative or descriptive writing is likely to incorporate more non-literal expressions than academic or informative writing will. Instructors should allow students to experiment with different styles of writing and understand how style affects expression and understanding.

Introducing, Developing, and Concluding a Text Effectively

Almost all coherent written works contain three primary parts: a beginning, middle, and end. The organizational arrangements differ widely across distinct writing modes. Persuasive and expository texts utilize an introduction, body, and conclusion whereas narrative works use an orientation, series of events/conflict, and a resolution.

Every element within a written piece relates back to the main idea, and the beginning of a persuasive or expository text generally conveys the main idea or the purpose. For a narrative piece, the beginning is the section that acquaints the reader with the characters and setting, directing them to the purpose of the writing. The main idea in narrative may be implied or addressed at the end of the piece.

Depending on the primary purpose, the arrangement of the middle will adhere to one of the basic organizational structures described in the information texts and rhetoric section. They are cause and effect, problem and solution, compare and contrast, description/spatial, sequence, and order of importance.

The ending of a text is the metaphorical wrap-up of the writing. A solid ending is crucial for effective writing as it ties together loose ends, resolves the action, highlights the main points, or repeats the central idea. A conclusion ensures that readers come away from a text understanding the author's main idea. The table below highlights the important characteristics of each part of a piece of writing.

Structure	Argumentative/Informative	Narrative
Beginning	Introduction *Purpose, main idea*	Orientation *Introduces characters, setting, necessary background*
Middle	Body *Supporting details, reasons and evidence*	Events/Conflict *Story's events that revolve around a central conflict*
End	Conclusion *Highlights main points, summarizes and paraphrases ideas, reiterates the main idea*	Resolution *The solving of the central conflict*

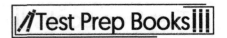

Reflecting on One's Own Writing Process

Teachers should create opportunities for students to evaluate both their own work and the work of their classmates. Teachers should reinforce the skills necessary for peer review, such as critical reading, revision skills, and collaboration. It's necessary to define the role of the peer reviewer as a reader, not an evaluator, so that students understand the goal is to offer helpful suggestions rather than grade the work like a teacher would. Students should learn that peer review is an essential step in the writing process. Revision strategies should be taught and the steps of the writing process reinforced.

Understanding Figurative Language

Whereas literal language is the author's use of precise words, proper meanings, definitions, and phrases that mean exactly what they say, *figurative language* deviates from precise meaning and word definition—often in conjunction with other familiar words and phrases—to paint a picture for the reader. Figurative language is less explicit and more open to reader interpretation.

Some examples of figurative language are included in the following graphic.

	Definition	Example
Simile	Compares two things using "like" or "as"	Her hair was like gold.
Metaphor	Compares two things as if they are the same	He was a giant teddy bear.
Idiom	Using words with predictable meanings to create a phrase with a different meaning	The world is your oyster.
Alliteration	Repeating the same beginning sound or letter in a phrase for emphasis	The busy baby babbled.
Personification	Attributing human characteristics to an object or an animal	The house glowered menacingly with a dark smile.
Foreshadowing	Giving an indication that something is going to happen later in the story	I wasn't aware at the time, but I would come to regret those words.
Symbolism	Using symbols to represent ideas and provide a different meaning	The ring represented the bond between us.
Onomatopoeia	Using words that imitate sound	The tire went off with a bang and a crunch.
Imagery	Appealing to the senses by using descriptive language	The sky was painted with red and pink and streaked with orange.
Hyperbole	Using exaggeration not meant to be taken literally	The girl weighed less than a feather.

Figurative language can be used to give additional insight into the theme or message of a text by moving beyond the usual and literal meaning of words and phrases. It can also be used to appeal to the senses of readers and create a more in-depth story.

Understanding Poetic Devices and Structure

Poetic Devices

Rhyme is the poet's use of corresponding word sounds in order to create an effect. Most rhyme occurs at the ends of a poem's lines, which is how readers arrive at the *rhyme scheme*. Each line that has a corresponding rhyming sound is assigned a letter—A, B, C, and so on. When using a rhyme scheme, poets will often follow lettered patterns. Robert Frost's *"The Road Not Taken"* uses the ABAAB rhyme scheme:

Two roads diverged in a yellow wood,	A
And sorry I could not travel both	B
And be one traveler, long I stood	A
And looked down one as far as I could	A
To where it bent in the undergrowth;	B

Another important poetic device is *rhythm*—metered patterns within poetry verses. When a poet develops rhythm through *meter*, he or she is using a combination of stressed and unstressed syllables to create a sound effect for the reader.

Rhythm is created by the use of *poetic feet*—individual rhythmic units made up of the combination of stressed and unstressed syllables. A line of poetry is made up of one or more poetic feet. There are five standard types in English poetry, as depicted in the chart below.

Foot Type	Rhythm	Pattern
Iamb	buh Buh	Unstressed/stressed
Trochee	Buh buh	Stressed/unstressed
Spondee	Buh Buh	Stressed/stressed
Anapest	buh buh Buh	Unstressed/unstressed/stressed
Dactyl	Buh buh buh	Stressed/unstressed/unstressed

Structure

Poetry is most easily recognized by its structure, which varies greatly. For example, a structure may be strict in the number of lines it uses. It may use rhyming patterns or may not rhyme at all. There are three main types of poetic structures:

Verse—poetry with a consistent meter and rhyme scheme
Blank verse—poetry with consistent meter but an inconsistent rhyme scheme
Free verse—poetry with inconsistent meter or rhyme

Verse poetry is most often developed in the form of *stanzas*—groups of word lines. Stanzas can also be considered *verses*. The structure is usually formulaic and adheres to the protocols for the form. For example, the English *sonnet* form uses a structure of fourteen lines and a variety of different rhyming patterns. The English *ode* typically uses three ten-line stanzas and has a particular rhyming pattern.

Poets choose poetic structure based on the effect they want to create. Some structures—such as the ballad and haiku—developed out of cultural influences and common artistic practice in history, but in more modern poetry, authors choose their structure to best fit their intended effect.

Understanding Effective and Ethical Research Practices

Identifying Relevant Information During Research

Relevant information is that which is pertinent to the topic at hand. Particularly when doing research online, it is easy for students to get overwhelmed with the wealth of information available to them. Before conducting research, then, students need to begin with a clear idea of the question they want to answer.

For example, a student may be interested in learning more about marriage practices in Jane Austen's England. If that student types "marriage" into a search engine, he or she will have to sift through thousands of unrelated sites before finding anything related to that topic. Narrowing down search parameters can aid in locating relevant information.

When using a book, students can consult the table of contents, glossary, or index to discover whether the book contains relevant information before using it as a resource. If the student finds a hefty volume on Jane Austen, he or she can flip to the index in the back, look for the word marriage, and find out how many page references are listed in the book. If there are few or no references to the subject, it is probably not a relevant or useful source.

In evaluating research articles, students may also consult the title, abstract, and keywords before reading the article in its entirety. Referring to the date of publication will also determine whether the research contains up-to-date discoveries, theories, and ideas about the subject, or whether it is outdated.

Evaluating the Credibility of a Print or Digital Source

There are several additional criteria that need to be examined before using a source for a research topic.

The following questions will help determine whether a source is credible:

Author
- Who is he or she?
- Does he or she have the appropriate credentials—e.g., M.D, PhD?
- Is this person authorized to write on the matter through his/her job or personal experiences?
- Is he or she affiliated with any known credible individuals or organizations?
- Has he or she written anything else?

Publisher
- Who published/produced the work? Is it a well-known journal, like National Geographic, or a tabloid, like The National Enquirer?
- Is the publisher from a scholarly, commercial, or government association?
- Do they publish works related to specific fields?
- Have they published other works?
- If a digital source, what kind of website hosts the text? Does it end in .edu, .org, or .com?

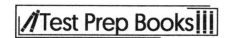

Bias
- Is the writing objective? Does it contain any loaded or emotional language?
- Does the publisher/producer have a known bias, such as Fox News or CNN?
- Does the work include diverse opinions or perspectives?
- Does the author have any known bias—e.g., Michael Moore, Bill O'Reilly, or the Pope? Is he or she affiliated with any organizations or individuals that may have a known bias—e.g., Citizens United or the National Rifle Association?
- Does the magazine, book, journal, or website contain any advertising?

References
- Are there any references?
- Are the references credible? Do they follow the same criteria as stated above?
- Are the references from a related field?

Accuracy/reliability
- Has the article, book, or digital source been peer reviewed?
- Are all of the conclusions, supporting details, or ideas backed with published evidence?
- If a digital source, is it free of grammatical errors, poor spelling, and improper English?
- Do other published individuals have similar findings?

Coverage
- Are the topic and related material both successfully addressed?
- Does the work add new information or theories to those of their sources?
- Is the target audience appropriate for the intended purpose?

Identifying Effective Research Practices

The purpose of all research is to provide an answer to an unknown question. Therefore, all good research papers pose the topic in the form of a question, which they will then seek to answer with clear ideas, arguments, and supporting evidence.

A *research question* is the primary focus of the research piece, and it should be formulated on a unique topic. To formulate a research question, writers begin by choosing a general topic of interest and then research the literature to determine what sort of research has already been done—the *literature review*. This helps them narrow the topic into something original and determine what still needs to be asked and researched about the topic. A solid question is very specific and avoids generalizations. The following question is offered for evaluation:

What is most people's favorite kind of animal?

This research question is extremely broad without giving the paper any particular focus—it could go any direction and is not an exceptionally unique focus. To narrow it down, the question could consider a specific population:

What is the favorite animal of people in Ecuador?

While this question is better, it does not address exactly why this research is being conducted or why anyone would care about the answer. Here's another possibility:

What does the animal considered as the most favorite of people in different regions throughout Ecuador reveal about their socioeconomic status?

This question is extremely specific and gives a very clear direction of where the paper or project is going to go. However, sometimes the question can be too limited, where very little research has been conducted to create a solid paper, and the researcher most likely does not have the means to travel to Ecuador and travel door-to-door conducting a census on people's favorite animals. In this case, the research question would need to be broadened. Broadening a topic can mean introducing a wider range of criteria. Instead of people in Ecuador, the topic could be opened to include the population of South America or expanded to include more issues or considerations.

Identifying the Components of a Citation

Citation styles vary according to which style guide is consulted. Examples of commonly-used styles include MLA, APA, and Chicago/Turabian. Each citation style includes similar components, although the order and formatting of these components varies.

MLA Style

For an MLA style citation, components must be included or excluded depending on the source, so writers should determine which components are applicable to the source being cited. Here are the basic components:

- Author—last name, first name
- Title of source
- Title of container—e.g., a journal title or website
- Other contributors—e.g., editor or translator
- Version
- Number
- Publisher
- Publication date
- Location—e.g., the URL or DOI
- Date of Access—optional

APA Style

The following components can be found in APA style citations. Components must be included or excluded depending on the source, so writers should determine which components are applicable to the source being cited.

The basic components are as follows:

- Author—last name, first initial, middle initial
- Publication date
- Title of chapter, article, or text
- Editor— last name, first initial, middle initial
- Version/volume
- Number/issue

- Page numbers
- DOI or URL
- Database—if article is difficult to locate
- City of publication
- State of publication, abbreviated
- Publisher

Chicago/Turabian Style

Chicago/Turabian style citations are also referred to as note systems and are used most frequently in the humanities and the arts. Components must be included or excluded depending on the source, so writers should determine which components are applicable to the source being cited. They contain the following elements:

- Author—last name, first name, middle initial
- Title of chapter or article—in quotation marks
- Title of source
- Editor—first name, last name
- Page numbers
- Version/volume
- Number/issue
- Page numbers
- Date of access
- DOI
- Publication location—city and state abbreviation/country
- Publisher
- Publication Date

Citing Source Material Appropriately

The following information contains examples of the common types of sources used in research as well as the formats for each citation style. First lines of citation entries are presented flush to the left margin, and second/subsequent details are presented with a hanging indent. Some examples of bibliography entries are presented below:

Book

- MLA

    Format: Last name, First name, Middle initial. *Title of Source*. Publisher, Publication Date.

    Example: Sampson, Maximus R. *Diaries from an Alien Invasion*. Campbell Press, 1989.

- APA

    Format: Last name, First initial, Middle initial. (Year Published) *Book Title*. City, State: Publisher.
    Example: Sampson, M. R. (1989). *Diaries from an Alien Invasion*. *Springfield, IL*: Campbell Press.
    Chicago/Turabian
    Format: Last name, First name, Middle initial. *Book Title*. City, State: Publisher, Year of publication.
    Example: Sampson, Maximus R. *Diaries from an Alien Invasion*. *Springfield, IL*: Campbell Press, 1989.

A Chapter in an Edited Book

- MLA
  Format: Last name, First name, Middle initial. "Title of Source." *Title of Container*, Other Contributors, Publisher, Publication Date, Location.
  Example: Sampson, Maximus R. "The Spaceship." *Diaries from an Alien Invasion*, edited by Allegra M. Brewer, Campbell Press, 1989, pp. 45-62.
- APA
  Format: Last name, First Initial, Middle initial. (Year Published) Chapter title. In First initial, Middle initial, Last Name (Ed.), *Book title* (pp. page numbers). City, State: Publisher.
  Example: Sampson, M. R. (1989). The Spaceship. In A. M. Brewer (Ed.), *Diaries from an Alien Invasion* (pp. 45-62). Springfield, IL: Campbell Press.
- Chicago/Turabian
  Format: Last name, First name, Middle initial. "Chapter Title." In Book Title, edited by Editor's Name (First, Middle In. Last), Page(s). City: Publisher, Year Published.
  Example: Sampson, Maximus R. "The Spaceship," in *Diaries from an Alien Invasion*, edited by Allegra M. Brewer, 45-62. Springfield: Campbell Press, 1989.

Article in a Journal

- MLA
  Format: Last name, First name, Middle initial. "Title of Source." *Title of Container*, Number, Publication Date, Location.
  Example: Rowe, Jason R. "The Grief Monster." *Strong Living*, vol. 9, no. 9, 2016, pp 25-31.
- APA
  Format: Last name, First initial, Middle initial. (Year Published). Title of article. *Name of Journal*, *volume*(issue), page(s).
  Example: Rowe, J. R. (2016). The grief monster. *Strong Living, 9*(9), 25-31.
- Chicago/Turabian:
  Format: Last name, First name, Middle initial. "Title of Article." *Name of Journal* volume, issue (Year Published): Page(s).
  Example: Rowe, Jason, R. "The Grief Monster." *Strong Living* 9, no. 9 (2016): 25-31.

Page on a Website

- MLA
  Format: Last name, First name, Middle initial. "Title of Article." *Name of Website*, date published (Day Month Year), URL. Date accessed (Day Month Year).
  Example: Rowe, Jason. "The Grief Monster." *Strong Living Online*, 9 Sept. 2016. http://www.somanylosses.com/the-grief-monster/html. Accessed 13 Sept. 2016.
- APA
  Format: Last name, First initial. Middle initial. (Date Published—Year, Month Day). Page or article title. Retrieved from URL
  Example: Rowe, J. W. (2016, Sept. 9). The grief monster. Retrieved from http://www.somanylosses.com/ the-grief-monster/html
- Chicago/Turabian
  Format: Last Name, First Name, Middle initial. "Page Title." *Website Title*. Last modified Month day, year. Accessed month, day, year. URL.
  Example: Rowe, Jason. "The Grief Monster." *Strong Living Online*. Last modified September 9, 2016. Accessed September 13, 2016. http://www.somany losses.com/ the-grief-monster/html.

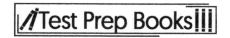

In-Text Citations

Most of the content found in a research paper will be supporting evidence that must be cited in-text, i.e., directly after the sentence that makes the statement. In-text citations contain details that correspond to the first detail in the bibliography entry—usually the author.

- MLA style - In-text citations will contain the author and the page number (if the source has page numbers) for direct quotations. Paraphrased source material may have just the author.
    - According to Johnson, liver cancer treatment is "just beyond our reach" (976).
    - The treatment of liver cancer is not within our reach, currently (Johnson).
    - The narrator opens the story with a paradoxical description: "It was the best of times, it was the worst of times" (Dickens 1).
- APA Style - In text citations will contain the author, the year of publication, and a page marker—if the source is paginated—for direct quotations. Paraphrased source material will include the author and year of publication.
    - According to Johnson (1986), liver cancer treatment is "just beyond our reach" (p. 976).
    - The treatment of liver cancer is not within our reach, currently (Johnson, 1986).
- Chicago Style - Chicago style has two approaches to in-text citation: notes and bibliography or author-date.
    - Notes – There are two options for notes: endnotes—provided in a sequential list at the end of the paper and separate from bibliography—or footnotes provided at the bottom of a page. In either case, the use of superscript indicates the citation number.
        - Johnson states that treatment of liver cancer is "just beyond our reach." [1]
        - 1. Robert W. Johnson, Oncology in the Twenty-first Century (Kentville, Nova Scotia: Kentville Publishing, 1986), 159.
    - Author-Date – The author-date system includes the author's name, publication year, and page number.
        - Johnson states that treatment of liver cancer is "just beyond our reach" (1986, 159).
        - Research shows that liver cancer treatment is not within our reach, currently (Johnson 1986, 159).

Integrating Information from Source Material

It can be daunting to integrate so many sources into a research paper while still maintaining fluency and coherency. Most source material is incorporated in the form of quotations or paraphrases, while citing the source at the end of their respective references. There are several guidelines to consider when integrating a source into writing:

The piece should be written in the author's voice. Quotations, especially long ones, should be limited and spaced evenly throughout the paper.

All paragraphs should begin with the author's own words and end with his or her own words; quotations should never start or end a paragraph.

Quotations and paraphrases should be used to emphasize a point, give weight to an idea, and validate a claim.

Supporting evidence should be introduced in a sentence or paragraph, and then explained afterwards: *According to Waters (1979)* [signal phrase], *"All in all, we're just another brick in the* wall" (p.24). *The wall suggests that people are becoming more alienated, and the bricks symbolize a paradoxical connection to that alienation* [Explanation].

When introducing a source for the first time, the author's name and a smooth transition should be included: *In Pink Floyd's groundbreaking album The Wall, Roger Waters argues that society is causing people to become more alienated.*

There should be an even balance between quotations and paraphrases.

Quotations or paraphrases should never be taken out of context in a way that alters the original author's intent.

Quotations should be syntactically and grammatically integrated.

Quotations should not simply be copied and pasted in the paper, rather, they should be introduced into a paper with natural transitions.

- o   As argued in Johnson's article...
- o   Evidence of this point can be found in Johnson's article, where she asserts that...

Practice Questions

1. Which of the following is an example of a rhetorical strategy?
    a. Cause and effect
    b. Antimetabole
    c. Individual vs. Self
    d. Ad hominem

2. Which of the following passages best displays clarity, fluency, and parallelism?
    a. Ernest Hemingway is probably the most noteworthy of expatriate authors. Hemingway's concise writing style, void of emotion and stream of consciousness, had a lasting impact, one which resonates to this very day. In Hemingway's novels, much like in American cinema, the hero acts without thinking, is living in the moment, and is repressing physical and emotional pain.
    b. Ernest Hemingway is probably the most noteworthy of expatriate authors since his concise writing style is void of emotion and stream of consciousness and has had a lasting impact on Americans which has resonated to this very day, and Hemingway's novels are much like in American cinema. The hero acts. He doesn't think. He lives in the moment. He represses physical and emotional pain.
    c. Ernest Hemingway is probably the most noteworthy of authors. His concise writing style, void of emotion and consciousness, had a lasting impact, one which resonates to this very day. In Hemingway's novels, much like in American cinema, the hero acts without thinking, lives in the moment, and represses physical and emotional pain.
    d. Ernest Hemingway is probably the most noteworthy of expatriate authors. His concise writing style, void of emotion and stream of consciousness, had a lasting impact, one which resonates to this very day. In Hemingway's novels, much like in American cinema, the hero acts without thinking, lives in the moment, and represses physical and emotional pain.

3. Autobiographies and memoirs are examples of what form of writing?
    a. Fiction
    b. Narrative
    c. Informational text
    d. Research papers

4. Rating scales, student logs, and the POWER method are effective assessment practices for what area of literacy development?
    a. Reading
    b. Writing
    c. Spelling
    d. Listening

5. Which effective writing area engages and connects with the audience, igniting emotion?
    a. Ethos
    b. Logos
    c. Pathos
    d. Kairos

Answer Explanations

1. A: The correct answer is cause and effect. A writer may use cause and effect as a strategy to illustrate a point in order to convince an audience. Choice *B* is a rhetorical device, not a strategy. Choice *C* refers to a narrative conflict, and Choice *D* is a logical fallacy.

2. D: This passage displays clarity (the author states precisely what he or she intended), fluency (the sentences run smoothly together), and parallelism (words are used in a similar fashion to help provide rhythm). Choice *A* lacks parallelism. When the author states, "the hero acts without thinking, is living in the moment, and is repressing physical and emotional pain," the words *acts*, *is living* and *is repressing* are in different tenses, and, consequently, jarring to one's ears. Choice *B* runs on endlessly in the first half ("Ernest Hemingway is probably the most noteworthy of expatriate authors since his concise writing style is void of emotion and stream of consciousness and has had a lasting impact on Americans which has resonated to this very day, and Hemingway's novels are much like in American cinema.") It demands some type of pause and strains the readers' eyes. The second half of the passage is choppy: "The hero acts. He doesn't think. He lives in the moment. He represses physical and emotional pain." For Choice *C*, leaving out *expatriate* is, first, vague, and second, alters the meaning. The correct version claims that Hemingway was the most notable of the expatriate authors while the second version claims he's the most notable of any author *ever*, a very bold claim indeed. Also, leaving out *stream of* in "stream of consciousness" no longer references the non-sequential manner in which most people think. Instead, this version sounds like all the characters in the novel are in a coma!

3. B: Narratives are personal accounts of a time period, event, or an individual, with the purpose of documenting, recording, or sharing such factual information. By contrast, fiction is a genre of writing that is fabricated. Informational texts are academic texts used to further a student's mastery of a given subject, and research papers are written reports students write to demonstrate their understanding of a given area of study that has been researched.

4. B: There are several effective assessments to evaluate a child's overall writing progress. Rating scales, student logs, and the POWER method are just some of these assessment methods. Although educators can create rating scales and student logs to assess and help students assess reading and spelling, the POWER method is specific to writing:

> P—Prewriting
>
> O—Organizing
>
> W—Writing a rough draft
>
> E—Evaluating
>
> R—Revise and Rewrite

5. C: Pathos refers to the author's appeal to the audience or reader's emotions. Ethos refers to the level of credibility of a piece of writing. Logos refers to the author's appeal to the audience or reader's logic. Kairos refers to the most opportune moment to do something. Therefore, the correct answer is pathos.

Oral Communication and Media Literacy

Oral Communication

Oral Versus Written Language

Oral language is characterized by the use of shorter sentences or fragmented sentences and slang. It is more concise than written language, and doesn't necessarily follow the rules of grammar. Its main focus is communication. Oral language learning comes before written language, so it can be more developed in students. Oral language is enhanced through tone, inflection, body language, and pitch. Written language tends to be more formal than oral language. It is typically composed of complete sentences and proper grammar, without the use of slang or fragmented sentences. Written language is typically chosen more carefully, with more precision, and may take more time to produce.

The Role of Cultural Factors in Oral Comunication

Students' oral language skills are influenced by their culture. Cultural factors such as families who speak multiple languages can impact the way a child's oral language develops. In some cases, children from a culturally-diverse background may not have the same oral language experience as other students, which can impact oral language development. Teachers should be prepared to provide support to students from culturally-diverse backgrounds and language experiences. Culture is acquired through observation and is shared among family members. It is passed from generation to generation and can adapt along the way. It is important for teachers to understand that what might be considered rude in one culture is quite the opposite in another. For example, some cultures believe that pointing is rude, while others see nothing wrong with it. Asking a child to point to a word in a text or in the classroom may be difficult if he or she has been taught this is unacceptable in his or her culture.

Using Effective Oral Communication

Identifying Techniques to Use in Collaborative Discussions
Effective oral communication requires the ability to express oneself clearly and diplomatically. It is imperative to teach students from a young age the value of respecting oneself and others, as well as the ability to keep an open mind during discussion and not to make things personal. Students should also be taught to keep the flow of discussion in alignment with the topic at hand and to listen actively as well as speak.

Age-appropriate Topics
Keeping topics *age-appropriate* is one way to stimulate productive conversation. It is important to consider the breadth of knowledge that an individual or group is likely to have. One of the primary objectives of conferencing in an academic setting is to challenge students into thinking critically. Choosing topics that are too advanced or beyond the realm of their knowledge would be an act in futility as they do not have the appropriate tools to engage in conversation. Similarly, topics that are too simple will not be beneficial as they will not be challenging. When choosing a topic, teachers should consider the average age of students, their vocabulary, their reading and writing skills, and life experiences they are likely to have.

Facilitating Appropriate Discussion Behavior

Once an appropriate topic has been chosen, discussions should be monitored to facilitate appropriate behavior. It is very important to stress that all perspectives will be welcome and respected and to make sure that student inquiries and responses are in alignment with that principle. The following are suggestions for facilitating appropriate discussion behavior in a group setting:

1. Cultivating an environment of inclusion and mutual respect

- Students should introduce themselves and be encouraged to address each other by name. "Icebreaker" games are an effective way to get students to know each other before engaging in any discussions.

- Allowing enough time for students to think about the topic and thoughtfully contribute to the discussion will encourage inclusion.

- The use of insulting or disrespectful language, tone, or body language should not be permitted.

- Students should be made aware of differences in cultural and social perspectives.

- Students should be encouraged to be mindful of the language they are using.

- Teachers should not make assumptions on how students will respond or behave based on their cultural, racial, or religious backgrounds.

- Everyone should have a chance to speak—e.g., teachers should not show favoritism towards a particular student or set of students or allow more tenacious students to dominate the discussion.

- Particular perspectives or ideas should not be verbally or nonverbally discouraged. Instead, students should be encouraged to think critically about what is being discussed and what they are saying.

- It's important not to rush students or make any student feel as though his or her comments and ideas are not important.

- Facilitators should not display a sense of superiority.

2. Keeping discussions productive

- Teachers should be explicit about the expectations or goals of the discussion and guide students back towards the topic if they get off track.

- Demonstrating what disrespectful behavior looks like at the start of the discussion can help establish clear expectations. Students should be reminded not to take things personally or to identify with any emotions they may experience from the discussion and, instead, approach the topics with logic.

- Ideas or counterarguments should be related to personal experiences or backed with evidence. Students should validate each other's ideas first before arguing in a respectful way, such as "I respect what you are saying," or "I understand where you are coming from."

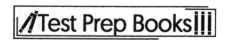

- Stereotyping and sweeping generalizations should be identified when used and subsequently avoided.

- If a student goes off on a tangent, he or she should be guided back to the primary topic or purpose by asking him/her to summarize what he/she is saying.

- If the discussion becomes heated or emotional, students should be encouraged to explore the real issue that is causing the emotions. The teacher might say, "I think there is a greater issue here that we should discuss openly and respectfully." Alternatively, students can be asked if they would like to take break and resume the discussion later. A teacher may also wish to bring up the differing values that are being displayed in the conference in an unbiased way so that students can recognize what they're truly arguing about.

- It's important that teachers avoid arguing with a student if the student attacks them. Acknowledging this kind of behavior only validates it.

3. Encouraging participants/guiding the flow of discussion

- For shy students, it's helpful to call on them by name and ask if they have any thoughts/feedback, while being nonjudgmental if they admit they don't know or don't have anything to say.

- Asking questions and requesting examples when students make a comment or present an idea helps guide the discussion flow.

- Writing student comments down and asking for other participants to elaborate on them will encourage more participation.

- Depending on the exercise, giving the students a topic or asking a student to present one will elicit participation.

- For students who have trouble participating in large groups, breaking up discussion into smaller groups will help them feel more comfortable.

Ensuring Accountability

One of the most challenging things about group discussions is ensuring that the students have prepared for it. For a discussion to be as productive as possible, students should be held accountable for completing their due preparation, such as homework, pre-class readings, or research. This can be done in numerous ways, such as by requiring the students to complete an at-home assignment and submit it electronically by midnight the previous night or on the day before. This assignment could be worth a significant grade to encourage students to complete it, and it could be in the following forms: responding to a question on an online discussion board, completing quizzes in reading comprehension, or answering true or false questions.

To ensure accountability during the discussion, students should be encouraged to participate by asking questions and asked to elaborate when something is unclear. Letting them take notes and leaving plenty of time for the formulation of thoughts and follow-up questions will increase accountability. After the discussion has ended, passing out a handout that students can fill out or having them summarize the discussion online are two beneficial strategies for accountability.

<u>Evaluating the Effectiveness of Strategies for Effective Discussions</u>
To increase student participation in discussion, teachers should consider the following strategies:

Asking students what they know about the topic and writing their responses on the white or blackboard, which creates an outline of what the students do and don't know as well as increases their self-esteem.

Having an anonymous question box where students can write down questions that can be read before or during the discussion, being careful not to react negatively to any questions, verbally or non-verbally, so as not to damage self-esteem

Allowing students to teach each other, proven as the most effective way to learn something is to teach someone else what has been learned—e.g., writing their own tests or homework, conducting one-on-one conferences

Dividing the class into smaller groups if students seem non-responsive, which helps shy students feel less intimidated and more comfortable in smaller settings

Allowing students to work together, which encourages them to interact with others and allows them to feel more comfortable with doing so when it comes time for group discussion

Asking students to create a topic to get them to initiate the conversation

Using games to make the discussion fun and motivate students to participate

The effectiveness of these strategies will depend entirely on the class. Teachers should use the assessment tools discussed previously to determine whether the techniques have been effective and adjust the teaching style accordingly.

Many of the above strategies can be used for one-on-one discussions as well. The most important things to keep in mind in keeping a student engaged and comfortable during a one-on-one discussion are as follows:

- Asking follow-up questions
- Clarifying any unclear or obscure questions or statements
- Never making the student feel unintelligent or inadequate
- Being as reassuring as possible, particularly if a student expresses insecurity in his or her abilities
- Being patient and allowing time for the student to sort out thoughts and ask necessary questions

Features of Oral Performances

Oral performance is an important part of any curriculum, as it presents an opportunity for students to become comfortable speaking in front of a group. As early as Kindergarten, students should be introduced to the skills of speaking and listening in a variety of contexts. Teachers can model and reinforce the necessary skills of oral communication such as speaking audibly, providing details, and answering questions. Students should have practice in a variety of age-appropriate situations from an impromptu sharing activity to a formal, prepared debate with a classmate. Oral presentation can enhance literacy through read aloud activities, and be an extension of the writing process when students present information they have compiled or written themselves. Oral presentations can be individual or collaborative, and include multimedia components. Students should also be able to identify the components of oral presentations, recognizing aspects such as a speaker's purpose, intended audience, and tone.

Types of oral performance are as follows:

Type	Features	Examples
Impromptu	Spur of the moment, no preparation	An interview, a sharing activity
Extemporaneous	Acknowledge the audience with few words, minimal prep time	Changing direction in a presentation to interest readers, responding to a question or interruption of the speech
Persuasive	Influence the audience's opinion, argue a point, provide evidence, preparation required	Prepared speech on a pre-determined subject
Expository	Inform and explain a topic, focuses on presentation of facts, requires prep time, includes organizational patterns like cause/effect, comparison	Prepared speech on a pre-determined subject
Interpretive	Interpret the deeper meaning of a piece of literature, prep time required to read and analyze source	Oral performance may or may not be prepared in advance of reading a piece of literature
Debate	Includes proposition and opposition format, often timed, prep time typically required on subject	Moderated debate between two individuals or two teams on a pre-determined subject

Developing Skills Necessary for Speaking, Listening, and Presenting that are Appropriate to Task, Purpose, and Audience

Instructing Students to Enhance Their English Language Literacy Development

Speaking, listening, reading, and writing are all intimately connected as essential elements of literacy development. As social beings, students begin to recognize that with effective literacy skills, their social, emotional, and physical needs can be met, and their curiosity can be satisfied. They also begin to learn that they can develop communication skills to answer questions that others pose. This can be an exciting and self-affirming realization for young students. In order to encourage literacy development, educators should ensure that all activities in the classroom involve meaningful language and literacy experiences. Each child learns at a unique pace and in a unique way. With this sensitivity in place, classroom activities should be as differentiated as possible.

Developing Listening Skills

Actively teaching good listening skills is essential in the classroom. Behaviors should not be expected that have not been taught. Students need to learn the difference between what an excellent listener does and what poor listening behaviors are. Good listening skills that should be taught include:

Focusing on the speaker, looking them in the eye, and choosing not to interrupt.

Looking at the speaker to indicate that the student is ready to hear what the speaker has to say and to pick up body language cues and facial expressions.

Giving nonverbal signals that the student is listening (e.g., nods, smiles).

Giving verbal signals that indicate interest in the speaker (e.g., repeating back what is heard to indicate understanding).

Subtly matching the energy and emotional level of the speaker to indicate understanding.

Choosing not to make side comments or to focus on other things occurring in the room.

Some strategies for teaching these skills in the classroom include, but are not limited to:

Providing pre-listening activities, such as teaching new vocabulary words, outlining what students will be hearing, distributing study guides or pre-listening questions, and teaching students the objectives of the listening activity beforehand.

Avoiding repeating directions multiple times. Teachers are often inclined to repeat steps and directions several times before allowing students to begin working. This is counterproductive because it teaches students that they do not have to listen the first time. Students should be taught that the teacher will say things only once and they are expected to listen, but they may ask for clarification. Students should also be taught to seek other sources of finding the instructions.

Modeling good listening and speaking skills in the classroom because students learn by watching and emulating others. Teachers need to consistently model choosing not to interrupt and focusing their full attention on the speaker. They also need to model speaking clearly with proper grammar and foster an environment in the classroom of good peer modeling as well.

Teaching students to take notes, write down questions, and report on or paraphrase what they have heard the speaker say. Students should be given active listening activities to complete during and after the listening task.

Giving students multiple methods to contribute to conversations. Some students are not inclined to speak in front of others. In such cases, it may be helpful to allow them to give other signals of understanding such as "thumbs up," "thumbs sideways," "thumbs down," or sign language for "yes" and "no" answers.

Encouraging the use of technology in the classroom to allow students to blog, tweet, or use quiz show-style games to indicate understanding of what they heard.

Developing Speaking Skills

Similar to listening skills, students also need to be taught speaking and presenting skills. Students need to learn such skills as:

- How to introduce themselves effectively
- How to make appropriate eye contact with listeners
- How to begin a conversation and keep it going

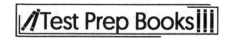

- How to interact with various types of audiences
- How to answer questions in an interview
- How to stand and deliver a speech with confidence
- How to ask for and answer questions during a presentation

The following strategies can help teach conversational and speaking skills:

Students can be taught to use "conversation enhancers" when working with others. Some examples are: "Really?" "Wow!" "That's interesting" "Tell me more about ..." "Can you say that in another way?" "Tell me what you are thinking ..." and "Can you add to my idea?"

Good conversational skills can be modeled as frequently as possible in one- to two-minute one-on-one dialogues with students. This is especially important for the introverted and shy students.

A safe speaking environment can be fostered by teaching good manners to listeners, and by challenging students who are disrespectful listeners to act in a different way.

Students should be asked open-ended questions that have no right or wrong answer and that invite lengthy answers instead of just "yes" or "no" responses.

"I don't know" should not be accepted for an answer. Students should be taught that their thinking is valued rather than whether they *know* something.

Students should be taught how to take turns in the classroom fairly and to not interrupt one another.

Students should be instructed not to read their presentations word for word, and to speak toward the audience instead of toward the project or PowerPoint slide.

Videos of good and poor presentations can be shown as models for students to critique.

Students should be taught to build in humor and good non-verbal communication into their presentations.

Students should be shown how to curb involuntary habits such as repeating themselves or saying "um" or "like" too much.

Task, Purpose, and Audience

Teaching students to present and speak to an audience involves teaching them how to structure a presentation so that it is appropriate for the task, purpose, and audience. *Task* is what the students are required to do with their presentation. *Purpose* is the reason for the presentation and how it will achieve the outcome of the task. *Audience* is whom the presentation is for, the population it is trying to reach, and why it is specifically for that group. Some presentation tips that teachers should impart to students are as follows:

- During student preparation, students should ask themselves: "Why am I giving this presentation?" "What do I want people to take away from the presentation?" and "How much does my audience already know about the topic?"

- Presentations should be structured with an effective introduction, covering each item on their agenda succinctly, and wrapping up with a memorable conclusion.

- Presentations should be given with clarity and impact. The audience won't remember everything a student presents, so he or she needs to highlight the key points clearly and concisely and then expand and illustrate as needed.

- Visual aids should be used to enhance the presentation without causing distractions – such as useless images and animated transitions between slides – from the information.

- Presentations should be given without memorization. Students should be charged with becoming more familiar with their content and to "test drive" the presentation beforehand.

- Appropriate pauses should be used during presentations to help the audience better absorb the information.

- Various techniques can be employed if there is a "stumbling point" or a piece of information is forgotten during the presentation.

Using Effective Speech and Presentation Delivery

Understanding Effective Delivery of a Speech or Presentation

Good public speakers all have several characteristics in common. It is not enough to simply write a speech, but it must also be delivered in a manner that is both engaging and succinct. The following qualities are inherent to good public speaking.

Confidence is possibly the most important attribute a speaker can have. It instills trust in the listener that the person knows what he or she is talking about and that he or she is credible and competent. Confidence is displayed by making brief eye contact—about 2-3 seconds—with different members of the audience to demonstrate that the speaker is engaged. It is also displayed in his or her tone of voice—strong, light-hearted, and natural. A nervous speaker can easily be identified by a small, quivering voice. Confidence is also conveyed by the speaker facing the audience; turning one's back may demonstrate insecurity.

Authenticity is another quality of an effective speaker, as it makes a person more relatable and believable to the audience. Speeches that are memorized word-for-word can give the impression of being inauthentic as the monologue does not flow quite naturally, especially if the speaker accidentally fumbles or forgets. Memorizing speeches can also lead to a monotonous tone, which is sure to put the audience to sleep, or worse, a misinterpreted tone, which can cause the audience to stop listening entirely or even become offended. Therefore, speeches should be practiced with a natural intonation and not be memorized mechanically.

Connection with the audience is another important aspect of public speaking. Speakers should engage with their listeners by the use of storytelling and visual or auditory aids, as well as asking questions that the audience can participate in. Visual and auditory aids could range from an interesting PowerPoint presentation to a short video clip to physical objects the audience can pass around to a soundtrack. The use of appropriate humor also allows the audience to connect with the speaker on a more personal level and will make the speech sound more like a conversation than a one-sided lecture. Speakers who are passionate about their subject inspire their listeners to care about what they're saying; they transfer their energy into the audience. This level of connection will encourage their listeners to want to be there.

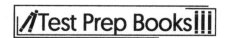

Succinctness and *purposeful repetition* ensures that the audience's attention remains focused on the message at hand. Repeating the overall point of the speech in different ways helps listeners remember what the speaker is trying to tell them, even when the speech is over. A speech that is longer than necessary will cause listeners to become bored and stop absorbing information. Keeping the speech short and sweet and leaving more time for questions at the end will ensure that the audience stays engaged.

There are many different styles a speaker can utilize, but the most important thing speakers should keep in mind is maintaining a connection with the audience. This will help ensure that the audience will remain open and focused enough to hear and absorb the message.

Evaluating the Advantages and Disadvantages of Different Media

Each visual aid has its advantages and disadvantages and should be used sparingly to avoid distracting the audience. Visual aids should be used to emphasize a presentation's message, not overwhelm it.

Microsoft PowerPoint is currently the most commonly used visual aid. It allows for pictures, words, videos, and music to be presented on the same screen and is essentially just a projection of a computer screen, allowing easy and quick access to all forms of media as well as the Internet. However, a PowerPoint presentation should not be overwhelmed with information, such as text-heavy slides, as audience members will spend more time reading the slides than listening to the speaker. Conversely, they may avoid reading it entirely, and the presentation will serve no purpose. A PowerPoint presentation that uses too many animations and visual elements may also detract from the presence of the speaker.

Handouts are a great way for the audience to feel more involved in a presentation. They can present lots of information that may be too much for a PowerPoint, and they can also be taken home and reviewed later. The primary disadvantage of handouts is that the audience may choose to read rather than to listen, thus missing the main points the speaker is trying to make, or they may decide not to read it at all. The best handouts are those that do not contain all the information of a presentation, but allow for the audience to take notes and complete the handout by listening or asking questions.

Whiteboards and *blackboards* are excellent for explaining difficult concepts by allowing the audience to follow along with a process and copy down their own version of what is being written on the board. This visual aid is best used to explain concepts in mathematics and science. The main problem with the board, however, is that there can be limited space, and if the presenter runs out of room, he or she will have to erase the content written on the board and will be unable to refer back to it later. He or she may also have to wait for the entire audience to write the information down, which slows down the presentation.

Overhead projectors are wonderful in that a speaker can use a prepared transparency and draw images or add words to emphasize or explain concepts. They can also erase these additions but still keep the original content if they wish to alter their method to fit the audience or provide further explanations. Similar to PowerPoint presentations, overhead projections should limit the amount of text to keep the audience focused on listening.

Physical objects are a useful way to connect with the audience and allow them to feel more involved. Because people interact with the physical world, physical objects can help solidify understanding of difficult concepts. However, they can be distracting if not properly introduced. If they are presented too early or are visible during the presentation, the audience will focus on the objects, wondering what purpose they may serve instead of listening to the speaker. Objects should instead be hidden until it is time to show them and then collected when they are no longer useful.

Videos are a great way to enliven a presentation by giving it sound, music, flow, and images. They are excellent for emphasizing points, providing evidence for ideas, giving context, or setting tone. The major issue with videos is that the presenter is unable to speak at this point, so this form of media should be used sparingly and purposefully. Also, overly-long videos may lose the audience's attention.

Effective public speakers are aware of the advantages and disadvantages of all forms of media and often choose to utilize a combination of several different types to keep the presentations lively and the audience engaged.

Presenting Information Clearly, Concisely, and Logically

All information should be presented with a clear beginning, middle, and end. Distinct organization always makes any work more clear, concise, and logical. For a presentation, this should involve choosing a primary topic and then discussing it in the following format:

> Introducing the speaker and the main topic
> Providing evidence, supporting details, further explanation of the topic in the main body
> Concluding it with a firm resolution and repetition of the main point

The beginning, middle, and end should also be linked with effective transitions that make the presentation flow well. For example, a presentation should always begin with an introduction by the speaker, including what he/she does and what he/she is there to present. Good transitional introductions may begin with statements such as *For those who do not know me, my name is...*, *As many of you know, I am...* or *Good morning everyone, my name is ___, and I am the new project manager*. A good introduction grabs the attention and interest of the audience.

After an introduction has been made, the speaker will then want to state the purpose of the presentation with a natural transition, such as *I am here to discuss the latest editions to our standard of procedure...* or *This afternoon, I would like to present the results of our latest findings*. Once the purpose has been identified, the speaker will want to adhere to the main idea announced. The presenter should be certain to keep the main idea to one sentence as too much information can confuse an audience; an introduction should be succinct and to the point.

Supporting information should always be presented in concise, easy-to-read formats such as bullet points or lists—if visual aids are presented during the presentation. Good transitions such as *Let's begin with...* or *Now to look at...* make the presentation flow smoothly and logically, helping listeners to keep ideas organized as they are presented. Keeping the material concise is extremely important in a presentation, and visual aids should be used only to emphasize points or explain ideas. All the supporting information should relate back to the main idea, avoiding unnecessary tangents.

Finally, a firm conclusion involves repeating the main point of the presentation by either inspiring listeners to act or by reiterating the most important points made in the speech. It should also include an expression of gratitude to the audience as well as transition to opening the floor for questions.

Evaluating a Speech

It is necessary for students to be able to effectively evaluate many components of a speech in order to comprehend its overall message. Point of view refers to the perspective from which a speech is presented. The reader should consider the author's stance on a subject, or his or her position. They should also consider the use of rhetoric or argument in order to deliver the message. A speaker may use causal analysis (the exploration of causes and effects), or analogical reasoning (making a comparison with familiar scenarios to explain new one) to present an argument. A speaker may also use evidence to support his or her point. The use of reasoning and rhetoric should be examined for their effectiveness in proving a point. Premises refer to the proposition on which an argument is based or for which a conclusion may be drawn. These are the facts of the argument that the speaker believes. These must be evaluated for truthfulness before a conclusion is drawn about the argument. Another important factor in the evaluation of a speech is word choice. This can help listeners understand the intended audience based on the language used. Tone and tone of voice can also influence the speaker's message. Students should be able to recognize different tones such as irony, sarcasm, or humor and what effects the tone has on the speaker's overall argument.

Presenting Findings and Supporting Evidence

Giving a speech requires knowing the components that make it effective for listeners. Depending on the subject matter and grade level, students must be able to present their own perspective on a subject using oral presentation techniques. It's important for students to use logical organization so the speech is easy to follow. Students should also be able to present facts and research in a way that shows their own perspective on the subject matter. The speaker should present any opposing viewpoints as a way of strengthening their own argument. This can be done through refuting these perspectives or pointing out their weaknesses. Students should know their audience and purpose before planning a speech, and consider them as they develop their viewpoint. It is necessary to consider what the audience knows and needs to know when developing an argument, and to consider how they may receive the message of the speech. Style should also be considered when giving a speech to be sure it is appropriate to the task. For example, a formal speech presenting a report on scientific findings would require a more formal style than an impromptu sharing activity in front of the group.

Delivering a Reflective Narrative

A reflective narrative is a memoir of a personal experience. A reflective narrative should identify a specific event or experience that had an impact on the writer. Potentially a lesson was learned or the writer was changed in some way from this event, and students should be able to convey the broader theme in the narrative. Typically, students can make connections to the incident and its meaning in the conclusion of the narrative. In order to make a reflective narrative interesting and meaningful to the reader, writers should include certain elements such as sensory language. Sensory language invokes all of the senses in order to paint a picture in the reader's mind. Students should also learn the skill of observation to reinforce descriptive elements of narrative writing. Other narrative techniques such as pacing and the use of dialogue should also be reinforced by teachers. For example, dialogue should be used sparingly, and only when the words spoken are very important. It can be used to show the relationship between characters as well.

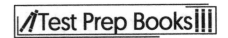

Media Literacy

Interpreting Media and Non-Print Text

In the 21st century, rhetoric is evident in a variety of formats. Blogs, vlogs, videos, news footage, advertisements, and live video fill informational feeds, and readers see many shortened images and snapshot texts a day. It's important to note that the majority of these formats use images to appeal to emotion over factual information. Online visuals spread more quickly and are more easily adopted by consumers as fact than printed formats.

Critical readers should be aware that media and non-print text carries some societal weight to the population. In being inundated with pictures and live footage, readers often feel compelled to skip the task of critical reading analysis and accept truth at literal face value. Authors of non-print media are aware of this fact and frequently capitalize on it.

To critically address non-print media requires that the consumer address additional sources and not exclude printed text in order to reach sound conclusions. While it's tempting for consumers to get swept away in the latest viral media, it's important to remember that creators of such have an agenda, and unless the non-print media in question is backed up with sound supporting evidence, any thesis or message cannot be considered valid or factual. Memes, gifs, and looped video cannot tell the whole, truthful story although they may appeal to opinions with which readers already agree. Sharing such non-print media online can precipitate widespread misunderstanding.

When presented with non-print media, critical readers should consider these bits of information as teasers to be investigated for accuracy and veracity. Of course, certain non-print media exists solely for entertainment, but the critical reader should be able to separate out what's generalized for entertainment's sake and what's presented for further verification, before blindly accepting the message. Increasingly, this has become more difficult for readers to do, only because of the onslaught of information to which they are exposed.

If a reader is not to fall prey to strong imagery and non-print media, he or she will need to fact-check. This, of course, requires time and attention on the reader's part, and in current culture, taking the time to fact-check seems counterproductive. However, in order to maintain credibility themselves, readers must be able to evaluate multiple sources of information across media formats and be able to identify the emotional appeal used in the smaller sound bites of non-print media. Readers must view with a discerning eye, listen with a questioning ear, and think with a critical mind.

Instructing Students on the Effective Use of Digital Media

Using Technology Tools for Effective Communication

Different technological tools serve different functions. To function in the developing world, students need to learn and understand *digital literacy*—the knowledge, dexterity, and critical thinking skills involved in using technology to create, evaluate, and present information. The best techniques for instructing students on choosing and using technological tools involve educating them on the advantages and disadvantages of each, demonstrating how to use them, breaking down their different aspects, assigning students homework or projects in which they will utilize different technological resources, and instructing them on when it is appropriate to use each kind.

The most common types of tools used for communication are as follows:

- Smartphones/apps
- Email
- Microsoft Office
- iMovie
- Skype
- Twitter
- Facebook
- Instagram
- Google Drive
- Various blogging websites
- Online bulletin boards
- Wikis

A good way to introduce students to varying technological tools is by using them in the classroom. It would be helpful to teach students how to use a PowerPoint presentation, for example, by giving a PowerPoint presentation. If a student asks a question to which the teacher does not know the answer, they can discover the answer together by using a reliable source on the Internet, projecting the process on the board, so that they can see exactly how it's done. Students can also receive homework and updates on school and classroom events through a personal blog or class bulletin board the teacher has designed so that they may become familiar with using online communication. Students can also be assigned to use personal blogs to practice and improve their writing skills.

The most effective method for learning new skills is a hands-on approach. Students can be educated on the pros and cons of each technological tool, but the best way for them to learn is to allow them to find out for themselves by assigning projects and asking them to give the reasoning behind choosing a specific tool. For example, they may be asked to do a project on some aspect of the Revolutionary War by choosing a media format. Ideas may include the following:

- Doing a presentation
- Filming and editing a video re-enactment of a great battle
- Writing a script in Microsoft Word or in a Google doc and having classmates act it out
- Creating Facebook statuses from the viewpoints of the forefathers in modern colloquial language
- Having a "Twitter war" between the British and the Colonials
- Asking various people to participate in a collaborative Wiki or Google Doc in which many people give their versions of aspects of the Revolutionary War
- Writing a blog narrating life as a soldier
- Posting photos of the signing of the Declaration of Independence

Students can then give their presentations to the classroom so that students can learn about the topic through different presentation styles.

Another way to engage students in using technology is to have them communicate with each other through the various methods of communication—e.g., starting a class Google Doc, creating a classroom Facebook group, or using a discussion board. This is also an excellent opportunity to encourage students to use Standard English through all methods of communication to enhance their writing skills and instill a sense of professionalism, which they will need throughout their lives.

For example, requiring that all students use complete sentences, proper spelling, and grammar through Facebook, Twitter, or blogs associated with homework or projects will encourage them to do so in their daily lives as well. Another example is requiring that students select tweets from their favorite celebrities or politicians, analyze their meaning and purpose, correct their grammar and spelling, and re-tweet them in the correct way. There are countless ways in which technology can be used in the classroom to enhance students' understanding of digital communication; all it requires is a little creativity.

Evaluating Technology-Based Strategies

It is hard to find a technological tool that will not be useful for students to explore. The more a student engages with the numerous different types of technology, the more digitally literate that student will become. Each type is effective and brings value to the table in its own way. When evaluating the effectiveness of a specific technology-based strategy, it's important to consider how this method is enhancing the student's digital literacy, as well as their critical thinking and communication skills. It is also necessary to evaluate the technology itself by asking relevant questions:

- Is it appropriate for the average age of the students in the classroom?
- Is it user friendly?
- Does it work consistently?
- Are there multiple ways to get help on learning how to use it?
- Are there trouble-shooting options?
- Does it have good reviews?
- Is it relevant to the content of the curriculum?
- Does it support and align to the learning objective?
- Is it more distracting than it is useful?
- Is it a tool that is/will be used often in the real world?
- Can it be used for more than one project or assignment?

One very effective teaching strategy is *collaborative learning*, in which two or more students work together to develop a project, work through an idea, or solve a problem. This method allows for students to play off each other's strengths and different experiences and learn how to communicate with their classmates to achieve goals. Technology can be used for collaborative learning in Google Drive, Skype, Google Hangouts, Neapod, Padlet, and Periscope, in creating PowerPoint presentations together, or by conducting surveys with websites like Survey Monkey.

Another effective teaching method is *discussion*, in which students are given a topic or create a topic themselves and then use technology to engage in discourse. This can be done via discussion boards, such as ProBoards or Boardhost, or done live through programs such as Skype or Hangouts. Discussion strategies are extremely effective for enhancing communication skills and digital literacy.

A third method is *active learning*, in which the student engages in activities such as reading, writing, or teaching the subject to another student. Blogging is a great way to encourage active learning as it provides a medium through which students can reflect on what they've learned and respond to comments posted by the teacher or other students. Most of the suggestions made in the previous section—making presentations, creating video re-enactments, writing scripts, having mock Twitter or

Facebook comment wars—are all forms of active learning. These types of activities solidify events, ideas, and skills in a student's mind in a way that memorization or flashcards do not as they utilize many different types of thinking and interaction.

One method that a teacher may employ depending on the class and circumstances is *distance learning*. Distance learning is any type of teaching method in which the student and teacher are not in the same place simultaneously. Many professors utilize distance learning through different kinds of technologies, including a live virtual lecture, computer simulations, interactive discussions, and virtual/audio learning environments. These strategies have their advantages in that one teacher can teach a large number of students and multiple locations, and students can communicate with fellow classmates across the globe.

Auditory learning is a strategy in which a student learns through listening. This typically happens via recorded lectures that can be downloaded as podcasts onto a classroom website, discussion board, or some other audio-simulated learning environment. *Visual learning* is learning through watching, in which ideas and concepts are illustrated through images, videos, or by observing a teacher complete a task, explain a concept, or solve a problem. This can be achieved through recorded videos, cartoons, virtual lectures, or by sitting in the classroom. Additionally, *kinesthetic learning* is active learning through physical interaction with an object or actively solving a problem, as opposed to passively listening or watching.

Every student has a different learning style which is unique to them—some learn better through listening while others learn better through doing. The best teaching methods employ all different learning strategies so that all the senses are engaged and every student has a chance at learning material based on their individual learning needs. Technology offers educators the tools do that.

The Impact of Media

Media sources can influence the way students experiences the world, and thus, their voice in their writing and communication. Visual images seen on television, the Internet, and in magazines, can have a powerful impact on the way children view themselves and the world. Teachers should consider the magnitude of media's impact on students, and assess whether they are being overexposed to negative images such as violence, sexuality, and alcohol or drug use. Steps should be taken to help students understand the role of the media and visual imagery in their self-concept, and to help promote a healthy self-image apart from these sources. Beyond the classroom, media impacts society at large. Teachers should encourage discussions about the influence of various media forms and messages on the culture and attitudes of the society in which they are displayed. It can be interesting and helpful to compare media from different countries, such as evaluating the similarities and differences in magazine ads from various countries. The marketing strategies and appeals can differ, reflecting different ideals and priorities.

Incorporating Media into Instruction

Media can be effectively incorporated into instruction before, during, and after students learn a concept. Media messages can be used to introduce a new concept or repeat and reinforce concepts already learned. Teachers should be aware that media messages can be interpreted differently by different students, and it is the teacher's role to help students process the intended concept. Media should be used in conjunction with more traditional instructional methods for optimal effectiveness and critical analysis.

Evaluating Students' Media Presentations

Like peer review in the writing process, students can also benefit from review of their media presentations. Effective review processes should be directed and specific, using questions that help students to identify the intended concepts of a lesson and to make sure the media message is delivered appropriately. Students should be able to identify the purpose of a classmate's presentation, and be clear about the purpose of their own presentations.

Legal Considerations

Teachers are subject to copyright, fair use, and liability laws like any other citizen. Materials used in the classroom should not violate these laws. It is the responsibility of the teacher to know the laws and abide by them in the reproduction and use of any classroom materials. This can be especially challenging with all of the resources readily available on the Internet. Teachers should be aware of and make use of the many free resources afforded to them as educators, such as texts and images in the public domain. Classroom use exemptions do exist for teachers and students to view a movie or perform a play, for example, but there are limitations that teachers should be familiar with before using such materials.

Aesthetic Effects of a Media Presentation

Media aesthetics include light, color, 2- and 3-dimensional space, time, motion, and sound. Knowing these elements of media can help students to create their own more effective presentations. Students should understand the role each of these elements in the effectiveness of media presentations. For example, playing music during a presentation can create a mood for the viewer, and elicit a desired emotion. It's also important for students to know how to manipulate aesthetics for desired effect in their own media presentations.

Integrating Multiple Sources and Formats of Information

Students should be able to solve problems and make decisions through the use of multiple informational sources. It is important for students to be able to analyze sources for credibility and relevance, evaluate them for any bias or inaccuracies, and ultimately synthesize them to generate an answer or make a decision. The more diverse the sources, the more comprehensive the answer or decision will be. One area where this is especially important is in Internet research. Students must be able to discern between many sources and choose the most reliable information to integrate. One way for students to glean an answer from multiple sources is through cross-referencing. When a fact is repeated in many credible sources, especially a variety of different types of sources, it can generally be accepted as true. Students should also know the criteria for evaluating a source's credibility, such as author credentials, peer-reviewed status, and timeliness of the information. As other media become more prevalent, such as videos and social media posts, students must also be able to identify what makes these types of sources credible and how to integrate them with more traditional sources.

Using Digital Media Strategically

Students can use digital media to make their presentations more effective. They should know how to integrate media that is appropriate to the intended audience, enhances purpose, and uses appropriate style and tone for the task. Digital media should be integrated strategically to be effective. Teachers can model this through their own presentations, and help students to recognize how digital media can spark an audience's interest, and highlight key facts. A well-placed video or photograph, for example, can illustrate a presenter's message and have a deeper impact on the audience than a simple lecture would. Students should understand the impact of visual, auditory, and interactive features in a presentation in order to deliver their message and keep the audience interested in the subject matter.

Practice Questions

1. Volume, articulation, and awareness of audience help with what practice?
    a. Effective instruction
    b. Communication
    c. Active listening
    d. Oral presentations

2. Offering a presenter with undivided attention and asking relevant and timely questions are examples of what skill set?
    a. Active listening skills
    b. Effective speaking
    c. Formal communication
    d. Informal communication

3. A student finds a digital first-hand accounts of an event. What type of source is this?
    a. Primary sources
    b. Secondary sources
    c. Direct sources
    d. Indirect sources

4. A student is struggling with reading aloud selected passages from books when giving oral book reports. When it is his turn to read to the class, the teacher offers an easier book she knows the student likes and is very familiar with. When the student reads aloud well and with enthusiasm, the teacher praises him to the class, then gives a more challenging book the next time. What is this called?
    a. Acknowledgement
    b. Providing feedback
    c. Encouragement
    d. Effective assistance

5. A student is struggling preparing his oral presentation on photosynthesis. Which of the following is NOT one of the tips the teacher should give to the student?
    a. Use descriptive language and make the speech verbose.
    b. Use purposeful repetition to emphasize key points.
    c. Use visuals and stories to connect with the audience.
    d. Solicit listeners for questions and build time in for them.

Answer Explanations

1. D: In order for oral presentations to be effective, the presenter's volume should match the size of audience and the location of the presentation. The presenter should also practice articulation—how clearly the words are being said. The third most important element of oral presentations is how well the presenter is engaging the audience. Making eye contact, moving around the room, and involving the audience, when appropriate, are all part of audience awareness skills.

2. A: Active listening skills are very important in all forms of communication, whether one is at home, among friends, in school, or at work. An active listener is one who pays close attention to what is being said, maintains eye contact, uses body language to indicate respect, asks relevant questions, and shares information that directly pertains to the subject.

3. A: Firsthand accounts are given by primary sources—individuals who provide personal or expert accounts of an event, subject matter, time period, or of an individual. They are viewed more as objective accounts than subjective. Secondary sources are accounts given by an individual or group of individuals who were not physically present at the event or who did not have firsthand knowledge of an individual or time period. Secondary sources are sources that have used research in order to create a written work. Direct and indirect sources are not terms used in literary circles.

4. B: Providing feedback is a way to build positive self-image and encourage success. A positive self-image is fostered by repeated success. Giving clear and effective feedback communicates to the student that her or his work is worthwhile, and that someone cares enough to review and consider it.

5. A: Being overly descriptive and verbose can make it difficult for listeners to follow a speech. It can get too long and boring, and more importantly, excessive description can muddle the focus of the speech. This tends to make a speech harder to follow and detract from the strength and clarity of the thesis or main point. Keeping the speech as succinct as possible, while still addressing and emphasizing the main points, will help keep listeners' attention and improve their comprehension.

Constructed Response

Directions

On the first constructed response, you will have sixty to ninety minutes to write an essay analyzing two passages with a similar topic. On the second constructed response, you will have forty-five to sixty minutes to write a constructed response of three assessment tasks responding to a student's draft. The first essay involves practice in synthesizing text. Synthesizing text means taking multiple texts and drawing conclusions from the information provided in them.

Brainstorming

One of the most important steps in writing an essay is prewriting. Before drafting an essay, it's helpful to think about the topic for a moment or two, in order to gain a more solid understanding of what the task is. Then, spending about five minutes jotting down the immediate ideas that could work for the essay is recommended. It is a way to get some words on the page and offer a reference for ideas when drafting. Scratch paper is provided for writers to use any prewriting techniques such as webbing, free writing, or listing. The goal is to get ideas out of the mind and onto the page.

Considering Opposing Viewpoints

In the planning stage, it's important to consider all aspects of the topic, including different viewpoints on the subject. There are more than two ways to look at a topic, and a strong argument considers those opposing viewpoints. Considering opposing viewpoints can help writers present a fair, balanced, and informed essay that shows consideration for all readers. This approach can also strengthen an argument by recognizing and potentially refuting the opposing viewpoint(s).

Drawing from personal experience may help to support ideas. For example, if the goal for writing is a personal narrative, then the story should be from the writer's own life. Many writers find it helpful to draw from personal experience, even in an essay that is not strictly narrative. Personal anecdotes or short stories can help to illustrate a point in other types of essays as well.

Moving from Brainstorming to Planning

Once the ideas are on the page, it's time to turn them into a solid plan for the essay. The best ideas from the brainstorming results can then be developed into a more formal outline. An outline typically has one main point (the thesis) and at least three sub-points that support the main point. Here's an example:

Main Idea

- Point #1
- Point #2
- Point #3

Of course, there will be details under each point, but this approach is the best for dealing with timed writing.

Staying on Track

Basing the essay on the outline aids in both organization and coherence. The goal is to ensure that there is enough time to develop each sub-point in the essay, roughly spending an equal amount of time on each idea. Keeping an eye on the time will help. If there are fifteen minutes left to draft the essay, then it makes sense to spend about 5 minutes on each of the ideas. Staying on task is critical to success, and timing out the parts of the essay can help writers avoid feeling overwhelmed.

Parts of the Essay

The *introduction* has to do a few important things:

- Establish the *topic* of the essay in original wording (i.e., not just repeating the prompt)
- Clarify the significance/importance of the topic or purpose for writing (not too many details, a brief overview)
- Offer a *thesis statement* that identifies the writer's own viewpoint on the topic (typically one-two brief sentences as a clear, concise explanation of the main point on the topic)

Body paragraphs reflect the ideas developed in the outline. Three-four points is probably sufficient for a short essay, and they should include the following:

- A *topic sentence* that identifies the sub-point (e.g., a reason why, a way how, a cause or effect)
- A detailed *explanation* of the point, explaining why the writer thinks this point is valid
- Illustrative examples, such as personal examples or real-world examples, that support and validate the point (i.e., "prove" the point)
- A *concluding sentence* that connects the examples, reasoning, and analysis to the point being made

The *conclusion*, or final paragraph, should be brief and should reiterate the focus, clarifying why the discussion is significant or important. It is important to avoid adding specific details or new ideas to this paragraph. The purpose of the conclusion is to sum up what has been said to bring the discussion to a close.

Don't Panic!

Writing an essay can be overwhelming, and performance panic is a natural response. The outline serves as a basis for the writing and helps to keep writers focused. Getting stuck can also happen, and it's helpful to remember that brainstorming can be done at any time during the writing process. Following the steps of the writing process is the best defense against writer's block.

Timed essays can be particularly stressful, but assessors are trained to recognize the necessary planning and thinking for these timed efforts. Using the plan above and sticking to it helps with time management. Timing each part of the process helps writers stay on track. Sometimes writers try to cover too much in their essays. If time seems to be running out, this is an opportunity to determine whether all of the ideas in the outline are necessary. Three body paragraphs are sufficient, and more than that is probably too much to cover in a short essay.

More isn't always *better* in writing. A strong essay will be clear and concise. It will avoid unnecessary or repetitive details. It is better to have a concise, five-paragraph essay that makes a clear point, than a ten-paragraph essay that doesn't. The goal is to write one-two pages of quality writing. Paragraphs should also reflect balance; if the introduction goes to the bottom of the first page, the writing may be going off-track or be repetitive. It's best to fall into the one-two page range, but a complete, well-developed essay is the ultimate goal.

The Final Steps

Leaving a few minutes at the end to revise and proofread offers an opportunity for writers to polish things up. Putting one's self in the reader's shoes and focusing on what the essay actually says helps writers identify problems—it's a movement from the mindset of writer to the mindset of editor. The goal is to have a clean, clear copy of the essay. The following areas should be considered when proofreading:

- Sentence fragments
- Awkward sentence structure
- Run-on sentences
- Incorrect word choice
- Grammatical agreement errors
- Spelling errors
- Punctuation errors
- Capitalization errors

The Short Overview

The essay may seem challenging, but following these steps can help writers focus:

- Take one-two minutes to think about the topic.
- Generate some ideas through brainstorming (three-four minutes).
- Organize ideas into a brief outline, selecting just three-four main points to cover in the essay (eventually the body paragraphs).
- Develop essay in parts:
- Introduction paragraph, with intro to topic and main points
- Viewpoint on the subject at the end of the introduction
- Body paragraphs, based on outline
- Each paragraph: makes a main point, explains the viewpoint, uses examples to support the point
- Brief conclusion highlighting the main points and closing
- Read over the essay (last five minutes).
- Look for any obvious errors, making sure that the writing makes sense.

14/25 00

Practice Test

Integrated Language Arts, Diverse Learners, and the Study of English

1. What is the structure of the following sentence?

    The restaurant is unconventional because it serves both Chicago style pizza and New York style pizza.

    a. Simple
    b. Compound
    c. Complex
    d. Compound-complex

2. The following sentence contains what kind of error?

    This summer, I'm planning to travel to Italy, take a Mediterranean cruise, going to Pompeii, and eat a lot of Italian food.

    a. Parallelism
    b. Sentence fragment
    c. Misplaced modifier
    d. Subject-verb agreement

3. The following sentence contains what kind of error?

    Forgetting that he was supposed to meet his girlfriend for dinner, Anita was mad when Fred showed up late.

    a. Parallelism
    b. Run-on sentence
    c. Misplaced modifier
    d. Subject-verb agreement

4. The following sentence contains what kind of error?

    Some workers use all their sick leave, other workers cash out their leave.

    a. Parallelism
    b. Comma splice
    c. Sentence fragment
    d. Subject-verb agreement

5. A student writes the following in an essay:

> Protestors filled the streets of the city. Because they were dissatisfied with the government's leadership.

Which of the following is an appropriately-punctuated correction for this sentence?

a. Protestors filled the streets of the city, because they were dissatisfied with the government's leadership.
b. Protesters, filled the streets of the city, because they were dissatisfied with the government's leadership.
c. Because they were dissatisfied with the government's leadership protestors filled the streets of the city.
d. Protestors filled the streets of the city because they were dissatisfied with the government's leadership.

6. What is the part of speech of the underlined word in the sentence?
   We need to come up with a fresh <u>approach</u> to this problem.

a. Noun
b. Verb
c. Adverb
d. Adjective

7. What is the part of speech of the underlined word in the sentence?
   Investigators conducted an <u>exhaustive</u> inquiry into the accusations of corruption.

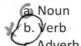

a. Noun
b. Verb
c. Adverb
d. Adjective

8. The underlined portion of the sentence is an example of which sentence component?
   New students should report <u>to the student center</u>.

a. Dependent clause
b. Adverbial phrase
c. Adjective clause
d. Noun phrase

9. What is the noun phrase in the following sentence?
   Charlotte's new German shepherd puppy is energetic.

a. Puppy
b. Charlotte
c. German shepherd puppy
d. Charlotte's new German shepherd puppy

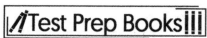

10. Which word choices will correctly complete the sentence?
    Increasing the price of bus fares has had a greater [affect / effect] on ridership [then / than] expected.

    a. affect; then
    b. affect; than
    c. effect; then
    d. effect; than

11. While studying vocabulary, a student notices that the words *circumference*, *circumnavigate*, and *circumstance* all begin with the prefix *circum–*. The student uses her knowledge of affixes to infer that all of these words share what related meaning?
    a. Around, surrounding
    b. Travel, transport
    c. Size, measurement
    d. Area, location

12. A student wants to rewrite the following sentence:
    Entrepreneurs use their ideas to make money.

He wants to use the word *money* as a verb, but he isn't sure which word ending to use. What is the appropriate suffix to add to *money* to complete the following sentence?

    Entrepreneurs _____ their ideas.

    a. –ize
    b. –ical
    c. –en
    d. –ful

monetize

13. A student reads the following sentence:
    A hundred years ago, automobiles were rare, but now cars are ubiquitous.

However, she doesn't know what the word *ubiquitous* means. Which key context clue is essential to decipher the word's meaning?

    a. Ago
    b. Cars
    c. Now
    d. Rare

14. A local newspaper is looking for writers for a student column. A student would like to submit his article to the newspaper, but he isn't sure how to format his article according to journalistic standards. What resource should he use?
    a. A thesaurus
    b. A dictionary
    c. A style guide
    d. A grammar book

15. A student encounters the word *aficionado* and wants to learn more about it. It doesn't sound like other English words he knows, so the student is curious to identify the word's origin. What resource should he consult?

    a. A thesaurus
    b. A dictionary
    c. A style guide
    d. A grammar book

16. Which domain is likely to be used by a website run by a nonprofit group?

    a. .com
    b. .edu
    c. .org
    d. .gov

17. Several generations ago, immigrants and locals in a region developed a simplified mixture of their two languages in order to carry out basic communication tasks. However, usage of this mixed language increased, and later generations passed it down to their children as their first language. These children are now speaking what kind of language?

    a. A pidgin
    b. A Creole
    c. A jargon
    d. A regionalism

18. Which of the following is true of Standard English?

    a. It is one dialect of English.
    b. It is the original form of English.
    c. It is the most complex form of English.
    d. It is the form that follows grammatical rules.

written

19. A teacher notices that, when students are talking to each other between classes, they are using their own unique vocabulary words and expressions to talk about their daily lives. When the teacher hears these non-standard words that are specific to one age or cultural group, what type of language is she listening to?

    a. Slang
    b. Jargon
    c. Dialect
    d. Vernacular

20. A teacher wants to counsel a student about using the word *ain't* in a research paper for a high school English class. What advice should the teacher give?

    a. *Ain't* is not in the dictionary, so it isn't a word.
    b. Because the student isn't in college yet, *ain't* is an appropriate expression for a high school writer.
    c. *Ain't* is incorrect English and should not be part of a serious student's vocabulary because it sounds uneducated.
    d. *Ain't* is a colloquial expression, and while it may be appropriate in a conversational setting, it is not standard in academic writing.

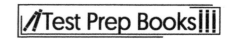

21. Which of the following is true of first language acquisition?
    a. Children need some instruction from parents or caregivers to learn a first language.
    b. Children first begin forming complete words when they are about two years old.
    c. Children experiment with the sounds of a language before they form words.
    d. Children have no language comprehension before they can speak.

22. Which of the following is true of second language acquisition?
    a. Students learn best through memorization of new vocabulary words.
    b. Second language acquisition follows the same stages as first language acquisition.
    c. Advanced fluency is achieved when the speaker has no accent in his or her second language.
    d. Second language learners experience a preproduction stage, during which they are unable to produce verbal expressions.

23. Which of the following would NOT be a recommended vocabulary teaching strategy?
    a. Focusing on specialized academic jargon that students will encounter in college
    b. Creating a word map to understand the connection between vocabulary terms
    c. Accessing prior knowledge when introducing a new area of vocabulary
    d. Providing examples of how to use terms inside and outside of class

24. Which of the following is an example of incidental learning in vocabulary development?
    a. After reading a story in class, the teacher provides students with a list of keywords to know from the text.
    b. While reading a novel for class, a student encounters an unfamiliar word and looks it up in the dictionary.
    c. As part of a writing assignment, students are instructed to utilize certain academic words and expressions in their essay.
    d. After getting back the results of a vocabulary exam, students are assigned to make personal study guides based on the words that they missed on the test.

25. A teacher is considering integrating some media sources like television and the Internet into his classroom, but he is unsure of how effective it will be. Which of the following is true about media literacy in language development?
    a. Instruction should focus only on professional media sources such as scientific journals and mainstream news publications to emphasize Standard English skills.
    b. In the twenty-first century, every student has access to and proficiency in using the Internet, so it is unnecessary to spend time on building skills in class.
    c. Students should explore media resources in their personal areas of interest to develop regular language habits in an enjoyable way.
    d. The Internet serves as a huge distraction for students and should not be part of instruction.

Literature, Reading Processes, and Skills for Reading Literary and Nonliterary Texts

1. Read the following poem then choose which option best expresses the symbolic meaning of the "road" and the overall theme?

Two roads diverged in a yellow wood,

And sorry I could not travel both

And be one traveler, long I stood

And looked down one as far as I could

To where it bent in the undergrowth;

Then took the other, as just as fair,

And having perhaps the better claim,

Because it was grassy and wanted wear;

Though as for that the passing there

Had worn them really about the same,

And both that morning equally lay

In leaves no step had trodden black.

Oh, I kept the first for another day!

Yet knowing how way leads on to way,

I doubted if I should ever come back.

I shall be telling this with a sigh

Somewhere ages and ages hence:

Two roads diverged in a wood, and I—

I took the one less traveled by,

And that has made all the difference—Robert Frost, "The Road Not Taken"

a. A divergent spot where the traveler had to choose the correct path to his destination
b. A choice between good and evil that the traveler needs to make
c. The traveler's struggle between his lost love and his future prospects
d. Life's journey and the choices with which humans are faced

2. Which option best exemplifies an author's use of *alliteration* and *personification*?
   a. Her mood hung about her like a weary cape, very dull from wear.
   b. It shuddered, swayed, shook, and screamed its way into dust under hot flames.
   c. The house was a starch sentry, warning visitors away.
   d. At its shoreline, visitors swore they heard the siren call of the cliffs above.

3. Read the following poem. Which option best depicts the rhyme scheme?

   A slumber did my spirit seal; A

   I had no human fears: B

   She seemed a thing that could not feel A

   The touch of earthly years. B

—from William Wordsworth, "A Slumber Did My Spirit Seal"

   a. BAC BAC
   b. ABAB
   c. ABBA
   d. AB CD AB

4. Read the following poem. Which option describes its corresponding meter?
   Half a league, half a league

   Half a league onward,

   All in the valley of Death

   Rode the six hundred.

   'Forward, the Light Brigade!

   Charge for the guns!' he said:

   Into the valley of Death

   Rode the six hundred.

—Alfred Lord Tennyson *"The Charge of the Light Brigade"*

   a. Iambic (unstressed/stressed syllables)
   b. Anapest (unstressed/unstressed/stressed syllables)
   c. Spondee (stressed/stressed syllables)
   d. Dactyl (stressed/unstressed/unstressed syllables)

5. This work, published in 1922, was a modernist piece that was banned both in the United States and overseas for meeting the criteria of obscenity. Taking place in a single day (June 16ᵗʰ, 1904), the novel contains eighteen episodes reflecting the activities of character Leopold Bloom in Dublin, Ireland. Originally written as to portray an Odysseus figure for adults, the structure of the work is often viewed as convoluted and chaotic, as its author utilized the stream of consciousness technique. Its literary reception was vastly polarized and remains so to this day, although modern critics tend to hail the novel as addressing the vast panoramic of futility within contemporary history.

The above passage describes which famous literary work?
a. James Joyce's *Ulysses*
b. Anne Sexton's poem "45 Mercy Street"
c. F. Scott Fitzgerald's *Tender is the Night*
d. George Eliot's *Middlemarch: A Study of Provincial Life*

6. In 1889, Jerome K. Jerome wrote a humorous account of a boating holiday. Originally intended as a chapter in a serious travel guide, the work became a prime example of a comic novel. Read the passage below, noting the word/words in italics. Answer the question that follows.

> I felt rather hurt about this at first; it seemed somehow to be a sort of slight. Why hadn't I got housemaid's knee? Why this invidious reservation? After a while, however, less grasping feelings prevailed. I reflected that I had every other known malady in the pharmacology, and I grew less selfish, and determined to do without housemaid's knee. Gout, in its most malignant stage, it would appear, had seized me without my being aware of it; and *zymosis* I had evidently been suffering with from boyhood. There were no more diseases after *zymosis*, so I concluded there was nothing else the matter with me.—Jerome K. Jerome, *Three Men in a Boat*

Which definition best fits the word *zymosis*?
a. Discontent
b. An infectious disease
c. Poverty
d. Bad luck

7. Read the following poem. Which option best describes the use of the spider?

> The spider as an artist
>
> Has never been employed
>
> Though his surpassing merit
>
> Is freely certified
>
> By every broom and Bridget
>
> Throughout a Christian land.
>
> Neglected son of genius,
>
> I take thee by the hand—Emily Dickinson, "Cobwebs"

a. Idiom
b. Haiku
c. ABBA rhyming convention
d. Simile

8. Which of the following is a <u>pre-reading</u> strategy used to support comprehension?
a. Skimming the text for content
b. Summarizing the text effectively
c. Organizing the main ideas and supporting details
d. Clarifying unfamiliar ideas in the text

9. Which best describes the plot in fiction?
a. What happens in the story or the storyline
b. Character development
c. The time and place of the story
d. The events in the story that are true

10. Which option best portrays *second person point of view*?
a. I went down the road, hoping to catch a glimpse of his retreating figure.
b. You, my dear reader, can understand loss and grief, too.
c. He left her standing there, alone to face the world.
d. There's nothing wrong with Margaret.

11. Which option best defines a *fable*?
a. A melancholy poem lamenting its subject's death
b. An oral tradition influenced by culture
c. A story with events that occur in threes and in sevens
d. A short story with animals, fantastic creatures, or other forces within nature

12. Which of the following describes the organizational pattern of chronological or sequence order?
    a. Text organized by describing a dilemma and a possible solution
    b. Text organized by observing the consequences of an action
    c. Text organized by the timing of events or actions
    d. Text organized by analyzing the relative placement of an object or event

13. Which phrase best completes the definition of a *memoir*?
    a. A historical account of a person's life written by one who has intimate knowledge of the person's life
    b. A historical account of a person's life written by the person himself or herself
    c. A fictional account about a famous person
    d. A nonfictional account about a famous person without factual reference

14. The statement below features an example of which of the following literary devices?
    Oh pity! Your high independence only reveals the immeasurable distance between us.

    a. Assonance
    b. Parallelism
    c. Amplification
    d. Hyperbole

15. Which poem belongs to the metaphysical literary movement?
    a. Emily Dickinson's "If I Should Die"
    b. Elizabeth Barrett Browning's "A Child Asleep"
    c. Andrew Marvell's "To His Coy Mistress"
    d. Sylvia Plath's "The Bell Jar"

16. Which word serves as the best example of the poetic device, *onomatopoeia*?
    a. Crackle
    b. Eat
    c. Provide
    d. Walking

17. Which term best defines a *sonnet*?
    a. A Japanese love poem
    b. An eight-line stanza or poem
    c. A fourteen-line poem written in iambic pentameter
    d. A ceremonious, lyric poem

18. Which literary school of thought developed out of structuralism in the twentieth century?
    a. Deconstruction
    b. Post-Structuralism
    c. Marxism
    d. Both A and B

19. Which phrase below best defines *inference*?
    a. Reading between the lines
    b. Skimming a text for context clues
    c. Writing notes or questions that need answers during the reading experience
    d. Summarizing the text

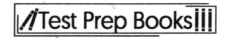

20. Which word best defines the prior knowledge a reader brings to the reading?
    a. Meta-cognitive
    b. Foreshadowing
    c. Schema
    d. Prediction

21. Which phrase best describes the purpose of nonfiction writing?
    a. To inform, entertain, or persuade readers
    b. To entertain, then to inform
    c. To convince readers they're wrong about the author's subject
    d. None of the above

22. Which phrase best defines *connotation*?
    a. An author's use of footnotes in his or her informational text
    b. Words or phrases that mean exactly what they say
    c. The author's use of allusion
    d. When an author chooses words or phrases that invoke feelings rather than a literal meaning

23. Which phrase below best defines the term *audience* as it is used in rhetoric?
    a. The group of readers to which the author is trying to appeal
    b. Students
    c. Subject matter experts
    d. Readers who already have formed subject matter opinions

24. Which of the below definitions is applicable to the *slippery slope* fallacy?
    a. Misrepresenting someone's argument
    b. Asserting that if one event occurs, the rest must follow as natural consequence
    c. Personal attack
    d. Using the opinion of the majority to sway the reader

25. How is it best for readers to approach non-print media critically?
    a. Assume sound bites are generally accurate
    b. Exclude printed text when approaching non-print media
    c. Become a subject matter expert on the topic at hand
    d. Address additional sources and not exclude printed text upon viewing non-print media

17/25

175

Written Communication

1. Which mode of writing aims to inform the reader objectively about a particular subject or idea and typically contains definitions, instructions, or facts within its subject matter?
    a. Argumentative
    b. Informative
    c. Narrative
    d. Descriptive

2. Editorials, letters of recommendation, and cover letters most likely incorporate which writing mode?
    a. Argumentative
    b. Informative
    c. Narrative
    d. Descriptive

3. The type of writing mode an author chooses to use is dependent on which of the following elements?
    a. The audience
    b. The primary purpose
    c. The main idea
    d. Both A and B

4. The rhetorical appeal that elicits an emotional and/or sympathetic response from an audience is known as which of the following?
    a. Logos
    b. Ethos
    c. Pathos
    d. None of the above

5. Which of the following refers to what an author wants to express about a given subject?
    a. Primary purpose
    b. Plot
    c. Main idea
    d. Characterization

6. Which organizational style is used in the following passage?
    There are several reasons why the new student café has not been as successful as expected. One factor is that prices are higher than originally advertised, so many students cannot afford to buy food and beverages there. Also, the café closes rather early; as a result, students go out in town to other late-night gathering places rather than meeting friends at the café on campus.

    a. Cause and effect order
    b. Compare and contrast order
    c. Spatial order
    d. Time order

7. Short, succinct sentences are best written for which of the following audiences?
    a. Adults or people more familiar with a subject
    b. Children or people less familiar a subject
    c. Politicians and academics
    d. University students

8. A student is starting a research assignment on Japanese-American internment camps during World War II, but she is unsure of how to gather relevant resources. Which of the following would be the most helpful advice for the student?
    a. Conduct a broad internet search to get a wide view of the subject.
    b. Consult an American history textbook.
    c. Find websites about Japanese culture such as fashion and politics.
    d. Locate texts in the library related to World War II in America and look for references to internment camps in the index.

9. Which of the following should be evaluated to ensure the credibility of a source?
    a. The publisher, the author, and the references
    b. The subject, the title, and the audience
    c. The organization, stylistic choices, and transition words
    d. The length, the tone, and the contributions of multiple authors

10. Which of the following is true of using citations in a research paper?
    a. If a source is cited in the bibliography, it is not necessary to cite it in the paper as well.
    b. In-text citations differ in format from bibliographic citations.
    c. Students should learn one standard method of citing sources.
    d. Books and articles need to be cited, but not websites or multimedia sources.

11. Which of the following is true regarding the integration of source material to maintain the flow of ideas in a research project or paper?
    a. There should be at least one quotation or paraphrase in every paragraph.
    b. If a source is paraphrased instead of being directly quoted, it is not necessary to include a citation.
    c. An author's full name must be used in every signal phrase.
    d. In-text citations should be used to support the paper's argument without overwhelming the student's writing.

12. Which citation style requires the inclusion of the author's last name, the title of the book or article, and its publication date in a bibliography entry?
    a. MLA
    b. APA
    c. Chicago
    d. All of the above

13. Which of the following qualities are necessary for effective speech delivery?
    a. Knowledge, erudite vocabulary, and conviction
    b. Charm, wit, and connection
    c. Confidence, authenticity, and succinctness
    d. Compassion, empathy, and tolerance

14. Which of the following components are advantageous and disadvantageous regarding the use of Microsoft PowerPoint presentations?
    a. They present information that can be taken home and reviewed later, but the audience may choose to read rather than listen.
    b. They allow the audience to follow along with the process of explaining difficult concepts and copy down their own version, but there is limited space that may need to be erased.
    c. They allow for pictures, words, and videos, but they can be distracting from the presence of the speaker.
    d. They allow for participants to interact with the physical world which helps solidify concepts, but they can be distracting if not properly introduced.

15. Which of the following should be considered before utilizing a technological device in the classroom?
    a. The age of the students
    b. Whether it is user friendly
    c. If it will be used in the real world
    d. All of the above

16. Which of the following refers to a teaching strategy in which two or more students work together to develop a project, work through an idea, or solve a problem?
    a. Listening
    b. Collaborative learning
    c. Active learning
    d. Discussion

17. A method of learning in which the student learns through physical interaction with an object is referred to as which of the following?
    a. Auditory Learning
    b. Visual Learning
    c. Kinesthetic Learning
    d. Distance Learning

18. Which of the following defines the stage of writing that involves adding to, removing, rearranging, or re-writing sections of a piece?
    a. The revising stage
    b. The publishing stage
    c. The writing stage
    d. The pre-writing stage

19. A research-proven approach to teaching writing that involves a short lesson, independent writing time, and sharing is known as which of the below?
    a. Writing workshop
    b. Teacher modeling
    c. The writer's notebook
    d. Freewriting

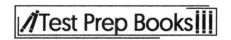

20. Which of the following is true regarding the most effective methods of teaching the writing process?
a. Instruction should be standardized so that all students should learn writing in the same way.
b. Feedback should be generalized, giving overall instruction for improvement instead of focusing on certain aspects of writing.
c. The most important way a student learns is by doing, so they should be given as many opportunities to write as possible.
d. Students should be compared to one another, so lower-achieving students can model their writing skills on those of more proficient students.

21. Which of the following is true of assessing student writing?
a. Students should only be given positive feedback so as not to make them feel discouraged.
b. Students should engage in peer assessments without instructor interference, to increase independent writing skills.
c. Writing assessments should always be holistic so students get the "big picture" of effective writing.
d. Writing assessments should be returned in a timely manner.

22. Which of the following is an evaluation tool that explicitly states the expectations of an assignment and breaks it down into components and evaluation criteria?
a. A one-on-one conference
b. An analytic rubric
c. A verbal feedback session
d. A discussion with peers

23. When it comes to class discussions, setting guidelines for the discussion, preventing distracting tangents, and refraining from arguing with students are examples of which of the following?
a. Cultivating an environment of inclusion and mutual respect
b. Keeping discussions productive
c. Encouraging participation
d. Ensuring accountability

24. If student participation in discussion is low, which of the following should be done to encourage more active participation?
a. Divide the classroom into smaller groups so that shy students will feel more comfortable speaking up.
b. Brainstorm ideas related to the topic on the board.
c. Allow students to lead discussion or suggest topics.
d. All of the above

25. Which of the following is NOT a strategy used to foster cultural awareness in the classroom?
a. Creating introduction cards that contain student background information
b. Assigning a family heritage project
c. Grouping students based on their backgrounds
d. Creating lessons related to important historic events in diverse cultures

Oral Communication and Media Literacy

1. A play contains both stage directions and dialogue. Which of the following statements shows how stage directions relate to the actors in a dramatic play?
    a. Stage directions reveal the importance of good lighting in a play.
    b. Dialogue reveals what an actor should say, while stage direction reveals how they should behave on stage.
    c. Stage directions are only the concern of the director, not the actors.
    d. Actors should pay equal attention to both stage directions and dialogue.

2. A student is asked to give a multimedia presentation of his research project on the solar system. Which of the following digital media tools could the student include to best enhance his presentation?
    a. A lecture on why Pluto isn't considered a planet anymore
    b. A model of the planets revolving around the Sun
    c. An interview with a science teacher on the planets
    d. A video showing how the planets revolve around the Su

3. Which of the following sources is likely considered the most credible?
    a. A website that appears on the first page of a Google search
    b. A social media post that has been shared over 100,000 times
    c. An online journal article that has been peer-reviewed
    d. A news report that appears on CNN

4. Which answer choice shows the accurate root of each of these words: transportation, multimedia, destruction, transmit?
    a. trans, multi, de, trans
    b. ation, media, tion, mit
    c. trans, multi, struct, trans
    d. port, multi, struct, mit

5. Which of the following correctly matches the affix, root, and suffix with the provided word?
    a. unreliable: unre – affix, lia – root, ble – suffix
    b. dehydration: de – affix, hydr – root, ation – suffix
    c. biology: bi – affix, olo – root, gy – suffix
    d. hypothermia: hyp – affix, other – root, mia – suffix

Use the following passage to answer questions 6-7

"An elderly gentleman of the amiable military type rushes into shelter, and closes a dripping umbrella. He is in the same plight as Freddy, very wet about the ankles. He is in evening dress, with a light overcoat. He takes the place left vacant by the daughter's retirement.

THE GENTLEMAN. Phew!

THE MOTHER [to the gentleman] Oh, sir, is there any sign of its stopping?

THE GENTLEMAN. I'm afraid not. It started worse than ever about two minutes ago. [He goes to the plinth beside the flower girl; puts up his foot on it; and stoops to turn down his trouser ends].

THE MOTHER. Oh, dear! [She retires sadly and joins her daughter].

THE FLOWER GIRL [taking advantage of the military gentleman's proximity to establish friendly relations with him]. If it's worse it's a sign it's nearly over. So cheer up, Captain; and buy a flower off a poor girl.

THE GENTLEMAN. I'm sorry, I haven't any change.

THE FLOWER GIRL. I can give you change, Captain,

THE GENTLEMEN. For a sovereign? I've nothing less.

THE FLOWER GIRL. Garn! Oh do buy a flower off me, Captain. I can change half-a-crown. Take this for tuppence.

THE GENTLEMAN[...]"Now don't be troublesome: there's a good girl. [Trying his pockets] I really haven't any change—Stop: here's three hapence, if that's any use to you [he retreats to the other pillar]."

"THE FLOWER GIRL [disappointed, but thinking three halfpence better than nothing] Thank you, sir.

THE BYSTANDER [to the girl] You be careful: give him a flower for it. There's a bloke here behind taking down every blessed word you're saying. [All turn to the man who is taking notes].

THE FLOWER GIRL [springing up terrified] I ain't done nothing wrong by speaking to the gentleman. I've a right to sell flowers if I keep off the kerb. [Hysterically] I'm a respectable girl: so help me, I never spoke to him except to ask him to buy a flower off me. [General hubbub, mostly sympathetic to the flower girl, but deprecating her excessive sensibility."

Excerpt From: George Bernard Shaw. "Pygmalion."

6. Which of the following examples is considered a stage direction?
    a. THE GENTLEMAN
    b. Oh, sir, is there any sign of its stopping?
    c. Trying his pockets.
    d. Oh, dear! [She retires sadly and joins her daughter].

7. What do the following stage directions and dialogue reveal about the flower girl's motivation?

"THE FLOWER GIRL [taking advantage of the military gentleman's proximity to establish friendly relations with him]. If it's worse it's a sign it's nearly over. So cheer up, Captain; and buy a flower off a poor girl."

    a. The flower girl is kind and wants to help the gentleman.
    b. She is very poor and needs help.
    c. She wants to be friendly to strangers.
    d. The flower girl is opportunistic and wants to manipulate the situation.

8. How can teachers best conduct a peer-review exercise for students?
    a. They can allow students to choose their own partners so they are comfortable
    b. They can ensure all students know that their role is to be an evaluator, not a reader
    c. They can provide students with a clear set of peer-review questions to answer
    d. They can allow students to opt out of the peer review if they are afraid to show their work

9. In which part of the writing process are peer reviews best utilized?
   a. Revision
   b. Prewriting
   c. Drafting
   d. Outlining

10. A student is asked to share about his weekend plans with the class without any preparation. This is an example of which type of oral presentation?
    a. Expository
    b. Debate
    c. Persuasive
    d. Impromptu

11. What is the defining trait of a tragedy?
    a. A heroine who has a problem to solve
    b. An unhappy ending
    c. An unlikely hero
    d. Use of a satirical tone

12. Which of the following scenarios constitutes unintentional plagiarism?
    a. A student who uses APA formatting instead of the required MLA formatting on a draft
    b. A student who copies a line of text from a website but does not provide any citation for it in the draft.
    c. A student who misspells some of the names of authors on the works cited page at the end of the draft
    d. A student who presents a complete reference list at the end of the document, but leaves out in-text citations in the draft

13. What is the major difference between voice and style?
    a. Voice refers to the author's personality while style refers to the words and the way they are written.
    b. Voice refers to tone of the writing and style refers to punctuation and grammatical choices.
    c. Voice can change in a writer's work while style tends to stay the same.
    d. Voice and style are essentially the same thing.

14. A student is giving a speech on global warming. Which of the following statements from the speech is an example of the student's stance?
    a. "I have serious concerns about climate change and how it will affect our future."
    b. "There are many ways to help slow climate change."
    c. "Global warming is a hot-button issue among politicians."
    d. "I have found some studies that refute global warming."

15. Why might a student bring up opposing viewpoints in a persuasive speech?
    a. To show that she has done her research
    b. To provide many different viewpoints on a subject
    c. To show that she is fair and balanced
    d. To refute those viewpoints and strengthen her own argument

Use the following excerpt to answer questions 16 and 17.

It would have been a difficult matter for Mr. Pontellier to define to his own satisfaction or anyone else's wherein his wife failed in her duty toward their children. It was something which he felt rather than perceived, and he never voiced the feeling without subsequent regret and ample atonement. If one of the little Pontellier boys took a tumble whilst at play, he was not apt to rush crying to his mother's arms for comfort; he would more likely pick himself up, wipe the water out of his eyes and the sand out of his mouth, and go on playing. Tots as they were, they pulled together and stood their ground in childish battles with doubled fists and uplifted voices, which usually prevailed against the other mother-tots. The quadroon nurse was looked upon as a huge encumbrance, only good to button up waists and panties and to brush and part hair; since it seemed to be a law of society that hair must be parted and brushed.

Excerpted from The Awakening by Kate Chopin

16. The word *quadroon* was a term used in the 1800s to refer to a person of both white and African ancestry. This information can be considered an example of which of the following?
    a. Dictionary skills
    b. Cultural context
    c. Political context
    d. Context clues

17. From what point of view is the passage told?
    a. Third person limited point of view
    b. Third person objective point of view
    c. First person point of view
    d. Second person point of view

18. A KWL chart is an example of which of the following?
    a. An orthography strategy
    b. A graphic organizer
    c. A context clue
    d. A rehearsal strategy

19. An author's choice to use flashbacks is an example of which of the following?
    a. Point of view
    b. Voice
    c. Plot structure
    d. Tone

20. Dimensions of a text that can be measured by a computer such as text cohesion are an example of which of the following?
    a. Qualitative dimensions
    b. Quantitative dimensions
    c. Language conventionality
    d. Reader and Task Considerations

Constructed Response Prompts

Constructed Response Prompt I

The following passages address related topics and develop themes that are related through their similarities and/or through their differences. In an essay to be read by an educator in the field of English, write an analysis of the two passages and use textual evidence as support. Your analysis should:

- Point out themes that connect to the two passages; and
- Show how both authors use literary elements or devices in each excerpt to develop and support these themes.

Excerpt from *Preface to Lyrical Ballads* by William Wordsworth (1800)

From such verses the Poems in these volumes will be found distinguished at least by one mark of difference, that each of them has a worthy *purpose.* Not that I always began to write with a distinct purpose formerly conceived; but habits of meditation have, I trust, so prompted and regulated my feelings, that my descriptions of such objects as strongly excite those feelings, will be found to carry along with them a *purpose.* If this opinion be erroneous, I can have little right to the name of a Poet. For all good poetry is the spontaneous overflow of powerful feelings: and though this be true, Poems to which any value can be attached were never produced on any variety of subjects but by a man who, being possessed of more than usual organic sensibility, had also thought long and deeply. For our continued influxes of feeling are modified and directed by our thoughts, which are indeed the representatives of all our past feelings; and, as by contemplating the relation of these general representatives to each other, we discover what is really important to men, so, by the repetition and continuance of this act, our feelings will be connected with important subjects, till at length, if we be originally possessed of much sensibility, such habits of mind will be produced, that, by obeying blindly and mechanically the impulses of those habits, we shall describe objects, and utter sentiments, of such a nature, and in such connexion with each other, that the understanding of the Reader must necessarily be in some degree enlightened, and his affections strengthened and purified.

Excerpt from Tradition and the Individual Talent by T.S. Eliot (1921)

If you compare several representative passages of the greatest poetry you see how great is the variety of types of combination, and also how completely any semi-ethical criterion of "sublimity" misses the mark. For it is not the "greatness," the intensity, of the emotions, the components, but the intensity of the artistic process, the pressure, so to speak, under which the fusion takes place, that counts. The episode of Paolo and Francesca employs a definite emotion, but the intensity of the poetry is something quite different from whatever intensity in the supposed experience it may give the impression of. It is no more intense, furthermore, than Canto XXVI, the voyage of Ulysses, which has not the direct dependence upon an emotion. Great variety is possible in the process of transmution of emotion: the murder of Agamemnon, or the agony of Othello, gives an artistic effect apparently closer to a possible original than the scenes from Dante. In the *Agamemnon,* the artistic emotion approximates to the emotion of an actual spectator; in *Othello* to the emotion of the protagonist himself. But the difference between art and the event is always absolute; the combination which is the murder of Agamemnon is probably as complex as that which is the voyage of Ulysses. In either case there has been a fusion of elements. The ode of Keats contains a number of feelings which have nothing particular to do with the nightingale, but which the nightingale, partly, perhaps, because of its attractive name, and partly because of its reputation, served to bring together.

Constructed Response Prompt II

Read the following writing assignment and student response carefully before beginning your assessment.

Writing Assignment

In a ninth-grade English class, a teacher assigns the following 45-minute in-class writing assignment to assess students' skills in persuasive writing:

> Think about social media in the world today and how it affects your peers' lives. Write a persuasive essay to a peer in which you are for or against heavy social media use. Be sure to:

- State your position
- Organize the argument in a coherent way
- Support your stance with reasoning and examples
- Use appropriate word choice

Student Response

People who share their lives on social media sites are edging into dangerous territory. Social media sites such as Facebook, Instagram, and Snapchat are black holes for those easily addicted to validation and acceptance. Society should be wary of allowing their kids to have open access to social media sites.

So many people feel a sense of joy at being "liked" or having a certain amount of friends or comments on their pages. This feeling may lead to a false sense of acceptance by peers, and the feeling that one has accomplished something. Friends post vacations, what they ate for lunch, who they are dating, and pictures of themselves and their families. They say that if it's not on social media, it didn't happen. Sharing so much personal information is an invasion of privacy and could prove dangerous. They think sharing personal pictures and details invites predators, cyberbullying, and identity theft.

People should take care to stay away from social media and get their validation and acceptance from entities that truly matter, like from themselves or a higher being. Being outside and getting exercise is a good alternative to staring at a screen all day. Those who get out and expand their worlds will definitely experience happier lives.

Task 1

Identify one strength in the student's response and explain how it makes the argument more effective. Provide specific examples from the response for support. Don't comment on grammar, usage, or mechanics.

Task 2

Identify one weakness in the student's response. Show how it inhibits the essay's effectiveness. Provide specific examples from the response. Don't comment on grammar, usage, or mechanics.

Task 3

Thinking about the significant weakness in the student's response in Task 2, develop one specific instructional activity that you as the English teacher would implement. Explain how the activity would address that particular weakness and why the activity would be effective.

185

Answer Explanations

Integrated Language Arts, Diverse Learners, and the Study of English

1. C: A complex sentence joins an independent or main clause with a dependent or subordinate clause. In this case, the main clause is "The restaurant is unconventional." This is a clause with one subject-verb combination that can stand alone as a grammatically-complete sentence. The dependent clause is "because it serves both Chicago style pizza and New York style pizza." This clause begins with the subordinating conjunction *because* and also consists of only one subject-verb combination. *A* is incorrect because a simple sentence consists of only one verb-subject combination—one independent clause. *B* is incorrect because a compound sentence contains two independent clauses connected by a conjunction. *D* is incorrect because a complex-compound sentence consists of two or more independent clauses and one or more dependent clauses.

2. A: Parallelism refers to consistent use of sentence structure or word form. In this case, the list within the sentence does not utilize parallelism; three of the verbs appear in their base form—*travel*, *take*, and *eat*—but one appears as a gerund—*going*. A parallel version of this sentence would be "This summer, I'm planning to travel to Italy, take a Mediterranean cruise, go to Pompeii, and eat a lot of Italian food." *B* is incorrect because this description is a complete sentence. *C* is incorrect as a misplaced modifier is a modifier that is not located appropriately in relation to the word or words they modify. *D* is incorrect because subject-verb agreement refers to the appropriate conjugation of a verb in relation to its subject.

3. C: In this sentence, the modifier is the phrase "Forgetting that he was supposed to meet his girlfriend for dinner." This phrase offers information about Fred's actions, but the noun that immediately follows it is Anita, creating some confusion about the "do-er" of the phrase. A more appropriate sentence arrangement would be "Forgetting that he was supposed to meet his girlfriend for dinner, Fred made Anita mad when he showed up late." *A* is incorrect as parallelism refers to the consistent use of sentence structure and verb tense, and this sentence is appropriately consistent. *B* is incorrect as a run-on sentence does not contain appropriate punctuation for the number of independent clauses presented, which is not true of this description. *D* is incorrect because subject-verb agreement refers to the appropriate conjugation of a verb relative to the subject, and all verbs have been properly conjugated.

4. B: A comma splice occurs when a comma is used to join two independent clauses together without the additional use of an appropriate conjunction. One way to remedy this problem is to replace the comma with a semicolon. Another solution is to add a conjunction: "Some workers use all their sick leave, but other workers cash out their leave." *A* is incorrect as parallelism refers to the consistent use of sentence structure and verb tense; all tenses and structures in this sentence are consistent. *C* is incorrect because a sentence fragment is a phrase or clause that cannot stand alone—this sentence contains two independent clauses. *D* is incorrect because subject-verb agreement refers to the proper conjugation of a verb relative to the subject, and all verbs have been properly conjugated.

5. D: The problem in the original passage is that the second sentence is a dependent clause that cannot stand alone as a sentence; it must be attached to the main clause found in the first sentence. Because the main clause comes first, it does not need to be separated by a comma. However, if the dependent

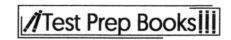

clause came first, then a comma would be necessary, which is why Choice C is incorrect. A and B also insert unnecessary commas into the sentence.

6. A: A noun refers to a person, place, thing, or idea. Although the word *approach* can also be used as a verb, in the sentence it functions as a noun within the noun phrase "a fresh approach," so B is incorrect. An adverb is a word or phrase that provides additional information of the verb, but because the verb is *need* and not *approach*, then C is false. An adjective is a word that describes a noun, used here as the word *fresh*, but it is not the noun itself. Thus, D is also incorrect.

7. D: An adjective modifies a noun, answering the question "Which one?" or "What kind?" In this sentence, the word *exhaustive* is an adjective that modifies the noun *investigation*. Another clue that this word is an adjective is the suffix *–ive*, which means "having the quality of." The nouns in this sentence are investigators, inquiry, accusations, and corruption; therefore, A is incorrect. The verb in this sentence is *conducted* because this was the action taken by the subject *the investigators*; therefore, B is incorrect. C is incorrect because an adverb is a word or phrase that provides additional information about the verb, expressing how, when, where, or in what manner.

8. B: In this case, the phrase functions as an adverb modifying the verb *report*, so B is the correct answer. "To the student center" does not consist of a subject-verb combination, so it is not a clause; thus, Choices A and C can be eliminated. This group of words is a phrase. Phrases are classified by either the controlling word in the phrase or its function in the sentence. D is incorrect because a noun phrase is a series of words that describe or modify a noun.

9. D: A noun phrase consists of the noun and all of its modifiers. In this case, the subject of the sentence is the noun *puppy*, but it is preceded by several modifiers—adjectives that give more information about what kind of puppy, which are also part of the noun phrase. Thus, A is incorrect. Charlotte is the owner of the puppy and a modifier of the puppy, so B is false. C is incorrect because it contains some, but not all, of the modifiers pertaining to the puppy. D is correct because it contains all of them.

10. D: In this sentence, the first answer choice requires a noun meaning *impact* or *influence*, so *effect* is the correct answer. For the second answer choice, the sentence is drawing a comparison. *Than* shows a comparative relationship whereas *then* shows sequence or consequence. A and C can be eliminated because they contain the choice *then*. B is incorrect because *affect* is a verb while this sentence requires a noun.

11. A: The affix *circum–* originates from Latin and means *around or surrounding*. It is also related to other round words, such as circle and circus. The rest of the choices do not relate to the affix *circum–* and are therefore incorrect.

12. A: Only two of these suffixes, *–ize* and *–en*, can be used to form verbs, so B and D are incorrect. Those choices create adjectives. The suffix *–ize* means "to convert or turn into." The suffix *–en* means "to become." Because this sentence is about converting ideas into money, money + *–ize* or *monetize* is the most appropriate word to complete the sentence, so C is incorrect.

13. D: Students can use context clues to make a careful guess about the meaning of unfamiliar words. Although all of the words in a sentence can help contribute to the overall sentence, in this case, the adjective that pairs with *ubiquitous* gives the most important hint to the student—cars were first *rare*, but now they are *ubiquitous*. The inversion of *rare* is what gives meaning to the rest of the sentence and *ubiquitous* means "existing everywhere" or "not rare." A is incorrect because *ago* only indicates a time frame. B is incorrect because *cars* does not indicate a contrasting relationship to the word *ubiquitous* to provide a good context clue. *C* is incorrect because it also only indicates a time frame, but used together with *rare*, it provides the contrasting relationship needed to identify the meaning of the unknown word.

14. C: A style guide offers advice about proper formatting, punctuation, and usage when writing for a specific field, such as journalism or scientific research. The other resources would not offer similar information. A dictionary is useful for looking up definitions; a thesaurus is useful for looking up synonyms and antonyms. A grammar book is useful for looking up specific grammar topics. Thus, Choices *A*, *C*, and *D* are incorrect.

15. B: A word's origin is also known as its *etymology*. In addition to offering a detailed list of a word's various meanings, a dictionary also provides information about a word's history, such as when it first came into use, what language it originated from, and how its meaning may have changed over time. A thesaurus is for identifying synonyms and antonyms, so *A* is incorrect. A style guide provides formatting, punctuation, and syntactical advice for a specific field, and a grammar book is related to the appropriate placement of words and punctuation, which does not provide any insight into a word's meaning. Therefore, Choices *A*, *C*, and *D* are incorrect.

16. C: The .org domain on websites is generally used by nonprofit groups or community organizations. A government website uses .gov, and .edu is used for educational institutions. Private companies and businesses use .com, so Choices *A*, *B*, and *D* are incorrect.

17. B: A utilitarian combination of two or more languages that springs up where different linguistic groups overlap is known as a pidgin; it is used for communication tasks but not as a first language. However, when that pidgin becomes entrenched in the culture and is then taught to children as their first, native language, it is known as a Creole. *C* and *D* are not correct because they both refer to vocabulary, not to entire languages. Jargon is the vocabulary of a specific field or industry, and regionalisms are the vocabulary of a specific place.

18. A: A dialect of a language refers to one version of that language that follows specific patterns of grammar, spelling, pronunciation, and vocabulary. In this sense, then, Standard English is simply one of many different dialects of English. Standard English is not the original form of English because the language has evolved considerably over the past several centuries and will most likely continue to do so in the future. Also, there is nothing that makes Standard English more complex or grammatical than other dialects of English. Although other dialects may deviate from the grammar used in Standard English, these dialects still follow their own predictable rules and patterns of grammar.

19. A: Slang refers to non-standard expressions that are not used in elevated speech and writing. Slang tends to be specific to one group or time period and is commonly used within groups of young people during their conversations with each other. Jargon refers to the language used in a specialized field. The vernacular is the native language of a local area, and a dialect is one form of a language in a certain region. Thus, *B*, *C*, and *D* are incorrect.

20. D: Colloquial language is that which is used conversationally or informally, in contrast to professional or academic language. While *ain't* is common in conversational English, it is a non-standard expression in academic writing. For college-bound students, high school should introduce them to the expectations of a college classroom, so *B* is not the best answer. Teachers should also avoid placing moral or social value on certain patterns of speech. Rather than teaching students that their familiar speech patterns are bad, teachers should help students learn when and how to use appropriate forms of expression, so *C* is wrong. *Ain't* is in the dictionary, so *A* is incorrect, both in the reason for counseling and in the factual sense.

21. C: In the babbling stage, children repeat simple syllables that will later form the building blocks of their first words, such as ma-ma and da-da. *A* is not a correct answer because children learn their first language simply by being exposed to it, without any formal instruction required. *B* is also incorrect because most children utter their first word by about one year old. Babies demonstrate understanding of language before they are able to actually form words themselves, so *D* is not correct.

22. D: This is the first stage of L2 acquisition, before the learner is ready to communicate in the target language. Both L1 and L2 acquisition clearly follow different stages, so *B* is incorrect. The final stage of L2 development, advanced fluency, does not require the speaker to have a native accent; rather, it refers to the stage at which the speaker encounters no difficulty in expression or comprehension in both conversational and academic settings; thus, *C* is incorrect. L2 learners benefit from a variety of instruction techniques, and students require both input—such as studying new vocabulary words—and output—actually using those words in productive language tasks—in order to develop new skills; therefore, *A* is also incorrect.

23. A: Although it is useful to introduce students to concepts they might encounter in a college classroom, making jargon the focus of instruction at the expense of vocabulary with more widely-applicable usage will not meet the needs of the majority of students in class. The other strategies are all appropriate ways to have students integrate new vocabulary into their existing knowledge structures and their everyday lives.

24. B: Incidental learning contrasts with direct instruction, wherein instructors direct students in the precise meaning of new vocabulary or call students' attention to important vocabulary skills in a given lesson. In incidental learning, students learn new vocabulary as they encounter unfamiliar terms during other learning tasks. In this case, *B* is the correct answer because the student uses a reading assignment as an opportunity to learn a new word. In all of the other answer choices, the instructor is the one guiding the students' attention towards specific vocabulary words.

25. C: Students should explore media resources in their personal areas of interest to develop regular language habits in an enjoyable way. Multimedia resources are a powerful educational resource and should be integrated into class instruction when possible, making *D* a poor answer choice. *B* is incorrect because it cannot be assumed that every student has regular access to the internet, and even students who do have home internet access may still need guidance in how to use it to find learning resources. *A* is incorrect because though it is useful to introduce students to academic and professional media sources, the diversity of media available means that these do not need to be the sole emphasis of instruction. Rather, it can be useful to help students explore areas of their own interest and build skills in how to apply language development concepts—e.g., reading comprehension skills, using context to learn new words, keeping a journal of new words and expressions, or formulating a reading response—both inside and outside of the classroom.

Literature, Reading Processes, and Skills for Reading Literary and Nonliterary Texts

1. D: Choice *D* correctly summarizes Frost's theme of life's journey and the choices one makes. While Choice *A* can be seen as an interpretation, it is a literal one and is incorrect. Literal is not symbolic. Choice *B* presents the idea of good and evil as a theme, and the poem does not specify this struggle for the traveler. Choice *C* is a similarly incorrect answer. Love is not the theme.

2. B: Only Choice *B* uses both repetitive beginning sounds (alliteration) and personification—the portrayal of a building as a human crumbling under a fire. Choice *A* is a simile and does not utilize alliteration or the use of consistent consonant sounds for effect. Choice *C* is a metaphor and does not utilize alliteration. Choice *D* describes neither alliteration nor personification.

3. B: The correct answer is ABAB. Choice *A* is not a valid rhyme scheme. Choice *C* would require the second and third lines to rhyme, so it is incorrect. Choice *D* would require the first and fifth lines rhyme, then the second and sixth. This is also incorrect as the passage only contains four lines.

4. D: The correct answer is dactyl. If read with the combination of stressed and unstressed syllables as Tennyson intended and as the poem naturally flows, the reader will stumble upon the stressed/unstressed/unstressed rhythmic, dactyl meter similar to a waltz beat. Choices *A*, *B*, and *C* describe meters that do not follow the dactyl pattern.

5. A: The correct answer is *A* as it is the only option that utilizes stream of consciousness technique in a novel format. Choice *B* is a poem by poet Anne Sexton, not a novel. Although Ms. Sexton's works were often criticized for their intimate content, this answer does not meet the question's criteria. Choices *C* and *D* are both incorrect. Both are novels, but not of the appropriate time period, country, or literary content.

6. B: The correct answer is an infectious disease. By reading and understanding the context of the passage, all other options can be eliminated since the author restates zymosis as disease.

7. D: The correct answer is simile. Choice *A* is incorrect because the poem does not contain an idiom. Choice *B* is incorrect since the poem is not haiku. Choice *C* is incorrect as it does not use the ABBA rhyming convention.

8. A: The correct answer is skimming the text for content. Skimming text for content is an important pre-reading strategy where readers identify important ideas and words without reading every line of the text. Summarizing text effectively, organizing main ideas and supporting details, and clarifying unfamiliar ideas in the text are all reading strategies to be used during or after reading a text.

9. A: The correct answer is "what happens" or the storyline. Choice *B* refers to characters in fiction. Choice *C* defines the setting. Choice *D* is incomplete. It may be partially true, but it isn't always the case. Most fiction is based on the imaginary.

10. B: The correct answer is *B* as the author is speaking directly to the reader and uses the pronoun *you*. Choice *A* uses first person point of view, which uses the pronoun *I*. Choice *C* uses third person point of view which utilizes pronouns such as *he*, *she*, or *we*. Choice *D* is unclear.

11. D: The correct answer is a short story with animals, fantastic creatures, or other forces within nature. Choice *A* defines an elegy. Choice *B* partially alludes to folklore. Choice *C* defines a fairytale.

12. C: The correct answer is text organized by the timing of events or actions. Chronological or sequence order is the organizational pattern that structures text to show the passage of time or movement through steps in a certain order. Choice *A* demonstrates the problem/solution structure. Choice *B* defines the cause/effect pattern. Choice *D* represents the spatial order structure.

13. A: The correct answer is a historical account of a person's life written by one who has intimate knowledge of the person's life. Choice *B* is not applicable since it is the definition of an autobiography. Choice *C* strictly refers to fiction and is not applicable to nonfiction. Choice *D* indicates that a memoir is not based on historical fact. In many instances, it is.

14. D: Hyperbole. Choices *A* and *B* are unrelated. Assonance is the repetition of sounds and commonly occurs in poetry. Parallelism refers to two statements that correlate in some manner. Choice *C* is incorrect because amplification normally refers to clarification of meaning by broadening the sentence structure, while hyperbole refers to a phrase or statement that is being exaggerated.

15. C: The correct answer is Andrew Marvell's "To His Coy Mistress." Emily Dickinson, Elizabeth Barrett Browning, and Sylvia Plath all belonged to different literary movements and contexts.

16. A: The correct answer is *crackle* as it is the only option that reflects the sound that the action would make. The other options do not.

17. C: The correct answer is a fourteen-line poem written in iambic pentameter. Choice *A* is incorrect as it incorrectly alludes to the haiku form. Choice *B* defines the octave poetic structure. Choice *D* defines what a poetic ode is.

18. D: The correct answer is that both Deconstruction and Post-structuralism developed in response to the Structuralism movement of the twentieth century. Choices *A* and *B* are incomplete answers as they do not complete both literary movements which encapsulate the response to Structuralism. Choice *C* is incorrect as Marxism was a response to the writings of Karl Marx and not in direct response to Structuralism.

19. A: Inferring is reading between the lines. Choice *B* describes the skimming technique. Choice *C* describes a questioning technique readers should employ, and Choice *D* is a simple statement regarding summary. It's an incomplete answer and not applicable to inference.

20. C: The correct answer is schema. Choice *A* is the name of a research-based strategy that asks the reader to decode text passages. Choice *B* is a literary device. Choice *D* is incorrect. It is part of reading instruction strategy, but not entirely applicable to a reader's prior knowledge he or she brings to the experience.

21. A: The correct answer is to inform, entertain, or persuade readers. Choice *B* may be partly true, but it is not wholly true. Choices *C* and *D* are incorrect.

22. D: The correct answer is when an author chooses words or phrases that invoke feelings other than their literal meaning. Choice *A* refers to footnoting, which isn't applicable, and Choice *C* refers to a literary device. Choice *B* defines denotation, which is conceptually the opposite of connotation.

23. A: The correct answer is the group of readers to which the author is trying to appeal. Choice *B* could be a partial answer, but it is incorrect. Choice *C* assumes authors only write for experts, so it is incorrect. Choice *D* is not true. Rhetoric tries to appeal to readers and tries to convince them of a thesis.

24. B: The correct answer is asserting that if one event occurs, the rest must follow as natural consequence. Choice *A* defines the strawman fallacy. Choice *C* alludes to ad hominem. Choice *D* defines the bandwagon fallacy.

25. D: The correct answer is to address additional sources and not exclude printed text when viewing non-print media. Choice *A* is an incorrect statement; readers should never assume sound bites are accurate. Choice *B* is also incorrect. Excluding print media when viewing non-print media is not being a careful consumer. Choice *C* is unlikely to occur.

Written Communication

1. B: The key word here is "inform," which is the primary purpose of all informative modes. They contain facts, definitions, instructions, and other elements with the objective purpose of informing a reader—such as study guides, instruction manuals, and textbooks. Choice *A* is incorrect because an argumentative mode contains language that is subjective and is intended to persuade or to inform with a persuasive bias. Choice *C* is incorrect as a narrative mode is used primarily to tell a story and has no intention of informing, nor is the language inherently objective. Choice *D* is incorrect as descriptive modes possess no inherent intent to inform, and are used primarily to describe.

2. A: Editorials, recommendation letters, and cover letters all seek to persuade a reader to agree with the author, which reflects an argumentative mode. Choice *B* is incorrect because the intent of the above examples is to persuade a reader to agree with the author, not to present information. Choice *C* is incorrect as the above examples are not trying to tell a story. Choice *D* is also incorrect because while the above examples may contain many descriptions, that is not their primary purpose.

3. D: Both the audience and primary purpose are important for choosing a writing mode. The audience is an important factor as the diction, tone, and stylistic choices of a written piece are tailored to fit the audience demographic. The primary purpose is the reason for writing the piece, so the mode of writing must be tailored to the most effective delivery method for the message. Choice *A* is incorrect because it only takes into account one of the aspects for choosing a mode and the audience, but leaves out the primary purpose. Choice *B* is incorrect for the same reason, except it only takes into account the primary purpose and forgets the audience. Choice *C* is incorrect as the main idea is the central theme or topic of the piece, which can be expressed in any form the author chooses. Because the mode depends on the reason the author wrote the piece, the main idea is not an important factor in determining which mode of writing to use.

4. C: Pathos is the rhetorical appeal that draws on an audience's emotions and sympathies. Choice *A* is incorrect as logos appeals to the audience's logic, reason, and rational thinking, using facts and definitions. Choice *B* is incorrect because ethos appeals to the audience's sense of ethics and moral obligations. Choice *D* is incorrect because *C* contains the correct answer; thus, the answer cannot be "None of the above."

5. C: The main idea of a piece is its central theme or subject and what the author wants readers to know or understand after they read. Choice *A* is incorrect because the primary purpose is the reason that a piece was written, and while the main idea is an important part of the primary purpose, the above elements are not developed with that intent. Choice *B* is incorrect because while the plot refers to the events that occur in a narrative, organization, tone, and supporting details are not used only to develop plot. Choice *D* is incorrect because characterization is the description of a person.

6. A: The passage describes a situation and then explains the causes that led to it. Also, it utilizes cause and effect signal words, such as *causes, factors, so,* and *as a result. B* is incorrect because a compare and contrast order considers the similarities and differences of two or more things. *C* is incorrect because spatial order describes where things are located in relation to each other. Finally, *D* is incorrect because time order describes when things occurred chronologically.

7. B: Children and less educated audiences tend to understand short, succinct sentences more effectively because their use helps increase information processing. Choice A is incorrect as longer, more fluid sentences are best used for adults and more educated audiences because they minimize processing times and allow for more information to be conveyed. Choices C and D are incorrect because there is no correlation between a given profession and a writing style; rather, it depends on how familiar the audience is with a given subject.

8. D: Relevant information refers to information that is closely related to the subject being researched. Students might get overwhelmed by information when they first begin researching, so they should learn how to narrow down search terms for their field of study. Both Choices A and B are incorrect because they start with a range that is far too wide; the student will spend too much time sifting through unrelated information to gather only a few related facts. Choice C introduces a more limited range, but it is not closely related to the topic that is being researched. Finally, Choice D is correct because the student is choosing books that are more closely related to the topic and is using the index or table of contents to evaluate whether the source contains the necessary information.

9. A: The publisher, author, and references are elements of a resource that determine credibility. If the publisher has published more than one work, the author has written more than one piece on the subject, or the work references other recognized research, the credibility of a source will be stronger. Choice B is incorrect because the subject and title may be used to determine relevancy, not credibility, and the audience does not have much to do with the credibility of a source. Choice C is incorrect because the organization, stylistic choices, and transition words are all components of an effectively-written piece, but they have less to do with credibility, other than to ensure that the author knows how to write. The length and tone of a piece are a matter of author's preference, and a work does not have to be written by multiple people to be considered a credible source.

10. B: In-text citations are much shorter and usually only include the author's last name, page numbers being referenced, and for some styles, the publication year. Bibliographic citations contain much more detailed reference information. B is incorrect because citations are necessary both in the text and in a bibliography. C is incorrect because there are several different citation styles depending on the type of paper or article being written. Rather, students should learn when it is appropriate to apply each different style. D is incorrect because all sources need to be cited regardless of medium.

11. D: The purpose of integrating research is to add support and credibility to the student's ideas, not to replace the student's own ideas altogether. Choice A is incorrect as the bulk of the paper or project should be comprised of the author's own words, and quotations and paraphrases should be used to support them. Outside sources should be included when they enhance the writer's argument, but they are not required in every single paragraph. Choice B is also incorrect because regardless of whether ideas are directly quoted or paraphrased, it is essential to always credit authors for their ideas. The use of the author's full name in every signal phrase is unnecessary, so Choice C is also incorrect.

12. D: Although there are differences between each formatting style, they all include the same basic components listed in the question for bibliography entries—the author's name, the title of the work, and its publication date. Therefore, the correct answer is all of the above.

13. C: Confidence, authenticity, and succinctness are the most important aspects of speech delivery as they instill trust in the audience and deliver a message succinctly, which reduces the likelihood that the audience's attention will wander. Choice A is incorrect as knowledge is important for a good speech, as is conviction, but appropriate vocabulary depends on the audience. The message could get lost if vocabulary is inappropriate or unfamiliar to the audience. Choice *B* is incorrect because though charm, wit, and connection could be useful, charming people may also be perceived as inauthentic and lose credibility with their audience. Choice *D* is incorrect because though compassion, empathy, and tolerance are all good qualities in a person and work well in certain speech topics, they are not inherent qualities that one must possess to deliver a good speech.

14. C: Microsoft PowerPoint is the medium that can present pictures, words, and videos because of its inherent digital format, but the vastness of the projection and presence of information can distract an audience from the presence of the speaker. Choice *A* is incorrect because handouts are print mediums that present information that can be taken home and reviewed later, and participants can choose to read rather than listen. Choice *B* is incorrect because blackboards, whiteboards, and overhead projectors allow for students to follow along with processes, but provide limited space. Choice *D* is incorrect because physical objects allow for participants to interact with the physical world, but they can be distracting if not properly introduced.

15. D: The age of the students is an important aspect to consider when using technology because many devices have basic requirements for motor and comprehension skills. User friendliness is important as not all students have the same amount of technological literacy. Teaching students to use a device that they will never use again is futile, so it's more practical to use technology that they will use in the real world. Choice *D* is the correct answer because it includes all of these aspects; Choices *A*, *B*, and *C* are incorrect because they only include one of the above aspects.

16. B: Collaborative learning is defined as a teaching strategy is which two or more students work together to learn something new. Choice *A* is incorrect because listening is not a teaching strategy so much as a learning strategy, and listening is required for most types of learning. Choice *C* is incorrect because active learning is when a student learns by doing, either by teaching another student or writing a summary. Two or more students coming together to learn actively, as opposed to one instructing the other, is more indicative of collaborative learning. Choice *D* is incorrect because although discussions may occur with two or more students, it does not usually include any form of active learning, such as creating a project or solving a problem.

17. C: One component of kinesthetic learning is students learning through physical interaction with something, such as a model or an interactive computer simulation. Choice *A* is incorrect as auditory learning is when a student learns through listening, such as listening to a lecture on a podcast. Choice *B* is incorrect because visual learning occurs when a student learns through watching or observing, such as an instructional video. Choice *D* is incorrect because distance learning occurs when the teacher and student are not in the same place and is achieved through technological means.

18. A: The revising stage involves adding, removing, and rearranging sections of a written work. Choice *B* is incorrect as the publishing stage involves the distribution of the finished product to the publisher, teacher, or reader. Choice *C* is incorrect because the writing stage is the actual act of writing the work, and generally does not including editing or revision. Choice *D* is incorrect as the pre-writing stage involves the planning, drafting, and researching of the intended piece.

19. A: The writing workshop is the teaching strategy involving a short lesson on how to write or to give the topic, an individual writing session, and then a sharing section in which the students read what they have written and listens to others. Choice *B* is incorrect because teacher modeling means being an example from which the students can imitate their writing and behavior. It requires that teachers be skilled writers themselves. Choice *C* is incorrect because the writer's notebook is the physical or digital

notebook where students write and store their work. And Choice *D* is incorrect because freewriting refers to giving students a set length of time to write on a subject without editing their ideas or expressions.

20. C: Giving the students many opportunities to write is the most effective way they learn to write, and the most effective learning occurs through doing. Choice *A* is incorrect because instruction should not be standardized; it should be individualized to fit different students' needs. Choice *B* is incorrect because feedback should be specific, not generalized, so that a student may focus on the parts of his or her writing that need work, while also recognizing what he or she is doing well in other areas. Choice *D* is incorrect because though it can be helpful for students to evaluate and discuss each other's work, it is important to avoid creating a culture of comparison and competition in the classroom, which can lead to lower morale and negatively affect relationships between students.

21. D: Writing assessments should be conducted and returned in a timely manner so that students can learn from their mistakes, which in turn helps them to avoid repeating the same errors and developing ineffective writing habits. Choice *A* is incorrect because though it is important to present criticism in a constructive and encouraging way, it is better to integrate positive feedback with suggestions for improvement. Choice *B* is incorrect because peer review can be an effective learning tool, but only when it is properly modeled and monitored by the instructor. Choice *C* is incorrect because, although a holistic approach is one way to approach writing assessments, it is not the only useful method; in some cases, students need to focus on one specific area of improvement.

22. B: An analytic rubric is an evaluation tool that explicitly states the expectations of an assignment and breaks it down into components. Choice *A* is incorrect because a conference is a discussion, not a tool. Choice *C* is incorrect because although verbal feedback may accompany a completed rubric, it is not the tool itself. Choice *D* is incorrect because a discussion with peers is not a tool, though it may incorporate evaluation.

23. B: Keeping discussions productive means that the instructor guides the flow of discussion to ensure adherence to the topic, which would entail preventing tangents and not engaging with the student should they wish to argue. Choice *A* is incorrect because cultivating an environment of inclusion and mutual respect involves letting everyone have a chance to speak, monitoring student behavior for respect and tolerance, and educating students on cultural differences. Choice *C* is incorrect because encouraging participation involves galvanizing the students by calling on them, writing their responses on the board, or having them create their own topic. Choice *D* is incorrect because ensuring accountability requires that students prepare for class participation by doing homework or taking quizzes, etc. and are held accountable by being assigned or deducted points.

24. D: Dividing students into smaller groups allows for shy students who are intimidated by a large group of people to feel more comfortable in participating. Allowing students to lead discussion or suggest topics gives them more responsibility while also encouraging them to prepare more for class and letting them choose topics that they are interested in. Brainstorming ideas together can give students a starting point when they do not feel confident or knowledgeable about speaking up on a topic. Therefore, *D*—all of the above—is the best answer.

25. C: As a non-example, *C* is correct because rather than grouping students based on shared backgrounds, instructors will offer more learning opportunities by encouraging them to interact with those from backgrounds that are different from their own. Creating introduction cards that contain the students' cultural background is a very enlightening way to get to know the students and demonstrate

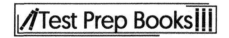

interest in them so they may feel compelled to mirror an instructor's interest and display curiosity towards others. Likewise, assigning family heritage projects encourage the students to examine their culture and then learn about other cultures in a safe and tolerant environment. Choice *D* is incorrect because it is another example of a strategy that allows students to expand their cultural knowledge.

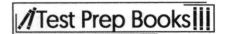

Oral Communication and Media Literacy

1. B: Stage directions in a play show the actors how they should behave and act, including their stage positions, mannerisms, and facial expressions. They can inform the actor how the character feels about what he or she is saying. While stage directions do include lighting, this isn't necessarily the concern of the actor. Directors are certainly concerned with stage directions, but actors should be as well. And while it is true that actors should be concerned with both dialogue and stage directions, this doesn't best state how stage directions relate to the actors in a play.

2. D: The best choice would be a video of the planets revolving around the Sun. This is a visual representation of the concept he is discussing in the presentation. A lecture, model, and interview are all helpful ways to learn, but they are not considered forms of digital media.

3. C: The most reliable source is the online journal because it has been peer-reviewed. Just because a source appears on the first page of a Google search, does not automatically make it reliable. Social media posts are typically not a reliable source of information, even if they have been shared many times. News reports on television must be carefully considered, as many news outlets provide biased information and their main purpose is to entertain viewers, not present reliable facts.

4. D: The correct answer is D as it shows the Latin root of each of these words. *Port* is the root of *transportation* and it means to carry. *Multi* is the root of *multimedia* and it means many. *Struct* is the root of the word *destruction* and it means to build. *Mit* is the root word of *transmit* and it means to send. *Trans* is incorrect because it is an affix meaning across. *De* is also an affix meaning the opposite. *Tion* is a suffix meaning the act or process.

5. B: The affix *de* means opposite, the root *hydr* means water, and the suffix *ation* means the act or process, so this is the correct answer. Unreliable does contain a root, affix, and suffix, but the root is *reli*, the affix is *un*, and the suffix is *able*. Both *biology* and *hypothermia* contain a root and suffix, but do not contain an affix, so they are incorrect.

6. C: [Trying his pockets] is the correct answer because it is not spoken dialogue; it is stage directions for the actor playing this part. It is contained in brackets so the actor knows this is not dialogue. THE GENTLEMEN is the name of a character, not a stage direction. Answer *B* is an example of spoken dialogue. Choice *D* includes both spoken dialogue and stage directions so this is also incorrect.

7. D: The stage directions and dialogue reveal that the flower girl is motivated to make a sale. The stage directions reveal that the flower girl wants to "take advantage" of the situation. The dialogue reveals that her overall goal is to make the sale when she says he should "buy a flower off a poor girl," manipulating the military gentleman. It is unlikely her goal is to help the gentleman based on these directions and dialogue. The flower girl may be poor, but this isn't revealed through this line from the play. She may be friendly to strangers, but only because she wants to make a sale.

8. C: Peer reviews are most effective when they are structured. Providing students with a set of peer-review questions will create structure in the activity. Allowing students to choose their own partners or to opt out of peer review are not proven strategies for peer conference success. Students should know that their role is not the evaluator, but a reader of the work. The teacher is responsible for evaluating and assessing student writing, not fellow students.

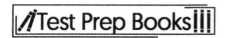

9. A: Peer conferencing should be used as part of the revision stage of the writing process. This is the stage where the draft is complete and students are looking for feedback on their writing. Using peer review before this stage, such as in the prewriting/outlining or drafting phase, doesn't make sense because students are not prepared to show their work. Writing the draft is necessary before any peer-review activities can be useful.

10. D: This is an example of an impromptu oral presentation because the student has not been given any preparation time, which is a hallmark of an impromptu presentation. Expository and persuasive oral presentations require preparations, and focus on the presentation of facts and an argument, respectively. A debate is between two people or teams, so it does not apply in this situation.

11. C: The defining quality of a literary tragedy is that it has an unhappy ending, usually where an important character dies. While a tragedy may include a heroine with a problem, this is not the defining trait. Heroes in tragedies typically have a tragic flaw. They may be unlikely, but this can occur just as often in comedy as in tragedy. Satirical tone is typically reserved for comedies.

12. D: When a student leaves out in-text citations, he or she may believe he has accurately cited his sources by providing a reference list at the end of the document. It may not occur to the student that it is also necessary to provide parenthetical citations for every sentence in the draft that comes from outside sources. While this is done unintentionally, it is still considered plagiarism. Using the wrong format of citation is not considered plagiarism. While it may not meet the standards of the assignment, the sources are still cited. The student in the second example has blatantly plagiarized an outside source, so this is considered intentional plagiarism. As long as there is a real attempt at citing sources accurately, misspellings are not considered plagiarism.

13. A: Voice is what makes the writing unique to the writer and style is the way a writer presents the information through words, sentence structure, and punctuation. Voice and tone are not the same and although punctuation is part of style, it is not its defining quality. Style is something that is developed over time and can certainly change throughout a writer's life, while voice tends to stay the same as it is what makes the writer who they are. Voice and style are related but certainly not the same.

14. A: A writer's stance is how he or she feels about the subject. In this case, the student is saying how she feels about global warming. Offering solutions to the problem, such as ways to help slow climate change, is not considered the writer's stance. Choice *C* provides more information about the topic, but does not make the writer's stance clear. The last example refers to research, and is not an example of writer's stance.

15. D: Introducing opposing viewpoints into a persuasive speech can be used as a way of identifying weaknesses and refuting these viewpoints. This can then strengthen the speaker's own argument. While research is important, opposing viewpoints aren't necessarily the type of research that would support a speaker's argument. Providing many views on a subject isn't the goal of a persuasive speech, not is being fair and balanced. If the speaker's goal is to persuade the audience, her viewpoint should be presented as the most correct and logical choice.

16. B: Knowing the definition of the word *quadroon* as it refers to a person living in the South in the 1800s is considered part of the cultural context of the novel. Knowing the meaning of this word offers readers insight into the characters and the setting. While a dictionary definition is helpful, it may not provide the cultural context of the word and its use in the novel. There isn't a political context offered by knowing the meaning of the word in this particular passage. Context clues would be helpful in figuring out what the quadroon nurse's duties were, but it doesn't offer any definition of the word *quadroon* nor its cultural context.

17. A: The passage uses third person limited point of view, with an unknown narrator telling the story from only one character's perspective, Mr. Pontellier. The narrator states his inner thoughts, so it cannot be considered third person objective, where the reader does not have access to any character's thoughts. There is no use of the personal pronouns "I, me, we, us, our" so it is not in first person point of view and there is also no evidence of second person pronouns like "you" or "your" in the passage.

18. B: A KWL chart is a graphic organizer that helps students in the writing process. It is not a strategy for learning to spell. It is not necessarily used as a context clue and is not related to rehearsal strategies in a dramatic play.

19. C: The way that a story is told refers to its plot structure. The use of flashback is a choice an author makes in the way the events are presented. Author's voice, tone, and point of view can be used in a flashback, but ultimately, the use of flashback is an example of an author's choice in plot structure.

20. B: Dimensions that cannot be measured by a human and only by a computer, such as text cohesion and word frequency, are considered quantitative dimensions. Qualitative dimensions are those that can be measured by readers. Language conventionality is an example of a qualitative dimension, and reader and task considerations are another measure that teachers can consider as they evaluate texts and match them to readers.

Dear TExES ELAR 7 - 12 Test Taker,

We would like to start by thanking you for purchasing this study guide for your TExES ELAR 7 - 12 exam. We hope that we exceeded your expectations.

Our goal in creating this study guide was to cover all of the topics that you will see on the test. We also strove to make our practice questions as similar as possible to what you will encounter on test day. With that being said, if you found something that you feel was not up to your standards, please send us an email and let us know.

We would also like to let you know about other books in our catalog that may interest you.

TExES Mathematics 7 - 12

This can be found on Amazon: amazon.com/dp/1628454350

TExES Social Studies 7 - 12

amazon.com/dp/1628454652

We have study guides in a wide variety of fields. If the one you are looking for isn't listed above, then try searching for it on Amazon or send us an email.

Thanks Again and Happy Testing!
Product Development Team
info@studyguideteam.com

Interested in buying more than 10 copies of our product? Contact us about bulk discounts:

bulkorders@studyguideteam.com

FREE Test Taking Tips DVD Offer

To help us better serve you, we have developed a Test Taking Tips DVD that we would like to give you for FREE. **This DVD covers world-class test taking tips that you can use to be even more successful when you are taking your test.**

All that we ask is that you email us your feedback about your study guide. Please let us know what you thought about it – whether that is good, bad or indifferent.

To get your **FREE Test Taking Tips DVD**, email freedvd@studyguideteam.com with "FREE DVD" in the subject line and the following information in the body of the email:

  a. The title of your study guide.

  b. Your product rating on a scale of 1-5, with 5 being the highest rating.

  c. Your feedback about the study guide. What did you think of it?

  d. Your full name and shipping address to send your free DVD.

If you have any questions or concerns, please don't hesitate to contact us at freedvd@studyguideteam.com.

Thanks again!

Made in the USA
Coppell, TX
18 April 2024

31459376R00116